FAITH

**APPLYING
FAITH IN
DAILY LIVING**

**WALTER
DAVITZ**

LAMB PUBLISHING, LLC

Copyright ©2017 Walter Davitz

Published by Lamb Publishing, LLC.
FAITH: Applying Faith In Daily Living / Walter Davitz

Library of Congress Control Number: 1-4071695611
ISBN: 978-0-9983908-1-9

Contact: lambpublishingllc@gmail.com

Scriptures marked KJV are taken from the KING JAMES VERSION (KJV): KING JAMES VERSION, public domain.

Scripture quotations which have brackets [ ] and / or bolded words are for the author's emphasis.

For foreign and subsidiary rights, contact: lambpublishingllc@gmail.com

Cover and Interior Design by D.E. West, ZAQ Designs / Dust Jacket Creative Services

Printed in the United States of America

LAMB PUBLISHING, LLC

If you like this book and would like to order more copies you can do it one of two ways.

First, you can order through Amazon.com. Type the following email address - https://www.amazon.com/Faith-Applying-Daily-Living/dp/099839081X If you order 2 or more the price with free shipping will be $12.74 ish each.

Second, If you would like, we can ship to you directly, but you will need to order 8 or more books to make it cost effective with the shipping. To order directly please contact us at lambpublishingllc@gmail.com
The price will be $10 for each book plus the shipping total (8 books is roughly $8 via media mail).

The book is also available on Amazon Kindle if you would like to purchase an electronic copy.

Thank you and God Bless!

CONTENTS

INTRODUCTION

My name is Walter Davitz and God has been working in my life for 60+ years revealing specific Bible verses to be used as a manual for describing faith and applying faith into my daily living. My hope is to share with you what God has revealed to me so that you learn what faith is and can actively apply it into your life.

Most of the premises shared in this book are what God has revealed to me. I have been sharing these premises with all God has brought my way. In the last few years, God has brought to me a few people who took the time to document the premises I share and work with me to expand upon them. This book on faith has been the work of a team of people who helped me co-author this book. These dear people are Carolyn Dozer, Joyce Brewer, Jim Leezer, and Richard Hecock. You will see in many instances we refer to other people in the book as we document their thoughts on the subject of faith. As you read you will also see we use the words "we" and "us" rather than I. This is on purpose as the book is a reflection of our agreement with what has been shared and the testimony of the Holy Spirit.

In this book, scripture has been extensively quoted because God's Word should always be the basis for everything we need to learn about in this world. The scriptures quoted in this book were copied and used by permission from an awesome study tool called e-sword. If you do not have this tool, we encourage you to get it from *http://www.e-sword.net*.

In addition, Appendix A lists the Strong's definitions of all the words we discuss throughout this book.

For an introduction with faith we leave you with the following thoughts:

Faith is like exercise to our bodies... it is personal and becomes stronger / deeper if used and weaker with neglect. You gain confidence and belief in what you can do as your muscles are strengthened.

Another analogy, faith is like a friendship... you feel close to someone you talk with often... your conversation is very free... explanations are unnecessary... you understand each other almost like you are thinking the same things. You gain confidence and belief in the person as you draw closer in your friendship.

ACKNOWLEDGEMENTS

I (Walter Davitz) would like to thank the team who helped document the thoughts which God has been revealing to me, organizing them and documenting them in this book.

The brothers and sisters in Christ who helped write the book are: Carolyn Dozer; Jim Leezer; and Richard Hecock

A special thank you to Joyce Brewer for the right side captions in the book.

As you read through this book you will find that we used the words we and us a lot. The reason for this is we as a collective team wrote the book together. When individual thoughts are presented we share who they are coming from.

We, the team, want to thank all those who have come before us. For Jesus, who came to this world to show us how to live, who died a brutal death as punishment for our sins, who is RISEN and SITS with God. For those who gave their hearts to God and allowed Him to fill them with His divine inspiration and do what He asked of them. From those, who under God's inspiration penned the Bible, to those who interpreted the Bible, to those who through the generations copied the Bible, to those who have written other books sharing the revelations God gave them so we can better understand His Word, to those who God gave musical ability to write hymns, praises, and worship, to those who were blessed to play the music created, and to those who sing the music. View this book as another tool in your arsenal to help you understand God better, to make scripture clearer, and to help you become more Christ like in a true Christian walk.

We also would like to thank all who helped proofed the book along with many other friends for their input.

We would love to hear from you if you have comments or questions. We will only be doing correspondence with email. You can contact us by email at *lambpublishingllc@gmail.com.*

SECTION I

The Purpose of Faith

Have you ever wondered what faith is? It seems like it is such a nebulous term which is thrown around by many, but most don't understand what it is. It has been called one of the foundations of being a Christian and even in the name "The Christian Faith". However, many or most Christians in today's world do not know what faith is. It has been misused. It has been taken advantage of. It has been abused. It has been claimed by many, owned by few, and understood by fewer.

This book on faith represents a life time of thoughts and scriptures which God has planted in me. I feel that God wants all Christians to understand faith and I have been spreading this understanding to all who God will allow. As with any great work dedicated to God and to help other Christians grow, it takes a team of people working together under God's direction. God has blessed me with a team of four other people who have come along side me, documented the thoughts and scriptures God has given me, expanded upon them, and working together developed this book. In some areas, God gave direction to one of us and we have called out their names specifically. However, through most of the book you will see most thoughts referred to as we, or us as we are in agreement with what is stated. As you read, we believe the Holy Spirit will also give testimony to what is stated and your faith will be increased.

It is my and the team's hope that God reveals to you what He has revealed to me. Not so that you know more, not that you can say you understand faith, but so you can become more Christ like and really make an impact on this world though His direction. We need Christians who have faith, praying for those that do not know Jesus as their savior, for our families, our leaders, and ourselves.

I leave you with this scripture to start your faith journey:

> *"And the LORD, he it is that doth go before thee; he*
> *will be with thee, he will not fail thee, neither forsake thee:*
> *fear not, neither be dismayed." - Deuteronomy 31:8*

I also want to open in prayer that God, the Great I AM, would meet you wherever you are at, that He would forgive you of any sins in your life, that He cleanse you, purify you, and that your heart would be open to receive HIS WORD as you read through this study. I pray that if you are in a storm, that God, our rock, fortress, and an ever present hope in our time of need, would clear your mind refocusing you on Jesus giving you direction, guidance, strength and courage to walk to Him even in the midst of the storm. May God richly bless you with the assurance of His love and the sufficiency of His grace. Amen.

Sincerely,
Walter Davitz

CHAPTER ONE

What is Faith?

I t never ceases to amaze me (Walter) how God has created us. Each year I get older and learn so much more about God as He reveals Himself to me. Often God creates a picture of what an end result will look like and gives that to us. He does this so we have something to dream / hope for to motivate us to move forward. The same is true with understanding faith. In this chapter we are going to define what faith is and figure out the components of faith so we have a good mental image of what faith is before we start on our journey of understanding faith. It will lead into what the rest of the book will be discussing.

> **Note:** *For our scripture, we are using the King James Version (KJV) from www.e-sword.net by permission, which is a downloadable app for one's computer or mobile device. We chose to use this tool since it provided the Strong's word definition reference numbers with full Strong's definitions and we could easily copy the scripture from there. If you do not have this tool we would encourage you to download it for your reference. For more information about Strong's please reference Appendix A. Appendix A also contains a listing of the other Strong's definitions for the words we will discuss in this book.*

Since there are so many definitions of faith floating around these days, let's go straight to scripture to see what it says about faith:

> *"Now faith*^{G4102} *is the substance* ^{G5287} *of things hoped for,*^{G1679} *the evidence*^{G1650} *of things not seen."*
> *– Hebrews 11:1*

We have bolded the words in this verse we need to discuss. The first word is *faith* and starting with the Strong's reference we see that it is Strong's G4102. Again in Appendix A you can look up the definition of faith, but for our purposes, faith means to be persuaded, or convicted to believe something, or in something. So, in simple terms, faith means I have been led to believe something is true.

The second word *substance*, Strong's G5287, means foundation. If we look at a house, the purpose of a foundation is to provide a stable base for something much heavier to rest on. It is built to hold the weight of a house, and to keep that house stable, level, prevent shifting and keep it from moving. A proper foundation is critical in order for one to continue building upon it.

The third item is the phrase *"things hoped for"*, Strong's G1679, and this phrase means to expect something. This may be confusing because in western culture we often say I wish something will happen, but there is a difference between hoped for and wished for. Hoped for is based on a confident expectation that what is hoped for will take place. Wishing on the other hand has the exact opposite connotation. If I wish for something, I do not reasonably expect that it will take place. In fact per *www.merriam-webster.com*, the word wish has the following definition: "to have a desire for something which is unattainable". When we wish for something our thinking tells us it is unattainable and therefore will not take place. Another way to state this : Hoped for is rooted in something which provides confidence the expectation will be fulfilled, where wishing is not rooted in anything and therefore it is not expected to happen.

The last word is *evidence,* Strong's G1650, and per Strong's it means proof. Again looking at the definition from *www.merriam-webster.com*, "proof is an act or process of showing that something is true".

Based on the definitions we just covered, we could translate Hebrews 11:1 to read this way: Now belief is the foundation of things expected the process of proving things not seen.

Hebrews 11:1 is a crucial verse in the Bible and in these few short words there is a wealth of depth to study and understand. It is full of assumptions that the one reading it understands the underlying principles (the foundation) and believes in each of these underlying foundational principles. To take this verse and not put context behind it, does an extreme amount of injustice to the purity of God's Word and what God intended for us to understand. The rest of this book is to explain the underlying principles of this verse to make them clear so we can truly believe, and in this statement we have our very first question. Truly believe in what? What are we to believe, and with this question we will explore all that God has revealed to me and my team about faith.

What are we to believe? This is an opened ended question which could be taken a thousand ways, but really if we think about it and really process this question there is only one belief we need to have. Our whole creation is built on this belief, we were created to understand this belief, our very existence relies on this belief, and when we die, where we end up is determined by this belief. The answer to our question is ***we are to believe in God***. The second question then could be one of two: why should

I believe in God, or what should I believe about God. The first question will be answered throughout this book so as you read, keep that question in the back of your mind so it can be answered. We are going to focus then on the second question what are we to believe about God. In this question comes the foundational underlying principles which Hebrews 11:1 assumes you have. These foundational principles are the following:

A That you are minding and paying attention to your thoughts/feelings and purposefully making sure they are in line with God.

B That you believe in who God is…our creator, our savior, the one and only God.

C That you have confidence in, assurance in, and reliance on God's character.

D That you have confidence in, assurance in, and reliance on God's character towards you (He has good planned for you).

E That you understand what God is telling you to do and believing it came from Him.

F That you act on what God is telling you (obedience).

As we discussed in Hebrews 11:1, belief has to have a foundation in order for one to expect something. The principles A through F are the foundation to one's belief. Let's look at these foundations another way:

We start to realize (by observation or conviction) that a higher being exists.

Then we understand the higher being is God and we start to believe in God.

Then we believe God created us and everything else.

We start to learn about God's character (who He is).

Then we believe God intends good towards us.

This leads to trusting in God (confidence in, assurance in, reliance on).

Because of trust, we want to listen to God and do what He wants (obedience).

Since we are doing what He told us to do, we can expect God to do what He said He would do.

These are the foundations Faith (belief) is built upon. With them we can have the "things hoped for" the things expected. Without them or if any one or more are missing, we only have an unattainable wish.

Here are our premises of faith:

- The substance (foundation) of faith is our belief in God, our thoughts of confidence in God, our confidence in His words concerning man and His promise to man.

> ## When we have faith in God, it is then we really learn to trust Him.

- The "evidence of things not seen" is God's spirit working in you and through you at the time of asking God for something He has led you to ask for.

- The "things hoped for" is the expectation God will fulfill the specific promises He has given you.

These premises allow us to believe God will do what He said He will do. Faith equals this belief.

Having stated the foundations of faith, let's take a look at them in summary form by reading more of Hebrews 11:

> "Through **faith**^{G4102} we understand that the worlds were framed by the word of God, so that things which are seen were not made of things which do appear."
> – Hebrews 11:3

So based on the above, through what we experience (5 senses interacting with God's creation), we know that there is a higher being that created the universe and that being is God.

> "By **faith**^{G4102} Abel offered unto God a more excellent sacrifice than Cain, by which he obtained witness that he was righteous, God testifying of his gifts: and by it he being dead yet speaketh." – Hebrews 11:4

The above is introducing the thoughts and feelings foundation. This passage has always troubled me (Rich). I thought for many years that Cain got the shaft. However, by reading the story closer, and through talking with Walter, I realized, or God gave me the thought, that God is a *JUST* God and is always telling us what He wants. Therefore both Able and Cain were told what God expected and Cain chose not to bring the sacrifice that God wanted. Why? We really don't know, but he chose to be disobedient none the less.

> ^{5} "By **faith**^{G4102} Enoch was translated that he should not see death; and was not found, because God had translated him: for before his translation he had this testimony, that he pleased God." ^{6} "But without **faith**^{G4102} it is impossible to please him: for he that cometh to God must believe that

he is, and that he is a rewarder of them that diligently seek him." – Hebrews 11:5 - 6

The above verses are introducing God's character and His character towards us. Trust / reliance on God is key to please God because without this we cannot even come to God. Coming to God is the first step because we need to be saved from our sins.

"By faith[G4102] *Noah, being warned of God of things not seen as yet, moved with fear, prepared an ark to the saving of his house; by the which he condemned the world, and became heir of the righteousness which is by faith.*[G4102]*" – Hebrews 11:7*

God Speaks to us through our thoughts. God expects us to act on those thoughts.

The above verse introduces understanding what God tells me to do something and then acting on that thought. In Genesis 6:14 God told Noah to build an ark. He also told Noah why. Because Noah believed in what God said and what God was going to do (God's promise), he did it and he saved his family in the process.

[8] *"By faith*[G4102] *Abraham, when he was called to go out into a place which he should after receive for an inheritance, obeyed; and he went out, not knowing whither he went."* [9] *"By faith*[G4102] *he sojourned in the land of promise, as in a strange country, dwelling in tabernacles with Isaac and Jacob, the heirs with him of the same promise:"* [10] *"For he looked for a city which hath foundations, whose builder and maker is God." – Hebrews 11:8 - 10*

In Gen 12:1 God told Abraham to leave Haran and go to a place that God would give him. God only promised to bless him at the time he left. Abraham knew God and trusted that God meant him good and did as God said. Again showing that there is a link between listening and acting on what we are told.

> *[11] "Through faith[G4102] also Sara herself received strength to conceive seed, and was delivered of a child when she was past age, because she judged him faithful who had promised." [12] "Therefore sprang there even of one, and him as good as dead, so many as the stars of the sky in multitude, and as the sand which is by the sea shore innumerable." – Hebrews 11:11 - 12*

We won't go into the details here but obviously there was action taken on Abraham and Sarah's part for the conception to take place. This action was the faith of both which started God's chosen people.

> *[13] "These all died in faith[G4102], not having received the promises, but having seen them afar off, and were persuaded of them, and embraced them, and confessed that they were strangers and pilgrims on the earth." [14] "For they that say such things declare plainly that they seek a country." [15] "And truly, if they had been mindful of that country from whence they came out, they might have had opportunity to have returned." [16] "But now they desire a better country, that is, an heavenly: wherefore God is not ashamed to be called their God: for he hath prepared for them a city." – Hebrews 11:13 - 16*

In the above verses, we get a glimpse of why the saints of the Bible believed even to death without seeing the end result. They believed because God showed them the end result, or spoke it into their minds via dreams, or visions in the form of a promise. They had confidence in God's word i.e., the thoughts God placed in their minds and they acted on them. They had confidence God would deliver on what he promised them even if it wasn't in their lifetime.

"By faith^{G4102} Abraham, when he was tried, offered up Isaac: and he that had received the promises offered up his only begotten son," [18] *"Of whom it was said, That in Isaac shall thy seed be called:"* [19] *"Accounting that God was able to raise him up, even from the dead; from whence also he received him in a figure."* [20] *"By faith^{G4102} Isaac blessed Jacob and Esau concerning things to come."* [21] *"By faith^{G4102} Jacob, when he was a dying, blessed both the sons of Joseph; and worshipped, leaning upon the top of his staff."* [22] *"By faith^{G4102} Joseph, when he died, made mention of the departing of the children of Israel; and gave commandment concerning his bones."* [23] *"By faith^{G4102} Moses, when he was born, was hid three months of his parents, because they saw he was a proper child; and they were not afraid of the king's commandment."* [24] *"By faith^{G4102} Moses, when he was come to years, refused to be called the son of Pharaoh's daughter;"* [25] *"Choosing*

The heroes of faith showed us how to live by faith.

They believed.

Without faith we have no belief.

11

*rather to suffer affliction with the people of God, than to enjoy the pleasures of sin for a season;" ²⁶"Esteeming the reproach of Christ greater riches than the treasures in Egypt: for he had respect unto the recompence of the reward." ²⁷"By **faith**^{G4102} he forsook Egypt, not fearing the wrath of the king: for he endured, as seeing him who is invisible." ²⁸"Through **faith**^{G4102} he kept the passover, and the sprinkling of blood, lest he that destroyed the firstborn should touch them." ²⁹"By **faith**^{G4102} they passed through the Red sea as by dry land: which the Egyptians assaying to do were drowned." ³⁰"By **faith**^{G4102} the walls of Jericho fell down, after they were compassed about seven days." ³¹"By **faith**^{G4102} the harlot Rahab perished not with them that believed not, when she had received the spies with peace." ³²"And what shall I more say? for the time would fail me to tell of Gedeon, and of Barak, and of Samson, and of Jephthae; of David also, and Samuel, and of the prophets:" – Hebrews 11:17 - 32*

The rest of the verses above just rise into a crescendo of what faith is. Each case tells of the person paying attention to the thoughts God gave them and then acting on them. Even down to Rahab who wasn't even part of God's chosen people, but because she believed the thoughts that God was putting in minds of the people of her city, she acted on those thoughts and helped the spies.

Let's look at her story:

⁹"And she said unto the men, I know that the LORD hath given you the land, and that your terror is fallen upon us, and that all the inhabitants of the land faint

*because of you." ¹⁰"For we have heard how the LORD
dried up the water of the Red sea for you, when ye came
out of Egypt; and what ye did unto the two kings of the
Amorites, that were on the other side Jordan, Sihon and
Og, whom ye utterly destroyed." ¹¹"And as soon as we had
heard these things, our hearts did melt, neither did there
remain any more courage in any man, because of you: for
the LORD your God, he is God in heaven above, and in
earth beneath." ¹²"Now therefore, I pray you, swear unto
me by the LORD, since I have shewed you kindness, that
ye will also shew kindness unto my father's house, and give
me a true token:" ¹³"And that ye will save alive my father,
and my mother, and my brethren, and my sisters, and all
that they have, and deliver our lives from death." ¹⁴"And
the men answered her, Our life for yours, if ye utter not
this our business. And it shall be, when the LORD hath
given us the land, that we will deal kindly and truly with
thee." – Joshua 2:9 - 14*

How did she know? She heard, she felt, she understood. The terror
was the dread that God placed on the hearts of the people of that land so
that Israel could attack and defeat them. These were thoughts planted in
the minds of the people of that land. Rahab was the only one that paid
attention to those thoughts and when given the opportunity, she trusted
in them and at the risk of her own life from her king, hid he spies. She did
this on the hope that they would in return grant her safety when the city
was destroyed. So she had faith that they would show her kindness and
the things she hoped for came to pass because of her obedience, trust and
confidence in what the spies promised which was a promise to her from
God since they swore by Him.

As we see faith described, we can only put our trust in the things *God promises us*. These promises may or may not be what we want, but they are always the best God has for us. Those who were honored in the list above, were those who put their wants aside and focused only on what God wanted, pursuing it with all their heart, soul, and mind. God sent His son Jesus to die a horrible and cruel death for the sole purpose of providing us a reconciliation of relationship with Him. He uses you and us to show others that relationship and create in them a desire to have the same relationship with Him. The relationship is built on trust, and trust can only come when both parties are on the same page with what is being given and received. If one of the parties is not on the same page, then trust is strained or maybe even broken. Do you desire to have such a solid relationship with God that no one and nothing can shake it? Do you desire to show others the passion of God's love towards us and the passion of our adoration of Him (His glory shining through you so that others only see Jesus when they see you and are inspired to have the same for themselves)? Can we even stop to imagine what our world would look like if all Christians pursued what God specifically promised them, putting aside our wants and only wanting what God has for us? The world would be changed, satan would fall, peace would reign and the Kingdom of God would be reflected on earth as it is in heaven. We hope that you want your name listed along with ours when God lists out the next list of those who He trusted with his very plans to save this world.

We have given an introduction of what faith is defined by the scriptures. These scriptures are truths which we will build on through the rest of this book so we can all have a faith that is unshakable, unbreakable, and powerful enough that satan and his minions cower before the church!

To make things easier as we progress through the book, let's put the foundations of faith in the form of a computer Boolean Logic statement...

FAITH = **A** and **B** and **C** and **D** and **E** and **F**.

Here are the statement variables (the foundational principles) in summary form:

A = minding and paying attention to your thoughts/feelings and purposefully making sure they are in line with God.

B = believing in God and who He is…our creator, our savior, the one and only God.

C = having confidence, assurance in, reliance on God's character.

D = having confidence, assurance in, reliance on God's character towards us (He has good planned for me).

E = understanding what God told me to do and believing it came from Him.

F = my obedience of acting on what God told me.

Computer Boolean Logic is a form of algebra in which all variables are normally reduced to True/False or On /Off. However, for our example, we are going to make them mean Exist (True/On) or Not Exist (False/Off). When you use the operator "and", it means all variables have to Exist or the whole statement does Not Exist. It changes the faith equation to either Exist or Not Exist. If I am confident with (A) my thoughts and feelings AND confident in (B) knowing who God is AND confident in knowing (C) God's character AND confident in knowing (D) God's character toward me, AND believe (E) what God tells me, AND act on that belief (F), then my Faith Exists. However, if any one or more of the variables do Not Exist then, the whole statement does Not Exist and therefore *my faith is non-existent.*

As we move through the book, we will be discussing each foundation principle as a variable in our Faith equation and explain why that principle has to exist for faith to be present.

At the end of each chapter we have selected a song which we feel sums up the chapter's content. If you like the songs, please consider purchasing them to support the artists.

We would like to end this chapter with an encouraging song called *"What Faith Can Do"*. We recommend that you go to *www.youtube.com* and in the YouTube search bar, search for *"What Faith Can Do by Kutless"* minus the quotation marks.

IN SUMMARY

We are using Hebrews 11:1 to define faith and we could translate it to read this way "Now belief is the foundation of things expected, the process of proving things not seen."

There are five foundational principles which allow one to have belief. These foundational principles represented by variables are:

A = minding and paying attention to your thoughts/feelings and purposefully making sure they are in line with God.

B = believing in God and who He is…our creator, our savior, the one and only God.

C = having confidence, assurance in, reliance on God's character.

D = having confidence, assurance in, reliance on God's character towards us (He has good planned for me).

E = believing what God told me and believing it came from Him.

F = my action of acting on those what God told me (obedience).

Using these variables faith can be represented in the following computer Boolean logic equation: **FAITH** = **A** and **B** and **C** and **D** and **E** and **F**, and when each variable is present (true) then one's faith exists. However if any one variable is absent (false) then one's faith does not exist.

Now that we have the foundational principles of faith, we are going to discuss each of the foundational principles in following Chapters 2 – 7. We are doing this to make each one easier to understand, comprehend, and to correct teachings that were never properly taught. As your faith becomes rock solid, you will then desire to know and do what God has created you for.

In the next chapter we will be discussing foundational principle (variable) **A** - minding and paying attention to your thoughts/feelings and purposefully making sure they are in line with God.

CHAPTER TWO

Thoughts and Feelings

As in most cases, all ends have a beginning. Since our first chapter dealt with the end of what we want our faith to be, even transcending our physical death like the patriarchs of old, we must now go back and start at the beginning and work our way to the end. So what is the beginning? Good question. We are glad you asked.

Well, first there are some definitions we need to get out of the way so that we are on the same page.

One – When we say Christian we are speaking of a person that believes in God, has confessed their sins, repented of their sins, and has accepted Jesus Christ as Lord and savior of their life, and is doing their best to live a Christ like life.

Two – When we say man or woman it is gender and age neutral. It means mankind.

Three – We will not capitalize satan as he does not deserve that respect.

Now that we are done with some simple definitions we need to talk about thoughts and feelings. Thoughts and feelings are variable A in our basic faith equation (**FAITH** = **A** and **B** and **C** and **D** and **E** and **F**).

The reason we are starting here rather than starting with God, is because we have to make sure we have the proper thoughts and feelings in our minds / hearts to truly ensure we are learning who God is.

Over the years, God has revealed to me (Walter) that thoughts and feelings are the beginning of everything. Our mind is full of thoughts. Some are good and some are not so good. Every Christian and non-Christian has both good and bad swimming around in their heads. I believe that satan cannot read our thoughts but he can plant suggestions and thoughts into our minds. Some thoughts come in what we see, hear, experience, etc. Some come from our natural desires, some from other people. The trick is discerning which thoughts are from God and which are from satan and which are from our natural self.

Let's look at some example scriptures, we captured by doing a search, for how the Bible defines "thought(s)". We found roughly 132 references to the word thought(s). We pulled out the scriptures which were more in general reference to man's frame of mine and God's. **Note**: the Strong's Word Definitions in Appendix A:

> *"And GOD saw that the wickedness of man was great in the earth, and that every imagination of the* ***thoughts***[H4284] *of his heart was only evil continually."*
> *– Genesis 6:5*

In the above verse, the word thoughts means man's thoughts, to plan or plot evil against one another and / or against God.

> [18]*"O LORD God of Abraham, Isaac, and of Israel, our fathers, keep this for ever in the imagination of the* ***thoughts***[H4284] *of the heart of thy people, and prepare their heart unto thee:"* [19]*"And give unto Solomon my son a perfect heart, to keep thy commandments, thy testimonies,*

and thy statutes, and to do all these things, and to build the palace, for the which I have made provision."
— 1 Chronicles 29:18 - 19

In the above verses, the same word and reference are used but the context here is for planning the building of God's temple and to keep his laws. So in this instance it is man's good thoughts toward fellow man and God.

*"The wicked, through the pride of his countenance, will not seek⁵ after God: God is not in all his **thoughts**."ᴴ⁴²⁰⁹*
— Psalms 10:4

The above Hebrew translation is negative and means man's evil plans.

*"How precious also are thy **thoughts**ᴴ⁷⁴⁵⁴ unto me, O God! how great is the sum of them!" — Psalms 139:17*

Another Hebrew word for thoughts showing they come from God. Here it means as a shepherd to protect his flock... or God's good plans for us.

*"For my **thoughts**ᴴ⁴²⁸⁴ are not your **thoughts**,ᴴ⁴²⁸⁴ neither are your ways my ways, saith the LORD."*
— Isaiah 55:8

Back to our first Hebrew word and again the context sets the word. Here the

Remember God's plan is not always our plan, but God's plan is always the best for us. God's plans always are to Glorify Him.

word is still plans and contrasts that God's good plans are not the same as our plans which can be good or evil.

> *"For as the heavens are higher than the earth, so are my ways higher than your ways, and my **thoughts**[H4284] than your **thoughts**."*[H4284] – Isaiah 55:9

Another Hebrew word which means idea. Here it conveys that God wants to share His ideas with man as one shares with a friend.

> *"For, lo, he that formeth the mountains, and createth the wind, and declareth unto man what is his **thought**,*[H7808] *that maketh the morning darkness, and treadeth upon the high places of the earth, The LORD, The God of hosts, is his name."* – Amos 4:13

Hebrew word to ponder or think about thoughts and that God's thoughts are communed to us to ponder or to think through.

> *"Casting down imaginations, and every high thing that exalteth itself against the knowledge of God, and bringing into captivity every **thought**[G3540] to the obedience of Christ;"* – 2 Corinthians 10:5

Greek action word stating to purposely take control over all our thoughts, feelings, ideas, intellect and subjugate them in obedience to what Christ wants. (For us to actively control these things rather than letting them control us.)

Here is a thought to ponder… I (Rich) was having a discussion with my wife on the difference between being a captive and a prisoner because the Bible distinguishes between the two. They came up with a prisoner in most cases is restricted in every way…they have no freedoms. However, a captive, although they are restricted to the rules of captivity, have freedom to move about, think, choices to be made, etc. Think of it in the old testament when the Assyrians came and took over the land, the whole Israel nation was under captivity either in the land or where they were deported to… but other than that and living by the governmental rules, they were free in almost every other respect. This verse is simply stating who is the captive… *it should be our thoughts, not us to be captive to our thoughts.*

> *"Among whom also we all had our conversation in times past in the lusts of our flesh, fulfilling the desires of the flesh and of the **mind**;G1271 and were by nature the children of wrath, even as others."*
>
> *– Ephesians 2:3*

In the NIV translation the word mind is translated as thought. In this verse due to the Adamic fall our minds are in a disposition of acting in evil until we are renewed by Christ.

Due to the Adamic fall, our minds are not in line with what God wants and are sometimes at war with what God wants. By the way if you have never heard of the term Adamic fall, this is when Adam and Eve sinned by disobeying God…both eating the fruit they were forbidden to eat and choosing it/each other over God. In doing this humans were given the ability to know good and evil (where they only knew the good existed before), and therefore we are each born into a sinful state due to the decision they made.

In addition to thoughts, there are feelings. We all have them. Again some come from God (like righteous anger), some from satan (like intense hatred) and most from ourselves – either our saved or natural state (love or envy). We need to discern where feelings are coming from.

The question then becomes, why are thoughts/feelings so important?

Key Point: *Because thoughts and feelings rule our lives. As much as we like to think we are logical beings, at our base core we are emotional beings and every thought feeling passes through our emotional center before it can be processed logically. How well we are able to contain an emotional response, to think through it, is called Emotional Intelligence. We follow our feelings and follow our thoughts. Therefore we must guard and watch our thoughts and feelings. We always want to make sure we are aware of the thoughts that are going through our mind to ensure that we are focused on the thoughts that are from God, or are good.*

The other thing with thoughts is to consider if some thoughts come from God then God is speaking to us through our thoughts. Many people complain that God never speaks to them or talks to them. However, they ignore the thoughts that God puts into their minds. Many of these thoughts deal with one's conscious and many people don't like how their conscious is dealing with them (like being convicted because they are sinning and need to stop) so they suppress or ignore those thoughts. If the thoughts were good or correcting, then those thoughts were from God and were ignored. God has been speaking to us our whole lives, but we are not listening or understanding which thoughts are from Him and which are not. By paying attention to our thoughts we can hear God speaking to us.

For example, maybe there is someone you have not spoken to in a while, not because of anything bad, but out of touch with them for a while and the thought comes out of nowhere that you should call them. Often times once you start talking, you find out that the other person really needed someone to talk with because of things going on in their life. You became a blessing because you called them. We have all been there…sometimes we listen and call, other times we do not call and find out later that our friend could have really used the encouragement from us (we missed out on a blessing to the friend and to us), or we find out that God had someone else call them (again we missed out on the blessing and someone else received it).

Another point to consider is often times when God is speaking to us, it is like Him speaking as a grown up to a 2 or 3 year old child. We, as the 2 or 3 year old, do not understand what God is saying. If you watch a parent talking to a 3 year old, the parent will go into a long discussion on why the child should, or should not do something. If you watch the child, they often times will get a glassy eyed look, or seem like what the parent is saying is a foreign language and they do not get any of it or only get the words they want to hear. I (Rich) have a 4 year old daughter. My wife and I work hard to explain to her that she needs to not run in the church. But she hears the word run and then takes off because she wants to run. This is what she wants to do and she basically ignores anything else we say and focuses on that. Often this is how we are with God. He is speaking to us with thoughts, but we only hear the words we want to hear based on what we want at the time. Then we go and do the thing we want and wonder why God does not seem to be in what we are doing. It is often because we did not listen to Him to begin with. We need to slow down and make sure we have a clear understanding of the thought and ask God clarifying questions to make sure that we do what He wants done.

Let's look at a very much quoted verse on this:

> *"And Jesus answered and said unto him, Blessed art thou, Simon Barjona: for flesh and blood hath not **revealed**[G601] it unto thee, but my Father which is in heaven." – Matthew 16:17*

Revealed, Strong's G601, means just what we would normally think. Peter's mind was opened and he understood…or more importantly God placed the thought in Peter's mind that Jesus was His son. Peter then acting in faith, told Jesus who He was and Jesus commended him for it saying that only God could have revealed that to him.

How do we know if a thought is from God, or from satan, or from ourselves. Good question and one that needed to be asked. Basically any thought or feeling that is contrary to scripture or is in conflict with scripture is not from God. For example, a thought that says I really hate my neighbor is not a thought from God. The 10 commandments speak against this and so does Jesus in the sermon on the mount when He says hating is the same thing as killing.

However the opposite is not necessarily true. The opposite is anything that takes us closer to God is from God. The reason this isn't always clear is, we as humans have the amazing ability to rationalize anything we want. So a thought that says, I need to buy a boat so that I can lend it to those in a ministry to use for their leisure, may be from God or may be from our own desire to own a boat. The boat is not the issue. The issue is where the thought is coming from. There is nothing wrong with a Christian owning a boat. There is nothing wrong with a Christian lending that boat to friends, or lending it to those in the ministry. It is wrong however, if I have a desire to have a boat, but really can't afford it, but buy a boat rationalizing it is God's will because I am going to allow those in the ministry to use it. Another example, if I have the money to buy a boat, but God told me to do something else with that money and I don't do that and buy the boat just because I wanted the boat. The issue is the attitude of the heart and the thoughts that are being produced by it, not whether or not you have a boat.

Now if you do not have a desire to have a boat and God clearly tells you to buy a boat, that is completely different. You are being obedient.

Consider Noah who God told to build an Ark. Noah worked on that ark for over 100 years. He was consistently obeying God for over 100 years.

Since we are on the topic, let's stop and make sure we are all on the same page with what thoughts from God are. When we say a thought or feeling is from God, it can come in many forms: it can come from His written word the Bible; it can be a revelation to you as you read and study the Bible; it can be a revelation by the Holy Spirit; it can be an external audible voice from a messenger angel or from Jesus (either seen or not seen); it could be a conviction or leading of the Holy Spirit coming from our soul into our minds; it could be an intense feeling driving you to do something that God would want done (a burden); it could even be the Holy Spirit physically manifesting Himself and taking control of you to do or say what needs to be said; it could be a vision; it could be dream; it could be an overwhelming peace sweeping over you; it could be God's presence settling down on you and you basking in His Glory; it could be some other way in which there is no shadow of doubt in your mind that God just visited with you; it could be something for you, or something God wants to intercede on / do for someone else; it could be that God is bringing your attention to a need that someone else or a group of people have so you can stand in the gap for them. We just wanted to take a moment to make sure we are not boxing God in, in any way. The above are just some experiences the team, who helped write this book, shared. We must mature and be mature by paying attention to our thoughts so that we know what God is saying.

We also need to make sure that we are protecting ourselves from thoughts and suggestions that satan is planting in our minds. satan, as we know, plants thoughts and feelings in our minds as well. Most of the time, these are thoughts of bitterness or hatred toward others. Often it is in response to something that they did which hurt us. We dwell on thoughts of revenge and hurting them back. These are not thoughts from God but from satan which we must watch for. We need to rebuke (defined in Strong's as forbid) these thoughts and focus on what God wants to tell us. satan will do everything in his power to overwhelm us with thoughts and feelings taking us away from where God is. It feels like we are drowning or washed away by them. If we take the bait, satan wins because that is what he wants from us. We mentioned we need to rebuke these thoughts. Rebuking is an active form of paying attention to the thoughts flowing through your mind. When you have a thought that you know is not of God, it is purposely acknowledging the thought was there, and as a child of Jesus, telling satan that the thought is not allowed to be in your mind (forbidding them). If you happened to think on the thought and a feeling came out of it, then it is to ask Jesus for forgiveness and then again claiming that we want to be Christ-like and telling satan that as a child of God that thought/feeling is not going to be allowed/tolerated in your mind. Telling satan he is not welcome there and must leave is the essence of scripture 2 Corinthians 10:5 which we quoted earlier… we must be actively monitoring our minds and hearts taking captive anything which is not of God and putting it out.

The final source of thoughts is our own desires. Our natural selves are in conflict with God until we receive his son Jesus as our personal savior. Even after that, we daily battle with thoughts and desires that our natural selves want. Maybe it is looking at an old habit we had and are still dealing with the habit's desires. Maybe it is an attitude that we deserve something that we really don't or that someone owes us something. Maybe it is looking a little too long at a particular person of the opposite sex and wondering what life would be like with them when we are married to someone else. All of these lead us down a path that is not where God wants us to go. We need to be aware of these thoughts too and rebuke them before they get a strong hold in our minds or become feelings in our heart.

A final note to consider which will be critical as we move into later chapters is that, just because we are dealing with a person, doesn't mean you are actually interacting with that person. If they do not have Jesus in their heart then they are an agent of satan and satan can cloud / take over their thinking. So when someone reacts harshly toward you, doesn't act right, is making decisions that are bad or wrong, or leading others down a path that is not correct, just remember it may not be them but satan through them.

The question we as Christians should always have when interacting with someone is, who are we speaking with? Are we speaking with the person or not? For an example in scripture let's look at Jesus and the man of the tombs:

> ²⁶ *"And they arrived at the country of the Gadarenes, which is over against Galilee."* ²⁷ *"And when he went forth to land, there met him out of the city a certain man, which had devils long time, and ware no clothes, neither abode in any house, but in the tombs."* ²⁸ *"When he saw Jesus, he cried out, and fell down before him, and with a loud voice said, What have I to do with thee, Jesus, thou Son of God most high? I beseech thee, torment me not."* ²⁹ *"(For he had commanded the unclean spirit to come out of the man. For oftentimes it had caught him: and he was kept bound with chains and in fetters; and he brake the bands, and was driven of the devil into the wilderness.)"* ³⁰ *"And Jesus asked him, saying, What is thy name? And he said, Legion: because many devils were entered into him."* ³¹ *"And they besought him that he would not command them to go out into the deep."* ³² *"And there was there an herd of many swine feeding on the mountain: and they besought him*

that he would suffer them to enter into them. And he
suffered them." [33] "Then went the devils out of the man,
and entered into the swine: and the herd ran violently
down a steep place into the lake, and were choked."
– Luke 8:26 - 33

What we want you to notice is the interplay that is going on in these verses. Jesus knew that the man was controlled by the demonic forces. The "man" came out to meet Jesus. Jesus didn't seek him out. The "man" started talking to Jesus. The "man" was asking what Jesus wanted with him. But the "man" was not in control. The verses say that the devils were the ones that were controlling the man. So even though Jesus was addressing and interacting with the "man", legion was the one doing all the talking and acting.

The point here is that anyone who is not a Christian, or more closely to the point, anyone who does not have Jesus as his own personal savior, can potentially be influenced, vexed, oppressed or even possessed by satan's demonic forces. We would contend that 99.9% are at least heavily influenced in some form. We base this on the fact that they do not have Jesus in their hearts to prevent satan from doing so. Whether giving you bad advice, or not being nice, or being rude, or someone in charge of you giving requirements that take you further from God rather than closer or making you choose between the two, are all influenced to outright possessed. These people are not in control of their thoughts, they get a thought and they act on it. Since the thought is not of God, then the thoughts can only come from the other two sources satan and one's natural self. In most cases, the thoughts are so subtle that you might never know that the person is being manipulated, but they are. And more than that, they are being used to lead you away from following God.

As a side note, we want to be clear, we are not to hate these people, we are to love them, pray for them, and share God's truth. We are not in a physical fight with them, we are in spiritual battle with what is influencing their minds. We need to battle on their behalf so they can be delivered. This is what Jesus is demonstrating here.

Continuing on, look at the following verses:

> [34] *"When they that fed them saw what was done, they fled, and went and told it in the city and in the country."* [35] *"Then they went out to see what was done; and came to Jesus, and found the man, out of whom the devils were departed, sitting at the feet of Jesus, clothed, and in his right mind: and they were afraid."* [36] *"They also which saw it told them by what means he that was possessed of the devils was healed." – Luke 8:34 - 36*

Obviously this was very disturbing to the "sane" people because they were not part of the conversation which was going on. But more importantly, they were not Christians either. The shepherds went and told the town officials to come see what is going on and intervene. They lost 2,000 of their assets and we are sure they were upset. In today's terms 2016 an adult pig is about $1.25 a pound undressed or so. If the average pig was 200 lbs, then they lost 2000 x 200 x 1.25 = $500,000.00 As you can see, this was a huge financial loss for the owners and the community.

Again these folks are not Christians, and they "think" let's go tell the officials and people of the town what happened. Then the people "think" we need to investigate this and intervene because this isn't right and we lost food supply. Who do you think came up with those thoughts? This is something to think about.

Further when they get there, they see the formerly possessed man now in his right mind or sane. In his sane state, he is right with God the way it was originally intended. He is sitting at Jesus' feet, we believe, listening to what Jesus is teaching him. Again as man was originally created to be.

So what should the town's people reaction been? It would be to bow down and worship Jesus as their lord and savior right? Wrong, their "natural" reaction comes out of our Adamic fall state. Where there is light, the darkness is exposed. What did Peter say to Jesus when Jesus gave them the first big catch? Luke 5:8 "When Simon Peter saw it, he fell down at Jesus' knees, saying, Depart from me; for I am a sinful man, O Lord." He didn't worship Jesus, he asked him to leave. Why? Because Peter was not saved yet. Jesus' light showed him he was sinful which made him afraid. So he asked Jesus to leave so that he could feel "normal" again.

What do the town's people do?

> [37]*"Then the whole multitude of the country of the Gadarenes round about besought him to depart from them; for they were taken with great fear: and he went up into the ship, and returned back again."* [38]*"Now the man out of whom the devils were departed besought him that he might be with him: but Jesus sent him away, saying,"* [39]*"Return to thine own house, and shew how great things God hath done unto thee. And he went his way, and published throughout the whole city how great things Jesus had done unto him." – Luke 8:37 - 39*

Right, they do the very same thing that Peter did. They recognized their sinful state, were afraid, and then asked Jesus to leave. These were either thoughts of fear from satan, or from their natural selves. They wanted things as "normal". The interesting thing here is that Jesus listened to their request and left. He didn't override them like he did with Peter and the demon possessed man.

Going back to the man, who was begging Jesus to leave him alone, now he wants to follow Jesus. Again he is in a healed state which was intended from creation. So naturally he wants to be with and follow Jesus. But Jesus sends him instead to be a witness for him in that area…or in better terms, to remain a light in that area of darkness.

Always remember anyone not for Jesus Christ is against Jesus Christ. If they are against Jesus (their natural state), then they are against you as a Christian. So when you are talking, working, etc. with a non-Christian, do not be surprised if you are really not interacting with that person but with whatever is controlling them. Again we say this to remind you we are not fighting with people, but with the powers and principalities of this dark world. We will discuss this more in Chapter 11.

We would like to close this chapter with the song *"Slow Fade"*. We recommend that you go to *www.youtube.com* and in the YouTube search bar, search for *"Slow Fade by Casting Crowns"* minus the quotation marks.

IN SUMMARY

We have learned some foundational truths:

1. Every human's natural state is to hate Jesus / God and to want him to depart due to the Adamic fall.

2. God is speaking to us all the time.

3. It is up to us to discern which thoughts we are to be paying attention to.

4. We need to know and focus on the thoughts that bring us closer to God and rebuke all the thoughts that are leading us away from God.

5. We always need to ask, are we dealing with the person or a spiritual influence on the person.

6. We must grow and mature.

This chapter dealt with variable **A** of our faith equation representing minding our thoughts and feelings. Remember our faith equation is **FAITH** = **A** and **B** and **C** and **D** and **E** and **F**.

In the next chapter we will be discussing who God is, variable **B**.

CHAPTER THREE

Who is God?

In this chapter we will be investigating variable **B** of our basic faith equation. Remember variable **B**, is believing in God and who He is…our creator, our savior, the one and only God.

The question, Who is God?, can be a deep theological discussion which takes us outside the parameters of this book. However, we do need to discuss some of the basic truths of God to continue laying a foundation of faith. To do this we will simply state some of the foundational scriptures about God.

Based on scriptures here are some things we know about God.

We know that God has always existed:

> *"I am Alpha and Omega, the beginning and the ending, saith the Lord, which is, and which was, and which is to come, the Almighty." – Revelation 1:8*

> *[13] "And Moses said unto God, Behold, when I come unto the children of Israel, and shall say unto them, The God of your fathers hath sent me unto you; and they shall say to me, What is his name? what shall I say unto them?"*
> *[14] "And God said unto Moses, I AM THAT I AM: and he*

said, Thus shalt thou say unto the children of Israel, I AM hath sent me unto you." ¹⁵*"And God said moreover unto Moses, Thus shalt thou say unto the children of Israel, The LORD God of your fathers, the God of Abraham, the God of Isaac, and the God of Jacob, hath sent me unto you: this is my name for ever, and this is my memorial unto all generations." – Exodus 3:13 - 15*

¹*"In the beginning was the Word, and the Word was with God, and the Word was God."* ²*"The same was in the beginning with God."* ³*"All things were made by him; and without him was not any thing made that was made." – John 1:1 - 3*

We know that God created everything (the whole universe) nothing existed before God created it other than God himself:

"In the beginning God created the heaven and the earth." – Genesis 1:1

"Who laid the foundations of the earth, that it should not be removed for ever." – Palms 104:5

"O LORD, how manifold are thy works! in wisdom hast thou made them all: the earth is full of thy riches." – Palms 104:24

¹⁹*"The LORD by wisdom hath founded the earth; by understanding hath he established the heavens."* ²⁰*"By his knowledge the depths are broken up, and the clouds drop down the dew." – Proverbs 3:19 - 20*

"Through faith we understand that the worlds were framed by the word of God, so that things which are seen were not made of things which do appear."
– Hebrews 11:3

God created time:

³"And God said, Let there be light: and there was light." ⁴"And God saw the light, that it was good: and God divided the light from the darkness." ⁵"And God called the light Day, and the darkness he called Night. And the evening and the morning were the first day."
– Genesis 1:3 – 5

"And God said, Let there be lights in the firmament of the heaven to divide the day from the night; and let them be for signs, and for seasons, and for days, and years:"
– Genesis 1:14

God created our planet earth and all living and non-living things in and on it:

⁶"And God said, Let there be a firmament in the midst of the waters, and let it divide the waters from the waters." ⁷"And God made the firmament, and divided the waters which were under the firmament from the waters which were above the firmament: and it was so." ⁸"And God called the firmament Heaven. And the evening and the morning were the second day." ⁹"And God said, Let the waters under the heaven be gathered together unto one place, and let the dry land appear: and it was so." ¹⁰"And God called the dry land Earth; and the gathering together of the waters called he Seas: and God saw that it was good." [11]*"And God said, Let the earth bring forth grass, the herb yielding seed, and the fruit tree yielding fruit after his kind, whose seed is in itself, upon the earth: and it was so."* [12]*"And the earth brought forth grass, and herb yielding seed after his kind, and the tree yielding fruit, whose seed was in itself, after his kind: and God saw that it was good."* [13]*"And the evening and the morning were the third day."* [14]*"And God said, Let there be lights in the firmament of the heaven to divide the day from the night; and let them be for signs, and for seasons, and for days, and years:"* [15]*"And let them be for lights in the firmament of the heaven to give light upon the earth: and it was so."* [16]*"And God made two great lights; the greater light to rule the day, and the lesser light to rule the night: he made the stars also."* [17]*"And God set them in the firmament of the heaven to give light upon the earth,"* [18]*"And to rule over the day and over the night, and to divide the light from the darkness: and God saw that it was good."* [19]*"And the evening and the morning were the fourth day."* [20]*"And God said, Let the waters bring forth abundantly the moving creature that hath life, and fowl that may fly above the earth in the open firmament of heaven."* [21]*"And God created great whales, and every living creature that moveth, which the waters brought forth abundantly, after their kind, and every winged fowl after his kind: and God saw that it was good."* [22]*"And God blessed them, saying, Be fruitful, and multiply, and fill the waters in the seas, and let fowl multiply in the earth."* [23]*"And the evening and* *the morning were the fifth day." ²⁴"And God said, Let the earth bring forth the living creature after his kind, cattle, and creeping thing, and beast of the earth after his kind: and it was so." ²⁵"And God made the beast of the earth after his kind, and cattle after their kind, and every thing that creepeth upon the earth after his kind: and God saw that it was good." – Genesis 1:6 - 25*

God created Man and called his creation good:

²⁶*"And God said, Let us make man in our image, after our likeness: and let them have dominion over the fish of the sea, and over the fowl of the air, and over the cattle, and over all the earth, and over every creeping thing that creepeth upon the earth." ²⁷"So God created man in his own image, in the image of God created he him; male and female created he them." ²⁸"And God blessed them, and God said unto them, Be fruitful, and multiply, and replenish the earth, and subdue it: and have dominion over the fish of the sea, and over the fowl of the air, and over every living thing that moveth upon the earth." ²⁹"And God said, Behold, I have given you every herb bearing seed, which is upon the face of all the earth, and every tree, in the which is the fruit of a tree yielding seed; to you it shall be for meat." ³⁰"And to every beast of the earth, and to every fowl of the air, and to every thing that creepeth upon the earth, wherein there is life, I have given every green herb for meat: and it was so." ³¹"And God saw every thing that he had made, and, behold, it was very*

good. And the evening and the morning were the sixth day." – Genesis 1:26 - 31

God created the Angels:

¹"Praise ye the LORD. Praise ye the LORD from the heavens: praise him in the heights." ²"Praise ye him, all his angels: praise ye him, all his hosts." ³"Praise ye him, sun and moon: praise him, all ye stars of light." ⁴"Praise him, ye heavens of heavens, and ye waters that be above the heavens." ⁵"Let them praise the name of the LORD: for he commanded, and they were created." ⁶"He hath also stablished them for ever and ever: he hath made a decree which shall not pass." – Psalms 148:1 - 6

God created Wisdom:

²²"The LORD possessed me in the beginning of his way, before his works of old." ²³"I was set up from everlasting, from the beginning, or ever the earth was." ²⁴"When there were no depths, I was brought forth; when there were no fountains abounding with water." ²⁵"Before the mountains were settled, before the hills was I brought forth:" ²⁶"While as yet he had not made the earth, nor the fields, nor the highest part of the dust of the world." ²⁷"When he prepared the heavens, I was there: when he set a compass upon the face of the depth:" ²⁸"When he established the clouds above: when he strengthened the fountains of the deep:" ²⁹"When he gave to the sea his decree, that the waters should not pass his commandment: when he appointed the foundations of the earth:" ³⁰"Then I was by him, as one brought up with him: and I was daily his delight, rejoicing always before him;" – Proverbs 8:22 - 30

God created satan:

[12]"Son of man, take up a lamentation upon the king of Tyrus [who most scholars agree is satan], and say unto him, Thus saith the Lord GOD; Thou sealest up the sum, full of wisdom, and perfect in beauty." [13]"Thou hast been in Eden the garden of God; every precious stone was thy covering, the sardius, topaz, and the diamond, the beryl, the onyx, and the jasper, the sapphire, the emerald, and the carbuncle, and gold: the workmanship of thy tabrets and of thy pipes was prepared in thee in the day that thou wast created." [14]"Thou art the anointed cherub that covereth; and I have set thee so: thou wast upon the holy mountain of God; thou hast walked up and down in the midst of the stones of fire." [15]"Thou wast perfect in thy ways from the day that thou wast created, till iniquity was found in thee." [16]"By the multitude of thy merchandise they have filled the midst of thee with violence, and thou hast sinned: therefore I will cast thee as profane out of the mountain of God: and I will destroy thee, O covering cherub, from the midst of the stones of fire." [17]"Thine heart was lifted up because of thy beauty, thou hast corrupted thy wisdom by reason of thy brightness: I will cast thee to the ground, I will lay thee before kings, that they may behold thee." [18]"Thou hast defiled thy sanctuaries by the multitude of thine iniquities, by the iniquity of thy traffick; therefore will I bring forth a fire from the midst of thee, it shall devour thee, and I will

bring thee to ashes upon the earth in the sight of all them
that behold thee." – Ezekiel 28:12 – 18

God is a triune God...meaning He is one operating as three, fully in agreement with each other:

From *www.merriam-webster.com* Trinity means "the unity of Father, Son, and Holy Spirit as three persons in one Godhead according to Christian dogma" or from another source "The union of three divine persons (or hypostases), the Father, Son, and Holy Spirit, in one divinity, so that all the three are one God as to substance, but three Persons (or hypostases as to individuality)."

The tri-personality of God is exclusively a Christian doctrine and a truth of Scripture. God in His existence as the Three-in-One and here are some scriptures for each:

God:

[10]"Ye are my witnesses, saith the LORD, and my
servant whom I have chosen: that ye may know and
believe me, and understand that I am he: before me there
was no God formed, neither shall there be after me." [11]"I,
even I, am the LORD; and beside me there is no saviour."
[12]"I have declared, and have saved, and I have shewed,
when there was no strange god among you: therefore ye are
my witnesses, saith the LORD, that I am God." [13]"Yea,
before the day was I am he; and there is none that can
deliver out of my hand: I will work, and who shall let it?"
– Isaiah 43:10 - 13

Jesus:

> *[1] "In the beginning was the Word, and the Word was with God, and the Word was God." [2] "The same was in the beginning with God." [3] "All things were made by him; and without him was not any thing made that was made." [4] "In him was life; and the life was the light of men."* — *John 1:1 - 4*

> *"I and my Father are one."* — *John 10:30*

> *[1] "God, who at sundry times and in divers manners spake in time past unto the fathers by the prophets," [2] "Hath in these last days spoken unto us by his Son, whom he hath appointed heir of all things, by whom also he made the worlds;" [3] "Who being the brightness of his glory, and the express image of his person, and upholding all things by the word of his power, when he had by himself purged our sins, sat down on the right hand of the Majesty on high;"* — *Hebrews 1:1 - 3*

Holy Spirit:

> *"And the earth was without form, and void; and darkness was upon the face of the deep. And the Spirit of God moved upon the face of the waters."* — *Genesis 1:2*

> *[16] "And Jesus, when he was baptized, went up straightway out of the water: and, lo, the heavens were opened unto him, and he saw the Spirit of God descending like a dove, and lighting upon him:" [17] "And lo a voice from heaven, saying, This is my beloved Son, in whom I am well pleased."* — *Matthew 3:16 - 17*

"And because ye are sons, God hath sent forth the Spirit of his Son into your hearts, crying, Abba, Father." – *Galatians 4:6*

Finally God created the Bible:

[16]*"All scripture is given by inspiration of God, and is profitable for doctrine, for reproof, for correction, for instruction in righteousness:"* [17]*"That the man of God may be perfect, throughly furnished unto all good works."* – *2 Timothy 3:16 - 17*

This is a Key point: *The Bible along with thoughts, feelings, and revelations from God help us to have faith in God. Since we know that God inspired the Bible, we can also trust that the Bible is true because God created and orchestrated it.*

How do we know if our thoughts, feelings and revelations are from God or not? He tells us in Hebrews 4:12 "For the word of God *is* quick, and powerful, and sharper than any two edged sword, piercing even to the dividing asunder of soul and spirit, and of the joints and marrow, and *is* a discerner of the thoughts and intents of the heart." His word, as we read, study, hear, research, dig into, etc. judges our heart and if we have peace, then we know it is from God. If we do not have peace, it is because God is telling us that what we are thinking/feeling is not of Him and we need to get that corrected.

We would like to end this chapter with one of the greatest songs ever written about God: ***"How Great Thou Art"***. We recommend that you go to *www.youtube.com* and in the YouTube search bar, search for *"How Great Thou Art by Carrie Underwood"* minus the quotation marks.

IN SUMMARY

We now know the following about God:

- He has always existed

- He created everything

- He created time

- He created earth and all that is on the earth

- He created mankind

- He created angels

- He create wisdom

- He created satan

- He exists in a triune form (God, Jesus, Holy Spirit)

- He created the Bible so that we can know Him.

Again to do a study on Who God Is, is outside of this book. In this chapter we simply laid some basic foundations of Who God Is to help us to be able to believe in Him so we can believe that He exists.

This chapter discussed variable **B** in our basic faith equation, **FAITH =** **A** and **B** and **C** and **D** and **E** and **F**.

In the next chapter we will look at variable **C**: God's character.

CHAPTER FOUR

God's Character

In this chapter we will be investigating variable **C** of our basic faith equation. Variable **C** is having confidence, assurance in, and reliance on God's character.

Before we get into this chapter, I (Rich) have a funny story, when this book was originally written for Walter, we had a one liner in the book to represent this variable. When the team read this, we decided it needed to be explained further. Well we have taken a one, or two line description and turned it into 13+ pages. We want to thank the team for pushing this further, thank God for His revealing, and thank Dr. Lester Sumrall for writing the book, "The Names of GOD…God's **Character** revealed through His Names". To continue the funny story, I (Rich) have the book by Dr. Sumrall and had read it many years before. I was stressing on where to even start to write about God's character and I happened to look one day at my wife's night stand and sitting there was Dr. Sumrall's book. Immediately the thought came into my head…"son why are you stressing, I have already provided you the starting point…you just need to use it". Praise God for His goodness. This chapter took more space than what we had intended, but we hope you are as blessed as we are through what God revealed.

How does one describe God's character? This is a tough one. How do we define God's character outside of our own life experience? Because our life experience can be positive or negative or both and/or could depend on the moment in time we are asked the question based on our thoughts, feelings, desires, choices, etc. To understand God's character we have to move outside of ourselves, we have to attempt to transcend into where God is. We cannot do this in ourselves, or by ourselves…we have to go to scripture to do it. As we stated in the previous chapter three, the Bible was created and orchestrated by God written through man. Therefore the best way to define God's character is to look into scripture to see what God says about Himself. He defines His character for us. God gave himself many different names in the Bible to describe His character along with countless analogies. However because this book is to define faith, we are going to limit the names we look at to the ones in this chapter.

Yahweh (Jehovah) – pronounced *yeh-ho-vaw*

God is Eternal.

This name is first used in Genesis 2:4 "These *are* the generations of the heavens and of the earth when they were created, in the day that the **LORD**[H3068] God made the earth and the heavens…" *The LORD* per Strong's H3068, means *self-Existent* or eternal/*Jehovah*

God Himself defines the root word of Strong's H3068 in Exodus 3:14 "And God said unto Moses, **I AM**[H1961] **THAT**[H834] **I AM:**[H1961] and he said, Thus shalt thou say unto the children of Israel, **I AM**[H1961] hath sent me unto you." Here the "*I AM*" H1961 means to exist or to have always been. So we can loosely translate "I AM THAT I AM" to…I exist Who/Which has always existed.

In *The Criswell Study Bible*, Dr. W. A. Criswell comments: "God exists in a way that no one or anything else does. His [supreme] nature is implied by His ever-present existence without beginning or ending. He is the only God who exists, and all other existence is dependent upon His uncaused existence." W. A. Criswell, ed., *The Criswell Study Bible* (Nashville: Thomas Nelson Publishers, 1979), p. 75.

This tells us a lot about God. He self exists, meaning He was not created. He has always been and will always be. He is the only absolute constant. Everything else that we know of, or have yet to discover was created by Him. Although some things He created are constants, they are not absolutes.

Since we brought up the word absolute, let's have a quick side bar discussion on this word to really drive the impact home of the above statement. *www.merriam-webster.com* defines the word absolute in the following ways:

(1*a):* free from imperfection : PERFECT

(1b): free from mixture : PURE

(2): completely free from constitutional or other restraint <*absolute* power>

(4): having no restriction, exception, or qualification

(5): UNQUESTIONABLE

(6*a*): independent of arbitrary standards of measurement

(7): FUNDAMENTAL, ULTIMATE

(8): perfectly embodying the nature of a thing

(9): being self-sufficient and free of external references or relationships

Let us restate what we stated about God using the references from Webster's definition of the word absolute: God is (1a) free from any imperfection, (1b) pure, (2) is not governed by anyone or anything but Himself, (4) has no restrictions, exceptions, or qualifications (like putting Dr. in front of His name implying a learned qualification), (5) is unquestionable (again going back to the fact that the Bible is the final authority), (6a) is independent of any arbitrary standards (because He set them), (7) is fundamental/ultimate (there is nothing else, He is the base of all), (8) is the perfect embodiment of everything, (meaning everything we know of through our senses screams out His existence to us), and (9) is self-sufficient and free from anything else in existence…not tied to anything else. By the way (BTW) I (Rich) love it when those that we normally think of refuting God actually prove who God is…(not Webster himself because I think he was a Christian, but all those that have come behind him and added/taken away from his work are not necessarily Christian)…kind of funny. God is absolute, and the only absolute that exists.

How exciting, fearsome, awe inspiring it is to know God…our finite minds and bodies are not fully capable of comprehending this name of God. Jim, a member of the team, said "I cannot wait to get to heaven so that I can fully understand His name!"

Jehovah-Elohim - pronounced *el-o-HEEM*

God is Triune.

The very first verse in the Bible contains the name Elohim and it reads Genesis 1:1 "In the beginning *God*[H430] created the heaven and the earth."

God, Strong's H430, is translated to the word Elohim and means gods or a plural form of God. This makes sense to us, as in Chapter Three we already spoke that God is Triune – made of 3 personalities if you will, but still one.

To go further Strong's H430 is derived from two other Strong's words: H433 meaning The Deity and H410 meaning Almighty (strong or mighty).

Putting this all together then, Elohim means the one and only God (especially when preferenced with Jehovah) who is All-mighty, or Almighty reflecting divine power (Majesty).

God is describing His character as the one and only God and He is the most powerful, strongest, mightiest being that has ever existed, or ever will exist. He is the one true God. He is the only god that deserves the worship from all of creation…no one/nothing else does.

Jehovah-Elyon - pronounced *el-yone*

The first verses in the Bible that declare this name are:

The Supreme Being. Deliverer.

> [18] *"And Melchizedek king of Salem brought forth bread and wine: and he was the priest of **the most high**[H5945] **God**."*[H410] [19] *"And he blessed him, and said, Blessed be Abram of **the most high**[H5945] **God**,*[H410] *possessor of heaven and earth:"* [20] *"And blessed be **the most high**[H5945] **God**,*[H410] *which hath delivered thine enemies into thy hand. And he gave him tithes of all."* – Genesis 14:18 - 20

The most high in Strong's H5945 means Supreme or The Supreme as a title of God. This name again declares that God is the supreme being of all which ever existed, exists or will exist.

Looking at the referenced verses Melchizedek (who many Jewish scholars think was Shem the son of Noah) came out to meet with Abram and blessed him. Melchizedek stated a couple more facts about God: He possesses everything in heaven and earth (which makes sense since

He created both) and that God is a deliverer…which again makes sense because everything is subjected to God. So God is the only one who can deliver someone from someone/something else which has a hold on them.

Another good example of this is in the book of Daniel 3:26 "Then Nebuchadnezzar came near to the mouth of the burning fiery furnace, *and* spake, and said, Shadrach, Meshach, and Abednego, ye servants of **the most high**[H5943] **God**,[H426] come forth, and come *hither.* Then Shadrach, Meshach, and Abednego, came forth of the midst of the fire."

Here, we see that King Nebuchadnezzar acted on a thought planted in his mind that he was the greatest and above all. He erects a statue in his honor and requires everyone to bow to it with penalties of death if they do not. Jewish men (Shadrach, Meshach and Abednego), who he had put in captivity and had elevated to high positions, did not bow and were thrown into a fiery furnace to die. However, God intervened and met them in the furnace to ***deliver*** them. The Strong's word H5943 is slightly different because it references the Chaldean version of (Supreme God). But the meaning is the same. When Nebuchadnezzar sees God's deliverance for these men, he confesses God's Supremeness and power above all other gods to deliver.

The Lord God is with us.

Jehovah-Shamah – pronounced *shawm*

Jehovah-Qârôb – pronounced *kaw-robe*

The Lord thy God desires to draw near us.

These two names of God, in our opinion, are closely linked to each other and describe more characteristics of God. The first one Jevohvah Shamah is found in Ezekiel 48:35 where the angel is describing to Ezekiel the new Jerusalem "It was round about eighteen thousand measures: and the name of the city from that day shall be, **The LORD is there.**"[H8033]

The LORD is there, as translated in Strong's H8033, simply means there…a place in time where God is. In the above verse God is stating that the city in which God will dwell will be called by the name "God is there"… or I exist who has always existed will be there. God is marking, if you will, this place with His presence. Here are some more verses that say similar things. Deuteronomy 16:11 "And thou shalt rejoice before the LORD thy God, thou, and thy son, and thy daughter, and thy manservant, and thy maidservant, and the Levite that is within thy gates, and the stranger, and the fatherless, and the widow, that are among you, in the place which the LORD thy God hath chosen to place his name **there**."[H8033]

In this verse, David is telling the Philistines that God has marked Israel as His territory because He is there… 1 Samuel 17:46 "This day will the LORD deliver thee [Goliath] into mine hand; and I will smite thee, and take thine head from thee; and I will give the carcases of the host of the Philistines this day unto the fowls of the air, and to the wild beasts of the earth; that all the earth may know that **there is**[H3426] a God in Israel."

In the end times God will come with a new earth and a new Jerusalem and dwell there:

> "And I heard a great voice out of heaven saying, Behold, the tabernacle of God is with men, and he will dwell with them, and they shall be his people, and God himself shall be with them, and be their God." – Revelation 21:3

> [22]"And I saw no temple therein: for the Lord God Almighty and the Lamb are the temple of it." [23]"And the city had no need of the sun, neither of the moon, to shine in it: for the glory of God did lighten it, and the Lamb is the light thereof." – Revelation 21:22 - 23

Now hold these thoughts and let's talk about the other name Jehovah-

Qârôb found in the following verses:

> *"The LORD **is nigh**[H7138] unto them that are of a broken heart; and saveth such as be of a contrite spirit."*
> *– Psalms 34:18*

> *"The LORD **is nigh**[H7138] unto all them that call upon him, to all that call upon him in truth." – Psalms 145:18*

The word nigh in Strong's H7138 is translated as near…the root word H7126 means to approach. So here God approaches to draw near those that call upon His name to seek His truth, and who are of broken heart.

Couple the above verses with the following verse Deuteronomy 4:7 "For what nation is there so great, who hath God **so nigh**[H7138] unto them, as the LORD our God is in all things that we call upon him for?"… meaning Israel is blessed to have GOD as their god because He has promised to draw near to them.

These two names together tell us that for Israel, God has put His name there/on them/has marked them and that He approaches them to be near them. However, we cannot stop there…this is the Old Testament and we now have the New Testament. Because Jesus came and extended His salvation to all mankind, He transformed What is marked (where God resides and what He is near) to WHO He resides in and has drawn near. Look at the following scriptures:

> *[15]"Whosoever shall confess that Jesus is the Son of God, God dwelleth in him, and he in God."[16]"And we have known and believed the love that God hath to us. God is love; and he that dwelleth in love dwelleth in God, and God in him."*
> *– 1 John 4:15 - 16*

Everyone that accepts Jesus as their savior (Christians) now have the name Jehovah-Shamah written on them because "God is there", (dwells in them) and they also have the name Jehovah-Qârôb written on them because God approached and drew near to them and He is now one with them in spirit. *Praise God that He worked a way to bring every man, woman, and child into His presence!!!*

El-Shaddai – pronounced *shad-dah'ee*

The name is first used in Genesis 17:1 "And when Abram was ninety years old and nine, the LORD appeared to Abram, and said unto him, I *am* **the Almighty**[H7706] God; walk before me, and be thou perfect."…and is translated as Almighty, Strong's H7706 meaning all powerful or all sufficient.

> The Almighty, All Powerful, All Sufficient.

Basically saying God is enough to meet all His own needs and therefore by default can also meet all the needs of His creation.

This is a comforting thought for us. As we know satan and our natural selves are always working to drive a wedge between God and us by having us doubt who God is and who we are in relation to God. (To be discussed in Chapter 9) However, by God's own name He is sufficient. He needs no one else to help Him. He is sufficient for us…we need no other but Him to help us. To really understand this, let's look at the definition of sufficient taken again from *www.merriam-webster.com*

"(1 *a*): enough to meet the needs of a situation or a proposed end"

"*(1b)*: being a sufficient condition"

"(2): QUALIFIED, COMPETENT"

And listing some of the Synonyms from Webster's: "SUFFICIENT, ENOUGH, ADEQUATE, COMPETENT, mean being what is necessary, or desirable. SUFFICIENT suggests a close meeting of a need. ENOUGH is less exact in suggestion than SUFFICIENT. ADEQUATE may imply barely meeting a requirement. COMPETENT suggests measuring up to all requirements without question or being adequately adapted to an end."

So again using God as the example, God is enough to adequately meet all the needs of His creation. (We would use the word abundantly rather than adequately but that is just us) He is competent or knows what is needed and when it is needed and has the requirements without question to meet the need.

But it gets even better…let's look at the next name.

Jehovah-Jireh - pronounced *j-ho-vaw jir-eh*

This name is only used once in the Bible and it deals with a test that God gave Abraham. The scripture reference revolves around God asking Abraham to sacrifice his son Isaac:

> **God will Provide, He supplies our needs.**

> [6] *"And Abraham took the wood of the burnt offering, and laid it upon Isaac his son; and he took the fire in his hand, and a knife; and they went both of them together."* [7] *"And Isaac spake unto Abraham his father, and said, My father: and he said, Here am I, my son. And he said, Behold the fire and the wood: but where is the lamb for a burnt offering?"* [8] *"And Abraham said, My son, God will provide himself a lamb for a burnt offering: so they went both of them together."* [9] *"And they came to*

the place which God had told him of; and Abraham built an altar there, and laid the wood in order, and bound Isaac his son, and laid him on the altar upon the wood." *¹⁰"And Abraham stretched forth his hand, and took the knife to slay his son." ¹¹"And the angel of the LORD called unto him out of heaven, and said, Abraham, Abraham: and he said, Here am I." ¹²"And he said, Lay not thine hand upon the lad, neither do thou any thing unto him: for now I know that thou fearest God, seeing thou hast not withheld thy son, thine only son from me." ¹³"And Abraham lifted up his eyes, and looked, and behold behind him a ram caught in a thicket by his horns: and Abraham went and took the ram, and offered him up for a burnt offering in the stead of his son." ¹⁴"And Abraham called the name of that place **Jehovahjireh:**ᴴ³⁰⁷⁰ as it is said to this day, In the mount of the LORD **it shall be seen**."*ᴴ⁷²⁰⁰
– Genesis 22:6 - 14

In Strong's H7200 *it shall be seen*, is translated as to see or seen. Jehovahjireh H3070 uses the root word H7200 and is translated I exist Who has always existed will see (remember Jehovah is the English form of Yahweh). The translators use the context around this name of God and fully translate it as "God will provide". Do you "see" it? (pun intended) I (Rich) didn't see it at first. I didn't understand how the translators made the jump from to see - to will provide. Since this is the only place it is mentioned in the Bible, it made it a little harder. However since we are talking about faith let's put what we have learned into practice to this point. Again, I did not get the translation. I said to myself, "I do not get the translation". The thought came into my head, "You should ask". So I acted on that thought and said "Father, I do not get this", I kept rolling it over in my mind and about 5 minutes later the following came to me as a thought from God:

So let's take this a step back and look at El-Shaddai and Jehovahjireh together… One could think of it this way El-Shaddai, Jehovahjireh or in English "I, the All-sufficient, exist Who has always existed will see". What will He see? He sees our needs. What will He do with our needs? ***HE WILL PROVIDE! Praise be to His name!*** God answered my thought with a thought which turned into a feeling of joy and praise!

God knows (sees or has seen) what our needs and wants are. He can sufficiently meet our needs even when we might not see it is Him because we are blinded to the situation or the desire we are in. He always provides just in time and at just the right time to prove He is in control and that we should rely on Him to provide. God does the miraculous in meeting the needs we cannot and would never be able to meet ourselves. When we praise Him for providing in those needs that we could never meet for ourselves (example reconciliation with God through salvation)… ***He is praised as THE ALMIGHTY!*** Amen!

One of the team members helping with this book made the statement "Sufficiency trumps abundance any day of the week". We always want abundance, but we live in the sufficiency of God.

If you were excited about Jehovah-Jireh wait until the next name…

Jehovah- Repheka - pronounced *raw-faw*

The scripture reference for this name is Exodus 15:26 "… If thou wilt diligently hearken to the voice of the LORD thy God, and wilt do that which is right in his sight, and wilt give ear to his commandments, and keep all his statutes, I will put none of these diseases upon thee, which I have brought upon the Egyptians: for I *am* the LORD that **healeth**[H7495] thee."

The word *healeth* H7495 is translated in Strong's as mend/cure/to make whole again. Here are some other references in the Bible to the same name:

> *2 "Bless the LORD, O my soul, and forget not all his benefits:"*
> *3 "Who forgiveth all thine iniquities; who healeth*H7495 *all thy diseases;"*
> *4 "Who redeemeth thy life from destruction; who crowneth thee with lovingkindness and tender mercies;"*
> *5 "Who satisfieth thy mouth with good things; so that thy youth is renewed like the eagle's." – Psalms 103:2 - 5*

God is the healer of all our diseases, physical and emotional and personal. Jesus makes us whole.

In these verses we see, God can heal us from all diseases. Note that in Exodus it came with conditions that we obey Him…more on this in Chapter 7. But the point here is that God is able to heal us of all diseases known and unknown. This is a physical healing.

Going further, Psalms 147:2 - 3 "The LORD doth build up Jerusalem: he gathereth together the outcasts of Israel." 3"He healeth **the broken**H7665 **in heart**,H3820 and bindeth up their wounds."

Here God is healing the broken in heart…what does that mean? Broken heartedness is usually an emotional wound or issue. So these verses state that God is a healer for our emotions or God can heal the emotional wounds/issues we have.

Further, Isaiah 30:26 "Moreover the light of the moon shall be as the light of the sun, and the light of the sun shall be sevenfold, as the light of seven days, in the day that the LORD bindeth up the breach of his people, and healeth the **stroke**H4273 of their wound."

This verse references the stroke of ones wound or the physical wounds that come in other ways. For example, something that we break or a cut whether it is an accident or intentionally caused by someone else. God is a healer of all wounds that we might receive.

And then just for kicks let's throw in these verses to drive the point home:

> ^{4} *"Surely he hath borne our* **griefs**,^{H2483} *and carried our* **sorrows**:^{H4341} *yet we did esteem him* **stricken**,^{H5060} **smitten**^{H5221} *of God, and afflicted."* ^{5} *"But he was wounded for our* **transgressions**,$^{H4480\ H6588}$ *he was bruised for our* **iniquities**:$^{H4480\ H5771}$ *the chastisement of our peace was upon him; and with his* **stripes**^{H2250} *we are healed."*
> *– Isaiah 53:4 - 5*

These verses are taken from Isaiah 53 which predict Jesus's coming and what His coming will do for mankind. Before translating this verse let us stop and share that Man is made of three parts, or lives in three realms: physical realm, emotional realm, and spiritual realm. Nothing hidden here these are just the three realms we live in. God made provisions to heal us in all three of these areas in the above scripture: Jesus (God) will take on our *griefs* (Strong's H2483 translated as diseases), *sorrows* (Strong's H4341 emotional wounds), *will be stricken and smitten* (Strong's H5060 and H5221 physical wounds), *bares our transgressions* (Strong's H6588 rebellious spirit against God (Adamic fall and our own attitudes toward God)), *bruised with our iniquities* (Strong's H5771 moral sins we personally commit), and because of what Jesus went through, the stripes beating death etc. we are *healed* (Strong's H7495 mended back together/cured/made whole again) when we accept Him as our personal savior.

God is the only healer…He is the one who has always existed, who sees, who provides, who can make us **COMPLETELY WHOLE AGAIN! That deserves an AMEN!!!** And again Praise be to GOD THE MOST HIGH and His goodness towards us and for all HE has provided for us!

Jehovah-Tsidqenu – prounounced *tseh-dek*

We see this name used in the scripture reference Jerimiah 23:6 "In his days Judah shall be saved, and Israel shall dwell safely: and this *is* his name whereby he shall be called, THE LORD **OUR RIGHT-EOUSNESS**."[H6664]

God is The Right (Just) One.

In this verse *our righteousness,* Strong's H6664, means "the right" in a natural, moral, and legal sense. It can also mean to be just. It is taken from the root word H6663 which means "to be right". How fitting with the ground work we have already laid so far. In the name Yahweh, we already discussed that God was absolute. This name takes God's absoluteness and applies it to His character of being right. He is the only being who is right naturally, morally and legally. You could read it in this way: I exist Who has always existed am The Right.

How good for God's creation that He is The Right One. In every sense naturally, morally, and legally He defines what is right because He is Right. His very being defines it. This is where God stands alone when we start talking about all the other "gods" who man has created. No other god in man's existence "defines" what is right. What is all the other gods downfall… their moral character? As a quick example look at the Greek gods like Zeus who was constantly having affairs with mortal women cheating on his god wife. Man in his sin was/is bringing God down to our level when we create our own gods and put man's characteristics on them. When we do this we think it is justice to be evil. However, God is not evil because by His own character He embodies being Right.

Not only does God define what is Right, but He also defines what is Clean.

Jehovah-Qâdôsh – prounounced *kaw-doshe*

The name Clean is seen in Psalms 99:9 "Exalt the LORD our God, and worship at his holy hill; for the LORD our God *is holy*."[H6918]

God is Clean (Holy).

The word *Holy* in Strong's H6918 is translated as sacred. The root word H6942 means "to be clean". These translations are telling us that God is Clean. Most often this is in relation to being ceremonially or morally clean. The word clean in American English has really been watered down. However, per *www.merriam-webster.com* there are a few definitions that get the point across that I will list:

"(1 *a*): free from dirt or pollution"

"*(1 b)*: free from contamination or disease"

"(2 *a*): PURE"

"(3 *a*): free from moral corruption or sinister connections of any kind"

"(4): ceremonially or spiritually pure"

From these definitions we can glean when God says He is clean, He is (1a) free from anything that is dirty or polluted, (1b) free from any contamination, (2a) pure, (3a) free from any moral wrong, and (4) ceremonially and spiritually pure. God defines what is clean, because He is Clean. This is why it was so important for the Israelites be clean because God wanted to be There among them...to draw them Near. However because of the Adamic fall, we by nature are not clean. So God instituted the whole sacrificial commandments to keep the Israelites clean (so they would be in clean standing) and He could live among them. Through the sacrifice of Himself (Jesus), today Christians are in a clean standing before God because His own blood covers us to make us clean.

In Chapter 3 describing Who God Is, we said that He created everything and it was good. He made **all** things clean because He is clean. However, with the Adamic fall, knowing good from evil came into play. What is evil? I (Rich) would contend that evil takes what God made as good, beyond the limits God placed on it, and at that point it becomes evil, or sinful because it is open rebellion against God. For example: food is good for us, but if we eat more of it than we should, going past the limits God set, then it becomes bad for us. Another one that is big in this day in age is sex...God created sex as good, but when it is taken past its limits, anytime it is done outside of a man and woman marriage, it is bad. Another good example... satan. God Himself says satan was created in perfection and beauty, ordained with every precious stone and meant to walk where none of the rest of creation was allowed to. But what happened, satan took what God created him to be past his limits and therefore became bad/evil. Because of this evil, this bad, this spoilage, satan was/is no longer clean and therefore God cast him out of the heavens. (Further explained in Chapter 11)

God is not evil. He contains no sin, He cannot because He is The Right and He is The Clean. He cannot stand evil, evil and God cannot be in the same place at the same time because evil is the opposite of being Right and being Clean. Evil is subjected to God and cannot stand in tandem, cannot stand with, cannot stand next to, cannot stand up against God. This is why in many encounters Jesus had with people they asked Him to leave… because they knew by His very being that He is The ONE who is Right and who is Clean.

Remember God is Absolute. His very existence defines what is Right and what is Clean.

Jehovah-Tsebaoth – pronounced *tseb-aw-aw*

> [45] "Then said David to the Philistine [Golaith], Thou comest to me with a sword, and with a spear, and with a shield: but I come to thee in the name of the LORD **of hosts**,[H6635] the God of the armies of Israel, whom thou hast defied."[46] "This day will the LORD **deliver**[H5462] thee into mine hand; and I will smite thee, and take thine head from thee; and I will give the carcases of the host of the Philistines this day unto the fowls of the air, and to the wild beasts of the earth; that all the earth may know that there is a God in Israel." – 1 Samuel 17:45 - 46

The Lord of Host (God of Battles) God fights on behalf of the Church and on behalf of us as individuals. He sees us through.

The definition for *hosts* Strong's H6635 means to amass (gather together) persons (things) and comes from the root word H6633 which implies amassing an army. With this name, God is telling us that He exists Who has always existed and is over all His army: the angels, the Israelites and Christians.

God Himself is captain of the army in His form of Jesus. We see this clearly stated in:

> [11] *"And I saw heaven opened, and behold a white horse; and he that sat upon him was called Faithful and True, and in righteousness he doth judge and make war."* [12] *"His eyes were as a flame of fire, and on his head were many crowns; and he had a name written, that no man knew, but he himself."* [13] *"And he was clothed with a vesture dipped in blood: and his name is called The Word of God."* [14] *"And the armies which were in heaven followed him upon white horses, clothed in fine linen, white and clean."* [15] *"And out of his mouth goeth a sharp sword, that with it he should smite the nations: and he shall rule them with a rod of iron: and he treadeth the winepress of the fierceness and wrath of Almighty God."* [16] *"And he hath on his vesture and on his thigh a name written, KING OF KINGS, AND LORD OF LORDS."*
> *– Revelation 19:11 - 16*

These verses from the book of Revelation show us that God does battle and He battles all who oppose Him. He battles for the Israel nation and for the church, His bride. Even down to the end of time, when the final battle will take place, God will lead out His armies to finish this battle between Him and evil forever... Praise God !!!

Another thing to take away from this characteristic of God is that He and His army never lose. In fact He does not just win, but He delivers (I Sam 17:46 above). Here are some Hebrew word translations for the word *deliver*, Strong's H5462, to snatch away; to give back; to turn back (as in time like before an event happened); to shut up or stop; to free; to restore;

to rescue; to retrieve; to ransom; to make the other yield; to pull off (strip away); to redeem; and to shield. Each of these is a different Hebrew word for deliver. God does all of these for us when we are with Him in the battles we face. ***Praise be to His Name JEHOVAH- TSEBAOTH***

We have looked at this name from a macro standpoint where God is the leader of hosts for the nation of Israel and for the church, but this name is much more personal than a corporate standpoint, God is the leader of armies to battle for you individually. Let us look at Hannah the Prophet Samuel's mom:

> *¹⁰"And she [Hannah] was in bitterness of soul, and prayed unto the LORD, and wept sore." ¹¹"And she vowed a vow, and said, O LORD **of hosts**,^H6635 if thou wilt indeed look on the affliction of thine handmaid, and remember me, and not forget thine handmaid, but wilt give unto thine handmaid a man child, then I will give him unto the LORD all the days of his life, and there shall no razor come upon his head." – 1 Samuel 1:10 - 11*

We see Hannah was in a bitter rivalry with Elkanah's other wife. This other woman, who was probably jealous that Elkanah loved Hannah more than he loved her, constantly provoked fights with Hannah reminding her that she had no children. This upset Hannah greatly. She called the other wife her adversary and she was in a great struggle. She asked the LORD of hosts to help her, to deliver her, her and her alone. She understood that although God is the leader of armies who battle for the nation of Israel and for the church, He also battles for us as individuals. She asks the leader of armies to help her. Stop and think about this statement, she was in a struggle, pain, hurt, and she asked/pleaded with God to deliver her from this. God in turn gave her a word through Eli and told her by this time next year she would have a son. She took God at His word and left in peace.

> [18] *"And she said, Let thine handmaid find grace in thy sight. So the woman went her way, and did eat, and her countenance was no more sad."* [19] *"And they rose up in the morning early, and worshipped before the LORD, and returned, and came to their house to Ramah: and Elkanah knew Hannah his wife; and the LORD remembered her."* [20] *"Wherefore it came to pass, when the time was come about after Hannah had conceived, that she bare a son, and called his name Samuel, saying, Because I have asked him of the LORD."* – 1 Samuel 1:18 – 20

She understood the word she received was a promise and she left that place waiting for God to deliver on that promise. This is another stop moment, not only did she ask/plead with God to help her, she trusted that God had her back. Even though she was going through all this, God had her back and she asked Him to come with all His armies, all His might to help her.

Let's then look at her worship when she dedicated Samuel to God:

> [1] *"And Hannah prayed, and said, My heart rejoiceth in the LORD, mine horn is exalted in the LORD: my mouth is enlarged over mine enemies; because I rejoice in thy salvation."* [2] *"There is none holy as the LORD: for there is none beside thee: neither is there any rock like our God."* [3] *"Talk no more so exceeding proudly; let not arrogancy come out of your mouth: for the LORD is a God of knowledge, and by him actions are weighed."*

⁴ "The bows of the mighty men are broken, and they that stumbled are girded with strength." ⁵ "They that were full have hired out themselves for bread; and they that were hungry ceased: so that the barren hath born seven; and she that hath many children is waxed feeble." ⁶ "The LORD killeth, and maketh alive: he bringeth down to the grave, and bringeth up." ⁷ "The LORD maketh poor, and maketh rich: he bringeth low, and lifteth up." ⁸ "He raiseth up the poor out of the dust, and lifteth up the beggar from the dunghill, to set them among princes, and to make them inherit the throne of glory: for the pillars of the earth are the LORD'S, and he hath set the world upon them." ⁹ "He will keep the feet of his saints, and the wicked shall be silent in darkness; for by strength shall no man prevail." ¹⁰ "The adversaries of the LORD shall be broken to pieces; out of heaven shall he thunder upon them: the LORD shall judge the ends of the earth; and he shall give strength unto his king, and exalt the horn of his anointed."
– 1 Samuel 2:1 - 10

We see she gives God all the glory. She praises Him. She recounts her deliverance. She speaks to all those who are oppressed and lets them know He is their God and they can ASK Him for help and He will bring His might and His armies to their rescue. **Praise God for His goodness to us!!!**

So we clearly see in these verses **God is the Lord of Hosts** for the nation of Israel, the Christian church and for us as individuals.

Side note: We are not sure if we were able to do the name Jehovah Tseboath justice and if this section is not making sense, we would suggest listening to the song *Whom Shall I Fear [God of Angel Armies]* sung by Chris Tomlin.

Jehovah-Nissi – prounounced *yeh-ho-vaw nis-see*

Moses the great man of God used this name to describe God's character in verse Exodus 17:15 "And Moses built an altar, and called the name of it **Jehovahnissi:**"H3071

Jehovahnissi is translated in Strong's H3071 as "The Lord is my Banner." The word banner comes from the root word

> The Lord is our Banner - Our lives should always shine for Him.

standard which goes back to the kingdoms and armies of old where they would have a long pole with a decorative cloth tied to it representing who they were. Even today most countries have a standard /banner/ flag (what we call it today) which represents the country. For example, the American Flag represents the United States of America (USA). It is made up of 13 stripes of alternating red and white. These stripes represent the original 13 English colonies that banded together and revolted against England. The blue represents union. The blue square contains 50 stars representing the 50 states that are bonded together in a union of laws and borders. So the American Flag has meaning in its design and represents the USA...a union of 50 states born out of 13 colonies banding together to gain independence from England. That is what the USA flag means. That is what represents the country of USA.

Moses calls the altar Jehovahnissi. He named the altar that name. If we look at the rest of the Exodus 17, Moses builds and names the altar after the Israelite community fights the Amalekites and defeats them. He builds an altar to give glory and honor to God for providing victory for the Israelite people and leaves the altar there as a *memorial* to all who pass signifying what God did for them. *Hold this thought for one paragraph as it is an important one.*

Going further into Exodus 20, God gives the Israelite people the Ten Commandments. After that God gives some instruction on altars… Exodus 20:24 "An altar of earth thou shalt make unto me, and shalt sacrifice thereon thy burnt offerings, and thy peace offerings, thy sheep, and thine oxen: **in all**[H3605] **places**[H4725] **where**[H834] **I record**[H2142] (H853) **my name**[H8034] **I will come**[H935] **unto**[H413] **thee, and I will bless**[H1288] **thee.**"

Let's focus on the bolded words. "…in all places where I record my name, I will come unto thee, and I will bless thee." God is saying everywhere the Israelite people will build an altar to Him (of remembrance of Him, giving Him praise, worship, sacrifices (to atone for sins) and peace sacrifices (thanks offering, peace offering, first fruits offering, etc.)) God would mark those spots as *memorials*, as Holy for the people to remember Him for who He is and for what He has done for them. The memorial would remind them of how *God had blessed them.*

So back to our thought that was held…what does this name of God mean to us as Christians? It means everything! We cannot be a Christian without God doing something for us! What has He done? He offered SALVATION to us…and when we accept His son Jesus as our savior we now become marked, we are no longer bound by rocks and dirt as an altar to remind us of God and what He has done, because we are LIVING memorials / altars /BANNERS reminding all who meet/ know/pass/see/ observe us of who GOD IS and what HE HAS DONE! Everything we say, do, act, react should be showing Jesus through us. We should be so full of Jesus, and He should be shining so brightly through us that anyone we come in contact with doesn't even notice we are there because all they can see is JESUS…**May He be the BANNER people see THROUGH YOU as well. AMEN!!!!**

Jehovah-Shalom – prounounced *yeh-ho-vaw shaw-lome*

Gideon one of the judges of Israel before there was a king, used this name to describe God's character. We can find this name in the following scriptures:

God is Peace.

> [22] *"And when Gideon perceived that he was an angel of the LORD, Gideon said, Alas, O Lord GOD! for because I have seen an angel of the LORD face to face."* [23] *"And the LORD said unto him, Peace[H7965] be unto thee; fear not: thou shalt not die."* [24] *"Then Gideon built an altar there unto the LORD, and called it Jehovahshalom:[H3073] unto this day it is yet in Ophrah of the Abiezrites."*
> – Judges 6:22 - 24

Strong's translates *Jehovahshalom* H3073 as Jehovah **IS** peace. This is made of two words, the one for Yahweh (Jehovah) we have already studied and then H7965 which means peace. The word peace gets its meaning from the root word H7999 which means "to *be safe* (in mind, body and/or estate)" which if you think it through; we can only have peace when we feel safe in every way. If we do not feel safe in all realms (physical, emotional, and spiritual) then we have no peace, we only have worry, fear, anxiety, etc.

Quick overview of the story, God sends an angel to speak to Gideon to have Gideon deliver the Israelites from the oppression of the coming raids from the Midianites and Amalekites. Gideon realized the experience for what it was and becomes fearful. Then God speaks to him directly and offers him PEACE that he will not die for hearing the message from God. What does Gideon do? He builds an altar (remember what we said in the name of Nissi) as a memorial/a testimony to his experience with the angel and what God promised. He called that memorial Jehovah IS peace. Meaning God is peace, He is the only one that can make one safe in mind, in body, and in estate (property). He extended His peace to Gideon, the Israelites, and extends His peace to us. God wants us to be at peace with Him…to be covered in His peace, which is why Jesus came to earth…but more about that when we discuss variable **D**.

What we find interesting in the story of Gideon is that Gideon built the altar and used the name of God BEFORE God did anything. Gideon believed God and acted on what God told him to do. Here are some highlights of what Gideon had to overcome: first he had to overcome his own people from his town who wanted to kill him for smashing down an idol; then he had to get people to believe him that God was going to deliver them from the invaders, then he had to rally an army, then God told him he had rallied too many 32,000, then God had him take 32,000 people down to 300, then God told him to take 300 against the invaders and defeat them. We are never told how many were with the invaders, but think about that, God said no to 32,000 people and took that number down to 300. That is not even one percent of what he started with…it is 20 people less than one percent. God could not have used Gideon if Gideon would not have taken God's character of peace to heart. This is applicable to us today. God is a God of miracles. He lives in the realm of the miraculous. He cannot use us in our own strength, we are insufficient. He uses what we have and adds Himself to it using all the names we have already studied. Again think about that…let it settle in…let it soak in deep into your soul because that is where peace is at. This is jumping ahead a little bit and will be explained further, but if you know God told you to do something, and you know beyond any shadow of doubt that God told you, then all you have to do is do, God will do the rest. *He extends His peace when we do what He wants…when we are obedient.* God told Joshua to be strong and courageous. We do not possess the ability to be strong and courageous, but we believe *when we do what God tells us, He GIVES us the strength and courage because now we are at peace.*

God IS peace!

Jehovah-Rachûm – prounounced *rakh-oom*

Jehovah-Chânan – prounounced *channûn*

God is Mercy.

God is Kindness / Compassion.

These two names are found in Psalms 103:8 "The LORD *is* merciful[H7349] and gracious,[H2587] slow to anger, and plenteous in mercy."

From Strong's, *merciful* H7439 is translated as compassionate with a root word of H7355 which means to fondle. Since the word fondle has such a negative connotation in our day in age, we looked up the meaning in *www.merriam-webster.com* and found the meaning, outside of a sexual connotation, is "to touch or handle (something) in a gentle way and/or to handle tenderly, lovingly, or lingeringly". As a father I (Rich) would equate this to when my wife, or I hold our children in a loving embrace, petting their head or stroking their back when hugging them. If you look at it in a parent to child relationship, the word would mean to communicate love toward another through touching outside of sexual intimacy.

The word *gracious* in Strong's H2587 means gracious, and comes from the root word H2603 meaning "to *bend* or stoop in kindness to an inferior".

Finally the word *mercy*, Strong's H2617, is translated as kindness.

We have defined the main words in this verse and now let's think through what they mean. God is compassionate…He wants to show love

73

to us in the same way that a parent would show love to a child. He is gracious…He doesn't just stand there over us like an overbearing person, He "bends" down like a parent getting down at eye level with their child to show closeness and contact with their child. Couple this with the name Qârôb "to draw near, or allow to approach" which shows He wants to be close to His creation. He wants to show us kindness. Just like a loving parent would do with their child.

To the team, these names prove that God did not simply create creation and then walk away and say, get to it. He wants to be there/draw near/ come down/bend/stoop from the heavens and get close to His creation to touch it/be in it/interact with it/hold it in his hands/embrace it/and show it who He is.

Look at what God was doing with His creation way back at the beginning, Genesis 3:8 "And they heard the voice of the LORD God walking in the garden in the cool of the day: and Adam and his wife hid themselves from the presence of the LORD God amongst the trees of the garden." This shows us that even in the beginning, God desired to commune with and be part of His creation. God walked in His creation seeking mankind out to be with them. God did this when He saved Noah, He did it with Abraham, He did it with the nation of Israel, and He did it with Jesus. With Jesus though, it all changed. With Jesus He was gracious (Chânan) (bended Himself into man's form and became one of us) so that He could show us in very real terms that He *is* there (Shamah), *is* approachable (Qârôb), and *is* compassionate (Rachûm) even allowing His creation to touch Him and to touch them back (physically, emotionally, and spiritually).

A lot of people who do not know God ask how can one man (Jesus) have had such a huge impact on the world from the time He was born until now…the answer is simple, ***nothing is the same after God touches it***.

We have come to the end of the discussing God's character, but we have one
more name to discuss. It is as important for
us to understand as the previous names we
have looked at. This one describes God's

God is Love.

character as love. The word for this is **Agapē**. Let's look at two scriptures
that speak to God being love:

> *"He that loveth not knoweth not God; for* **God**[G2316]
> *is*[G2076] **love.**[G26] *– 1 John 4:8*

And

> *"...we have known and believed the love that God
> hath to us.* **God**[G2316] *is*[G2076] **love;**[G26] *and he that dwelleth
> in love dwelleth in God, and God in him." – 1 John 4:16*

The interpretation for *love* is Strong's G26 and means love. But not
necessarily in the terms we think of it today. We have to dig deeper into the
meaning. Going further G26 has a root of G25 which means again love.
We have not gotten much traction yet. ☺ We need to go and compare the
word of G5368 to get an understanding of what the word love is trying
to convey. Strong's G5368 says the following: "*have affection* for (denoting
personal attachment, as a matter of sentiment or feeling; while G25 is
wider, embracing especially the judgment and the *deliberate* assent of the
will as a matter of principle, duty and propriety: the two thus stand related
very much".

So what does this mean? Good question, let's explore. We believe the
key here is in the G5368 explanation of the word love. It breaks love into
two pieces the heart and the mind. The heart represents passion, desire,
affection, longing for something, or someone. The mind represents as the
Strong's explanation "the *deliberate* assent of the will as a matter of principle,
duty and propriety". So the word Agapē brings both pieces together into

one word. Think of it this way, when we "fall in love" it is all from the heart there is little logical processing going on in the brain other than focusing on the desire of the heart. However as Dr. Gary Chapman explains in his books about the five love languages, when the "in love, or falling in love" feelings wear off, then our minds (logical part if you use that loosely) takes over and we make a choice ("a *deliberate* assent of the will") to love the person.

Per the scriptures above then, God is Agapē. God is Love. He again defines love, because He is love. And He loves **ALL** His creation with all His passion, desire, feelings, affections, longings with all His deliberate will. But if we just stopped here, we would only be talking about mankind's love. God's love is more than that. Look at the names Yahweh (Jehovah) and Qâdôsh, which both mean pure. We are not pure, we are only pure when we are clothed in Jesus' shed blood. It covers us to make us pure. However, God IS pure. This means, **God is the purest form of love.** There is no malice, no evil intent, no harboring resentment, no ulterior motive that God has against His creation. His love is pure and in the purest form.

We saved this name for last as it is the prelude and bridge into the next variable of our equation…God's Character towards man. However, before we jump to the next chapter, let's hold this thought and summarize what we have learned in this chapter.

I (Rich) have been wondering how does one capstone such wonderful revelations? I have been sitting here at my computer listening to 104.9 FM The River, a Christian radio station, while writing the chapters for variables **B**, **C**, and **D** and heard the song, *"Your Great Name"*. We recommend that you go to *www.youtube.com* and in the YouTube search bar, search for *"Your Great Name by Natalie Grant"* minus the quotation marks. Or another good one to listen to is *El-Shaddai* sung by Amy Grant

IN SUMMARY

God is: self-existent; Eternal; Almighty; one and only Divine Power; Supreme Being; Deliverer; desires to be with us; desires to be near us; All Sufficient; All Powerful; our Provide;, our Healer; Right; Just; Clean; Holy; Pure; Lord of the Hosts; God of battles; our Banner; Peace; Mercy; Kindness; Compassion; and Love, in fact He is everything to all mankind.

- We now know this about God's character:
- Yahweh has **always** existed
- Elohim **is** in three forms (God, Jesus, Holy Spirit)
- Elyon **is** The Supreme
- Shamah **is** There (or wants to be there with us)
- Qârôb **is** Near (approachable)
- Shaddai **is** Almighty
- Jireh **is** the Provider
- Repheka **is** the Healer
- Tsidqenu **is** Right
- Qâdôsh **is** Clean
- Tsebaoth **is** Over All
- Nissi **is** the Banner
- Shalom **is** Peace
- Rachûm **is** Compassionate (wants to hold)
- Chânan **is** Gracious (bends to our level)
- Agapē IS LOVE

This chapter discussed variable **C** (God's Character) in our basic faith equation of **FAITH** = **A** and **B** and **C** and **D** and **E** and **F**.

We hope this chapter blessed you as much as it has us! Now to the chapter on how His character is reflected to mankind.

CHAPTER FIVE

God's Character Toward Mankind

In this chapter we will be investigating variable **D** of our basic faith equation. Variable **D** is having confidence, assurance in, reliance on God's character toward mankind–specifically you and I.

For myself (Rich), this is the variable that started the discussions with Walter and ultimately led to this book. Walter and I were standing just outside of the door of the sanctuary one day while our pastor was talking about Faith and explaining that God can do anything. When I (Rich) heard this statement, I turned to Walter and said *"I know God can. I know He can do anything because He is God. Nothing is too small or impossible for Him. That has never been my issue. My issue comes in with this... I know He can, but will He? Why would He? Why would He care?"* I have to admit that, if I remember correctly, I was frustrated about something I was praying for and not getting an answer on. To be honest I do not exactly remember what it was, but I do remember that after listening to Walter, I was not praying in faith because I did not understand what faith was. I believe this was in 2007. For two years, I listened to Walter explain what he had learned over the last 60+ years about faith, as often as I could. The thought came to me one day in the summer of 2009, the revelations Walter has been given needed to be documented so that a wider audience can truly understand faith and pray in faith. Because of that thought, we documented Walter's thoughts into this book. (THANK YOU team !!!)

So let's really get to the nitty gritty of the questions I (Rich) had: 1) Will God do it? 2) Why would God do it? and 3) Why would God care about what I am asking?

Let's first go back to creation and restate a foundational truth: God created everything and *He saw that everything was GOOD*! Did you hear that ring in your mind? He did not create everything ok. He did not create everything somewhat. He did not create everything and when done say I messed up, let me start over, He didn't say some of the things were good and others were not…He created everything and *HE saw it was ALL GOOD*!, Genesis 1:31 "And God **saw**[H7200] everything that he had made, and, behold, *it was* **very**[H3966] **good**.[H2896] And the evening and the morning were the sixth day. In the prior verses to 31 it states "God saw that *it was* very good." Strong's translates the word *good* as H2896 which means good. However, the root word H2895 means "to be good" So what is being said in the prior verses in Genesis 1 and in this verse, God saw it was good or that creation embodied good. It was good in the purest sense of the word because as we stated before, God is pure. Further, if you remember, the name of God, *Jireh* (will provide), has the root word of Strong's H7200 which means to see. So when it says "God **saw**[H7200] that *it was* good.", we could translate that as God was constantly looking over His creation and ensuring that it was all good, pure, that anything missing was provided for. We wanted to lay this foundational truth because it is an important base on what God thought of mankind when we were created. He saw mankind and called us GOOD.

So the funny thing here, and what I (Rich) did not know at the time is, most of the names of God we studied in the prior chapters already answered my 3 questions. Let's look at them again:

- Shamah - **is** There

  God wants to be there with us, just like He used to be in the beginning with Adam and Eve. He is among us. After Jesus, for Christians, He is there in us. We are now one with Him.

- Qârôb - **is** Near

  God allows us to approach Him. In Old Testament it was through the priests and through sacrifice of animals. Only then could He approach the Israel community. After Jesus, He approaches us inviting us into salvation. After Salvation, He is now in us and because we are covered in Jesus blood we can approach God. (What an awesome truth!)

- Shaddai - **is** Almighty

  God is sufficient to meet our needs, and many times our wants. He is the only one that can do both, and through Jesus, meets our biggest need of being back in relationship with Him.

- Jireh - **is** the Provider

  God is constantly watching us, not to see if we are bad and then to punish us, but rather to meet our needs. Not only is He sufficient to meet our needs, but He proactively watches over us to meet our needs at just the right time to show us and the world His character towards mankind. He wants to show us that He is watching over us and wants to provide for us. Our problem is we do not pay attention to where our blessings are coming from.

- Repheka - **is** the Healer

  God is the only one who can make us whole again physically/emotionally/spiritually, and whole in relationship with Him again through Jesus. He wants us to be whole, He created us to be whole, He wants to restore us to wholeness in Him.

• Tsidqenu - **is** Right

God set down for us what is right, to define it for us, to give example through Jesus' life, so we know how to live within the proper limits. I (Rich) once heard this explanation on why God has commandments for us to follow. I apologize to the person I heard it from because it was 20+ years ago and I do not remember who said it, but this has stuck with me since I heard it. "When man complains to God on why He has commandments (rules) that we must follow, it is like a train complaining it is limited to the tracks it must run on. Think about that…when a train derails it is a bad thing, it is a mess, it can be very dangerous depending on what the train is pulling. When we take ourselves off of God's tracks (His law, precepts, wisdom, commandments, rules, etc.) our life becomes like a train that is derailed…a great big and sometimes a disastrous mess to ourselves and others. Then someone has to come back in and repair all the damage and get the train back on the tracks again. When we hit rock bottom, God is there waiting for us, and helps us get back on our tracks to be what He created us to be." When we are on God's tracks for our life, we can do what we need to do with full assurance that God has us headed in the right direction with minimum friction.

• Qâdôsh - **is** Clean

God is pure and free from any imperfection from a moral and ceremonial standpoint. He has defined for us what is clean and what is not clean. Again this goes back to His laws, commands, precepts, wisdom, "rules" which set for us the limits we are to live within. This is beyond telling us what not to do or what we can't do, it is to tell us what we can and should do to live a life pleasing to Him. To be clean, so Jesus can shine through us and touch those around us who do not know Him. It is awesome to know He already thought of what we would need to know, give it to us, and then provide the Holy Spirit to guide us with our conscious to let us know when we are going to make a bad choice.

- Tsebaoth - **is** Over All

    This name again tells us that God is over all His hosts, over all His army and commander of His army. It extends from the spiritual realm from God and His angels to our realm as Christians for fighting the injustices of the world both physically and spiritually helping those who are not able to help themselves. God is with us in the battles we face and helps us win them as He walks beside us. The saying "people do not care how much you know until they know how much you care" rings true here. People see how much God cares for them through you, and I. He uses us to share Himself and then because of what we do and what we show, they can be led to a saving knowledge of Jesus Christ. Again reference the song "Whom Shall I Fear".

- Nissi - **is** the Banner

    This word is to show what God has done. God has already done an amazing thing for us with the crucifixion and resurrection of Jesus. He provided us with a way to be in relationship with Him again. It was freely given, all we need to do is accept it. This word also is used to reflect all the things God has done for us personally as memorials for us. Why do we need these memorials? Good question, we believe it is to help us remember how God is with us and to use them so that we can increase our faith. If I can trust that God has done one thing for me, then I can rely on what He did in the past for Him to meet the next need I have, even if it is bigger than the last one. That is a building block of faith.

- Shalom - **is** Peace

  God is Peace…complete, nothing else needed, peace. God extends His peace to us. Peace that penetrates into our being physically, emotionally, and spiritually. When we are at peace with God and ourselves, we can extend His peace to others in such a way that it is healing…not just a rest or a break but total peace regardless of what is going on around us. I (Walter) had a dream recently in which I saw a Christian family going about their day inside a circle of light that shown on them like an upside down cone. It was revealed to me that the light was coming down from God and creating a safe area in which the family went about their day. Outside of the light boundaries, there was evil, chaos, malice and forces that wanted to destroy the family, but the family was not even aware of those forces. They simply went through their day and walked where they wanted to walk and the light moved the other things out of their way as they went. This is the peace that God extends to us.

- Rachûm - **is** Compassionate

  God wants to hold and embrace us like a loving parent to a child. The Bible says we are heirs of God. Meaning we are sons and daughters of God. We are princes and princesses of God. He touches our hearts in a very real way when we worship, pray, meditate, and focus on Him. He lets us know He is with us.

- Chânan - **is** Gracious

  God continues to bend down to our level to show us how much He cares about us. He walked in the garden with Adam and Eve, walked and talked with Abraham, showed Himself to Moses, ate with the Israelite leaders, encouraged Joshua, allowed Himself to come in human form as Jesus living and walking among us experiencing everything we experience to know all we have to deal with, and finally, when we accept Jesus as our savior, He lives within us so that we can become one with Him. I have never heard nor read of any other god that has done so much on its part to be with mankind than Yahweh

• Agapē - IS LOVE

Let's talk about this one in more depth. So how much does God love us?

> [16]" *For God so loved the world, that he gave his only begotten Son, that whosoever believeth in him should not perish, but have everlasting life.*" [17]"*For God sent not his Son into the world to condemn the world; but that the world through him might be saved.*" – John 3:16 - 17

The whole intent of God sending Jesus was for restoring to us what we lost in the garden, namely oneness with God...to be in right relationship with Him again. God did not have to do this. For that matter, He didn't have to do anything. He could have just stood back and left us to be. But He didn't. He created us to be in relationship with Him. He singled out the Israelite people first and then through Jesus He extended this relationship to all mankind.

The apostle Paul says the following about God and His love towards us:

> [38]"*For I am persuaded, that neither death, nor life, nor angels, nor principalities, nor powers, nor things present, nor things to come,*" [39]"*Nor height, nor depth, nor any other creature, shall be able to separate us from the love of God, which is in Christ Jesus our Lord.*" – Romans 8:38 - 39

Wow, think of what Paul is saying here…nothing, **nothing, We** *are saying nothing* that has ever existed; or that will ever exist; whether physical, emotional, spiritual; whether a being or an inanimate object *can separate God's LOVE toward us.* His love is always there, it is always extended, it is always real. As man we can: try to grieve God; try to hate God; try to turn our back on God; try to force others or manipulate others away from God; have our governments try to outlaw God; and if Jesus were here today, we could treat Him like He was treated the day He was crucified… *BUT* we cannot do anything to change **HIS LOVE TOWARD US!** *Praise God for being Agapē!*

If this were not enough, the apostle John wrote the words of Jesus for our future eternity. God doesn't just love us now He wants us to be with Him in eternity:

> ² "In my Father's house are many mansions: if it were not so, I would have told you. I go to prepare a place for you." ³ "And if I go and prepare a place for you, I will come again, and receive you unto myself; that where I am, there ye may be also." – John 14:2 - 3

From our understanding, in Jesus' day, when a man and woman were engaged to be married, the man went to his father's house and added on a room to the house for he, and his bride. He had no contact with his fiancée until his father felt the room was complete enough to shelter the couple. When this took place, the father released the man to go get his fiancée and bring her to the home where they were married and then entered the room to consummate the marriage. They then stayed in the addition to raise their family. Jesus is telling the disciples, that not only does God love us in the present, but Jesus has gone to heaven to prepare for us rooms, ROOMS

IN GOD'S HOUSE, so that when God is ready, we can live with Him in eternity. God wants our relationship with Him to last forever. Praise God!

Are you catching yet what God's character is toward mankind… toward us? Are you starting to gain confidence in, assurance in, and reliance on the fact that God's character toward us is for our good? What a glorious revelation to understand within our limits, how much God cares for us! What He truly thinks of us. What He has already done for us and what He wants to do for us. He has our backs just like He had Hannah's back.

Let's finish with one more scripture Jeremiah 29:11 "For I know the thoughts that I think toward you, saith the LORD, thoughts of peace, and not of evil, to give you an expected end." We could read this scripture as: I know the intentions that I think for you, says the LORD, intentions that are friendly not evil, to give you an expected end. God is always thinking of us. He is thinking thoughts of peace not thoughts of evil. He has an end for us…this is or can be translated as prosperity, reward, lengthy future. He is wanting to give us an expected future. Now this is not name it claim it….This is not meaning that God is going to grant you money or riches or health or anything like that during your life on earth. It simply means that God has a plan for our future and He is constantly thinking thoughts on inviting us into that future. We believe this is in us finding our Spiritual Gifts and then using them under God's direction, His thoughts speaking to us, to become Christ like and to be an example for others while we are on earth. To some this may mean giving all they have to help others. To some this may mean leading others. To some this may mean instructing others. To some this may mean leaving home to help others. To some this may mean staying in a bad job to be a light to that work place. To some this may mean having bad health so that they may be a light to others that are in bad health. To some this may mean being a modern day Job. See not all of the above are good things according to human standards, but to God's standards the safest place we can be is smack dab in the center of His will no matter what else is going on around us. This is because He has promised that His intentions toward us are good not evil and the plan is His not ours.

The kicker here is that God can only invite us into it. He very rarely if ever forces us. Remember the train analogy, His intentions/plans are the track leading to the end He wants/needs us to fulfill. We can choose to jump track, but just like a train derailing, we end up doing the major damage to our lives and those that are close to us. But if we accept His invitation and stay on His tracks moving forward, we get the one thing we were created to have… ONENESS with GOD.

Every person is born with two voids in their life. The first one is to accept Jesus as their personal savior. The second is to become Christ like so God can put us where needed to show others who He is.

> God's plan is for us to fulfill the life He wants us to have. He gives us a choice to stay on track or not. He rarely forces us.

Some that are reading this book are jumping up and down for God's character toward us; however, there are some that are reading this that have been or are in a derailment state. We want to encourage you before ending this chapter…God is a god of *redemption*. God is a god of *restoration*. Don't believe us…then look at the names God uses to describe Himself, He: is there with us, is approachable for us, wants to embrace us, bends Himself down to us, is able to sufficiently meet our needs, provides for us, to wholly heal us, clearly shows us what is right and clean, is over all for us, shows us memorials of what He has done for us, brings us complete peace, and is determined to passionately **LOVE *YOU*** no matter what… NO MATTER WHAT! Do you see it, do you understand, our whole existence is to be one with God, in right relationship with Him, completely His, and He will do and has done everything He can do to make that happen. Even when the first three of four of mankind turned their backs on him (Adam, Eve, Cain), even though He punished them/us for their acts, even then, He already provided the plan for us to be back in relationship with Him. HE REDEEMED US. HE ALREADY REDEEMED US! That is provided for, and in His redemption, HE RESTORES US. We were all BOM's (Big Ole Messes) before salvation…We are all derailed trains…*every one of us*… We are born as BOM's…with no hope. BUT God already provided the cure to RESTORE US back into relationship with HIM. It doesn't matter if at this very moment you are right with God, if you are far from God, if you have been in a derailment and not been restored, or if you are just going off the tracks…HE is right there next to you, knelt down, with His arms outstretched toward you, ready for you to turn and see Him and fall into His embrace, just like a child who is hurt/scared/ sick/frustrated/ sorry/sad/happy/excited does with a loving parent. Turn…do you hear me…TURN…I said…TURN to HIM and let HIM LOVE YOU WITH ALL HIS CHARACTER TOWARD YOU!!

So I (Rich) never did answer my questions. Before we close out this chapter, let's answer them:

Will God do it? ——
Yes! Because He created me, and He called ME GOOD!

Why would God care about what I am asking? —— *Because His very character states that He does.*

Why would God do it? ——
Because by His very word, HE CANNOT LIE

Praise be to God for showing us so clearly who He is, His character and His character towards us so that we can have confidence in, assurance in, reliance on Him… that we can **TRUST HIM**.

We would be remise if we do not take a moment to discuss becoming saved or rededicating your life to God. Becoming saved means that you have admitted you are a sinner, believing that God sent His son Jesus Christ to die on a cross shedding His blood to cover your sins, making a conscious choice to turn away from sin (repenting), inviting Jesus/accepting Him to come into your heart, and finally confessing Jesus as Lord of your life. If you have prayed this prayer to God, and are making a conscious choice to be a follower of Jesus (a Christian), then we want to welcome you as a new brother or sister in Christ. Praise be to God there is another name written in heaven.

We would like to end this chapter with the song *"One Thing Remains"*. We recommend that you go to *www.youtube.com* and in the YouTube search bar, search for *"One Thing Remains by Kristian Stanfill"* minus the quotation marks.

IN SUMMARY

We now know this about God's Character towards us:

- We know that when He created creation, He saw it as GOOD.

- We know He sent Himself to die for us and to be raised from the dead to redeem and restore us.

- We know that nothing can separate us from HIS LOVE.

- We know that He wants us to be with Him forever.

- We know that He is constantly thinking good intentions for us.

We know by His names He: is there with us, is approachable for us, wants to embrace us, bends Himself down to us, is able to sufficiently meet our needs, provides for us, to wholly heal us, clearly shows us what is right and clean, is over all for us, shows us memorials of what He has done for us, brings us complete peace, and is determined to passionately and deliberately **LOVE** *YOU*.

We have been studying the basic foundational truths of faith. We have now looked at the following variables **A** minding our thoughts/feelings/ desires, **B** who is God, **C** God's character, and **D** God's Character for us. Remember our basic faith equation is **FAITH** = A and B and C and D and E and **F**.

May you be blessed by what we have learned so far…this has been good, but oh there is so much more…let's look at variable **E** as we continue through our faith equation.

CHAPTER SIX

Faith: "Things Hoped For"

In the prior chapters we have laid a very firm foundation of faith. Like any foundation, it is made to be strong to support what is built upon it. God, by His very nature, built the foundation for us by giving us thoughts, sharing who He is, sharing what His character is, and what His character towards us is. Praise God for the awesome revelations that He has given to be used as the sub foundation, if you will, to what we continue to discuss. The next few chapters move from the foundation which is immovable and unchangeable, to focus on us as man and how we build upon that foundation. So just like any foundation which is meant to be built upon, let's build some more with the second to last variable of our basic faith equation **E**. Variable **E** is believing in what God says.

Before we get started though, let's stop and make sure we are all on the same page with the statement "what God says" or another way to state it "what and how has God spoken to you". We need to restate what we said in Chapter 2 quickly reminding ourselves what we defined. When we say God told us or says something, it can come in a few forms: it can come from His written word the Bible; it can be a revelation to you as you read and study the Bible; it can be a confirmation to you of a thought/revelation by the Holy Spirit; it can be an external audible voice from a messenger angel or from Jesus (either seen or not seen); it can be a thought that God places in our minds; it could be a conviction or leading of the Holy Spirit coming from our soul into our minds; it could be an intense feeling driving you to do something that God would want done; it could even be the Holy Spirit physically manifesting Himself and taking control of you to do or say what needs to be said or done; it could be a vision; it could be dream; it could be an overwhelming peace sweeping over you; it could be God's presence settling down on you and you basking in His Glory; it could be some other way in which there is no shadow of doubt in your mind that God just visited with you; it could be something for you or something God wants to intercede on/do for someone else; it could be that God is bringing your attention to a need that someone else or a group of people have so you can stand in the gap for them. We just wanted to take a moment to make sure we are not boxing God in, in any way. The above examples are just some experiences the team, who helped write this book, shared. There may be more which we have not experienced that others have. When we speak of "what God says" it is a very loose interpretation of "saying" something.

Having said the above, believing in what God says really starts with a question...why would I believe in something God says? I (Walter) was sharing the following scriptures in one of the team's review sessions and, as a case in point, let's look at Abraham:

> [1]"Now the LORD had said unto Abram, Get thee out of thy country, and from thy kindred, and from thy father's house, unto a land that I will shew thee:" [2]"And I will make of thee a great nation, and I will bless thee, and make thy name great; and thou shalt be a blessing:" [3]"And I will bless them that bless thee, and curse him that curseth thee: and in thee shall all families of the earth be

blessed." ⁴"So Abram departed, as the LORD had spoken
unto him; and Lot went with him: and Abram was
seventy and five years old when he departed out of Haran."
– Genesis 12:1 - 4

And then

"By faith Abraham, when he was called to go out into
a place which he should after receive for an inheritance,
obeyed; and he went out, not knowing whither he went."
– Hebrews 11:8

Let's process these scriptures. God spoke to Abraham. Then Abraham believed what God said. Why would Abraham do this? Was it that Abraham approached God asking Him for a promise land? Or maybe Abraham said to himself, "You know I want a large land inheritance and I want my offspring to be God's chosen people so I am going to ask God just that."? Maybe Abraham felt God "owed" him? Maybe Abraham thought he could manipulate God and force God to do this? Maybe Abraham was a name it, claim it person? Maybe he thought because his father Nahor made it halfway to where God wanted the family, that he could inherit it? However, it is none of these. None of these bring faith. None of these inspire, encourage, uplift, or even praise God in any way shape or form. Why...because all of the above come from mankind's thinking, not from God.

So again we have not answered the question...why would Abraham believe what God said? We believe it is all the foundation that has already been laid. God created Abraham to be an example for others and He revealed Himself through Abraham to others. We believe, even though it is not explicitly stated in the Bible, Abraham had a relationship with God.

Abraham understood where the thoughts were coming from, he understood who God was, he must have had a basic understanding of God's character, and he believed or trusted that God's character was meant for his good. Further God revealed to me (Walter) these scriptures:

> ^{13}*"For when God made* **promise**^{G1861} *to Abraham, because he could swear by no greater, he sware by himself,"* ^{14}*"Saying, Surely blessing I will bless thee, and multiplying I will multiply thee."* ^{15}*"And so, after he had patiently endured, he obtained the promise."* ^{16}*"For men verily swear by the greater: and an oath for confirmation is to them an end of all strife."* ^{17}*"Wherein God, willing more abundantly to shew unto the heirs of promise the* **immutability**^{G276} *of his counsel, confirmed it by an oath:"* ^{18}*"That by two* **immutable**^{G276} *things, in which it was impossible for God to lie, we might have a strong consolation, who have fled for refuge to lay hold upon the hope set before us:"* ^{19}*"Which hope we have as an anchor of the soul, both sure and stedfast, and which entereth into that within the veil;"* ^{20}*"Whither the forerunner is for us entered, even Jesus, made an high priest for ever after the order of Melchisedec." – Hebrews 6:13 - 20*

These scriptures give us the solidity of what God was intending and what Abraham was receiving from God's intent. In verse 13 what God told Abraham was meant as a promise and was received as a promise by Abraham. Then in verse 17 not only did God make a promise, He confirmed the promise swearing by Himself to fulfill it...the oath. The author of Hebrews then states in verse 18, if we take the fact that God's character/nature is immutable (unchangeable/ always is the same, even from the beginning, as we have laid as a foundation in the previous chapters) and that in His character He cannot lie, then the promise which was made and the oath which confirmed it *WILL BE FULFILLED.*

Did you catch the statement? This is the main point, the most key point. This is the whole crux of this book and why it was written, to correctly explain what faith is and what it is not. *IF GOD SAYS IT, IT WILL BE FULFILLED! AND,* we do not stop here, because stopping here leaves faith hanging. This is why the author of Hebrews does not stop, he continues his sentence to expand on what this means for us. He goes on to say, because of God's character, His promise and His oath, we can Hebrews 6:18b–19a "…lay hold upon the **hope**^{G1680} set before us: Which *hope* we have^{G2192} as an anchor of the soul, both sure and stedfast…".

Oh man this is starting to really get good! I am about to get my PRAISE ON! What did we start this book with? Do you remember? We started this book with the scripture Heb 11:1 "Now **faith**^{G4102} is the substance **of things hoped for,**^{G1679} the evidence of things not seen."

Do you see it? Do you see what God did? God not only defined faith for us in Hebrews, but He defined the word HOPE. What are the "things hoped for" (Strong's G1679)? They are the promises and the oaths of GOD based on the immutability of His character!

Specifically for Abraham, what are the "things hoped for"? They are found in Hebrews 6:14 "Saying, Surely blessing I will bless thee, and multiplying I will multiply thee." Based on the information that he had, Abraham believed God. He trusted God. He had confidence in God and what God wanted for him and his family. HE BELIEVED in what GOD SAID because he BELIEVED IN GOD! As we saw at the beginning of this chapter, this is what Hebrews 11:8 is saying, Abraham believed in what God said, not the end result, not in what Abraham wanted, he believed in what God said, God's promise, God's oath because he believed IN GOD.

It was the one thing that carried Abraham, it anchored his soul, he was sure and steadfast, because he believed in GOD and therefore what GOD SAID would COME TO PASS!

Just like the other saints of old: Noah; Joesph; Moses; Samuel; David; Solomon; Daniel; Disciples, Paul, etc.; this is where we need to be. We need to be shaken apart from all the lies we have been fed for so many years. We need to remove / clean away the fluff and get back to the bare bones and ask one simple question... WHAT HAS GOD SPECIFICALLY TOLD ME? Not what do you desire, not what do you want, not what do you wish for, not what do you think about, not what deliverance you need, not what situation you are in, not whatever other thought is roaming freely in your mind that is from your natural self or even implanted by satan. No. No, there is only one question, WHAT HAS GOD TOLD ME? Then and only then do you have a choice. That choice is as simple, or as hard as we make it. The choice is: do you believe what God told you or not? Will you trust Him? Will you have confidence in Him? Do you believe in Him? Will you let Him "have this", will you let it go, will you let HIM WORK?

Let's look at two examples in the Bible that really drive this point home. The first example is in Luke:

> [1] *"Now when he had ended all his sayings in the audience of the people, he entered into Capernaum."* [2] *"And a certain centurion's servant, who was dear unto him, was sick, and ready to die."* [3] *"And when he heard of Jesus, he sent unto him the elders of the Jews, beseeching him that he would come and heal his servant."* [4] *"And when they came to Jesus, they besought him instantly, saying, That he was worthy for whom he should do this:"* [5] *"For he loveth our nation, and he hath built us a synagogue."* [6] *"Then Jesus went with them. And when he was now not far from*

the house, the centurion sent friends to him, saying unto him, Lord, trouble not thyself: for I am not worthy that thou shouldest enter under my roof." ⁷"Wherefore neither thought I myself worthy to come unto thee: but say in a word, and my servant shall be healed." ⁸"For I also am a man set under authority, having under me soldiers, and I say unto one, Go, and he goeth; and to another, Come, and he cometh; and to my servant, Do this, and he doeth it." ⁹ When Jesus heard these things, he marvelled at him, and turned him about, and said unto the people that followed him, I say unto you, I have not found so great faith, no, not in Israel." ¹⁰"And they that were sent, returning to the house, found the servant whole that had been sick." – Luke 7:1 - 10

And the second example is found in the following scriptures in Mark:

²²"And, behold, there cometh one of the rulers of the synagogue, Jairus by name; and when he saw him, he fell at his feet," ²³"And besought him greatly, saying, My little daughter lieth at the point of death: I pray thee, come and lay thy hands on her, that she may be healed; and she shall live." ²⁴"And Jesus went with him; and much people followed him, and thronged him." ²⁵"And a certain woman, which had an issue of blood twelve years," ²⁶"And had suffered many things of many physicians, and had spent all that she had, and was nothing bettered, but rather grew worse," ²⁷"When she had heard of Jesus, came in the press behind, and touched his garment. ²⁸"For she said, If I may touch but his clothes, I shall be whole." ²⁹"And

straightway the fountain of her blood was dried up; and she felt in her body that she was healed of that plague." [30] *"And Jesus, immediately knowing in himself that virtue had gone out of him, turned him about in the press, and said, Who touched my clothes?"* [31] *"And his disciples said unto him, Thou seest the multitude thronging thee, and sayest thou, Who touched me?"* [32] *"And he looked round about to see her that had done this thing."* [33] *"But the woman fearing and trembling, knowing what was done in her, came and fell down before him, and told him all the truth."* [34] *"And he said unto her, Daughter, thy faith hath made thee whole; go in peace, and be whole of thy plague."* [35] *"While he yet spake, there came from the ruler of the synagogue's house certain which said, Thy daughter is dead: why troublest thou the Master any further?"* [36] *"As soon as Jesus heard the word that was spoken, he saith unto the ruler of the synagogue, Be not afraid, only believe."*
– Mark 5:22 - 36

So between the examples, there are three people that are very sick. In fact they are so sick that the centurion, Jairus (a father), and the woman were very worried. They had a lot on the line by going to Jesus. The centurion represents the Roman occupation and oppression of the Jewish people and by him asking a Jew for help, it may have meant his command. Jairus was a synagogue leader, meaning he was part of either the Pharisees or Sadducees both of which hated Jesus and had even stated that anyone who confessed Jesus would be put out of the synagogue (they would be cut off from all community and family, an outcast). The woman, if we understand biblical culture, was not allowed in crowds without exclaiming in a loud voice that she was unclean so that everyone else would not touch her and therefore also become unclean. But yet they recognized that Jesus had the answer they needed. They had a *thought* that if they went to Jesus, maybe, just maybe He would help them. Why, because whether they wanted to admit it or not, they knew Jesus was from *God* and they knew Jesus *cared*. (Again the foundations we have already laid) Two of them ask Jesus to come and heal the one they were interceding for. *(On a quick side note here, note the servant and the daughter are not active participants of what is being done here. All is being done third party on their behalf in one case remotely and the other in person. The point to take away in this side note is that we can intercede on behalf of others even if they do not want it.)* And what does Jesus do? In both cases, He consents and goes. Now let us ask you, what did it mean when Jesus consented and went with them? Did it mean Jesus was going to go and look over the situation and say, "Sorry man, I cannot help". Or maybe "Sorry but if you would have come sooner, maybe I could have done something", or "Hey man, I just wanted to see the situation and then make a determination before committing to anything"? NO. Jesus consented and went. That very act was a promise that He was going to heal. Why? Because that is why they came to Him, it was implied in the questions will you come and heal. It wasn't will you come, it was will you come AND heal. Why would Jesus go if He was not going to heal? It would make no sense. It would not glorify God. It would not show the people that Jesus was God. It would discredit all He had done and said to that point. By the very nature of saying He would go with them, **HE MADE A PROMISE** to heal and by moving and going He made **AN OATH**, that it would be fulfilled.

Let's talk through the rest of Jairus first. I do not know about you but for me (Rich) Jairus represents me and how I approach faith. I know God can, but will He act on my behalf. Jairus knew he had no right to go to

Jesus to ask for healing, but he knew Jesus could heal his daughter. His question, while at Jesus feet was really, will you come Jesus and heal my daughter? Jesus consents and goes. I know this may be a little dramatic flair, but can you feel Jairus' relief? He asked Jesus and as he had hoped and wished, Jesus consented to go. I bet he did a long wheeeewwww under his breath when they started. Hope was revived, they might just make it to the house in time, if they hurry and do not delay. Then all of a sudden, Jairus' hopes are jarred back to reality. Jesus all of a sudden stops. Why? Well there is someone else that needs His help. Someone else that also came with hope of all hopes that if she could just touch Jesus' clothes, just get close enough to lay hold of Him in just the slightest of way, she will be healed. She does not even consider herself worthy to ask. But God is no respecter of persons. He, as Jehovah Chânan (gracious), takes time to stop and acknowledge the woman and allows her to testify of God's goodness. And here is Jairus with little to no time left, standing there waiting... I can only imagine what is running through his mind: Jesus we do not have much time, Jesus, please hurry; Jesus, why are you dealing with her when you said you would come with me first; Jesus, why are you helping her over me. And the second biggest challenge to our faith takes place. What happens? *TIME PASSES...* time for us is such a killer of faith, because we do not pay attention to what GOD TELLS US. But he holds his tongue. Then satan enters the picture, ups the ante, and Jairus' worst fears come to reality. He is told before Jesus can get to his daughter, that she has indeed died. If I were Jairus, I would start to cry, out of loss, out of frustration, out of holding out in pride before going to Jesus, in Jesus for not moving fast enough, of just knowing that I was so close to Him doing something for me; out of the fact that it was my fault for not doing something sooner. But before he can even start, Jesus turns to him and says Mark 5:36b "Be not afraid, only **believe**."[G4100], have faith (to put trust in). Only believe, **only** believe, **only believe**... in what? His daughter is dead, what is left to believe in? Ahh… and here is the issue that I (Rich) have struggled with for so many years and am still processing through. It is what God has revealed to Walter and what Walter has been sharing with anyone who will listen to him. I, like Jairus, do not listen to what GOD SAYS. I am so caught up in the moment, in the struggle, in the need/want/desire/heart cry, that I hear what God says, but do not *listen* to what God says. What did Jesus say to Jairus? Jesus said He will go with Jairus. Again we know by Jesus consenting and going, He was making a promise and an oath that He would heal the daughter. And at this point we run into the gap between the physical and the spiritual. We see what is happening in the physical, but we do not understand the spiritual. Jesus made a promise and oath to Jairus. To Jesus this was a done deal. Everything else that happened in the physical is irrelevant to the promise and oath. Time, sickness, distance, hurt, other's opinions, anyone else holding up Jesus, anything else that is said, even death itself are all **irrelevant**. Jesus made a promise. He confirmed it by going. *AND HE FULFILLED IT!!!!!!!* Do you hear… **HE FULFILLED IT!** He went to the house and healed the daughter. What was Jairus supposed to believe in / to have faith in / to put his trust in? The healing? No… *He was supposed to believe in Jesus. He was supposed to believe Jesus would do what **He said** He would do.* That is faith. That is variable **E**. That is the only thing we should ever believe in, what GOD tells us!

As an opposite end of the spectrum, I (Walter) believe the centurion story represents where we as Christians are supposed to be in our faith. Why? Look at the story. He asks, not even going himself, but sending others on his behalf. Jesus consents and starts heading to the home to heal. But what does the centurion do? He sends other servants to Jesus to tell Him that he is not worthy to have Jesus come into his home. Now think about that statement. The Romans were in power. They were the occupying rulers. The centurion could have demanded, forced, beaten, brought under guard, arrested, etc. Jesus, and had Him come to heal the servant. However, he does not, he asks, and then he lets Jesus know before He can get there, that he knows Jesus is the true authority in play and simply asks Jesus to *say the word*. He knows if Jesus simply commands the servant to be healed, he will be healed. Jesus already committed to coming with the intent to heal. It was the same promise, same oath Jairus had, but the centurion believed it and rather than have Jesus come, he simply asked Jesus to speak the promise into fulfillment.

WOW… let that sink in… simply speak it. What belief! No wonder that Jesus was so amazed. Jesus makes the statement no one in all Israel has that faith. This is variable **E** in its purest form. God says and I believe! That should be our motto. This should be one of the things which defines Christians as different from everyone else. This should be one of the things which defines Christianity as different than any other "religion". God speaks and I believe. Nothing more. Nothing less. Not name it claim it, not if I do this will you do…, not if I am good then…, not God owes me, not I have strayed away and there is no hope, not I am too lost, not "will He"?… no none of that… only simple pure belief, confidence in, trust in what God says. That is all… That is variable **E**. That is where we need to be. That is where we need to grow. That is where we need to look.

One of the team members who has helped with this book, Jim, has a modern day experience like the centurion. Jim and his wife have been praying for the salvation of one of their family members. After both of them being in much distress over this issue, they went to the altar to pray and give this burden to God. Jim shared with the team later that when he and his wife got up from the altar, they were filled with complete peace. Jim shared that it was like God had spoken to them both that He had this. It was in His hands and it is a done deal. Now the family member hasn't accepted Jesus as their savior yet, BUT, the promise and oath have already been spoken to Jim and his wife. Now all they need to do is *believe in GOD* that He will do what He promised. Updating this statement the family member and 3 additional others have come to a saving knowledge of Jesus Christ. Praise God for His goodness of fulfilling His promises!

And then there is one more thing that comes... variable **F**, my action of acting on what God told me (obedience).

We would like to end this chapter with the song **"We Believe"**. We recommend that you go to *www.youtube.com* and in the YouTube search bar, search for *"We Believe by NewsBoys"* minus the quotation marks.

IN SUMMARY

This is what we know about believing what God says:

- We need to understand when God is speaking.

- We need to *listen* to what God says.

- When God says something that is specifically to us, we need to receive what is told as a promise and an oath that He will fulfill it.

- We need to apply the promise and oath as "things hoped for".

- We need to take the "things hoped for" and let them become anchors for our souls to be firm and steadfast.

- We take all of what we have learned so far, and we need to believe in GOD that He will fulfill the promise and oath.

Again this chapter described variable E believing in what God says in our basic faith equation is **FAITH** = **A** and **B** and **C** and **D** and **E** and **F**.

In the next chapter we will look at our final variable in the basic faith equation… **F** which is taking action and doing what God says.

CHAPTER SEVEN

Faith: "Ready, Set, Action"

As we are starting to see the definition of faith coming together there is one more element to our basic definition of faith and that is **F** acting on what God told us.

Let's first look at what James say about faith without action:

> *"What doth it **profit** ^{G3786}, my brethren, though a man say he hath faith, and have not **works** ?$^{G2041\ (G3361)}$ can faith save him?" – James 2:14*

Works, Strong's G2041, means to toil, or to state it another way it means putting effort into doing something. This passage of scripture introduces us to one of the debates that has been going on ever since Jesus's death. Can I believe without doing anything with that belief? Funny that almost 2,000 years later nothing much has changed we still deal with the same questioning. Maybe that is why God had James write the passage.

Let's read the rest of the passage:

> ^{15}*"If a brother or sister be naked, and destitute of daily food,"* ^{16}*"And one of you say unto them, Depart in peace, be ye warmed and filled;" notwithstanding ye give them not those things which are needful to the body; what doth*

*it profit?" ¹⁷"Even so faith, if it hath not works, is dead, being alone." ¹⁸"Yea, a man may say, Thou hast faith, and I have works: shew me thy faith without thy works, and I will shew thee my faith by my works." ¹⁹"Thou believest that there is one God; thou doest well: the devils also believe, and tremble." ²⁰"But wilt thou know, O vain man, that faith without works is dead?" ²¹"Was not Abraham our father justified by works, when he had offered Isaac his son upon the altar?" ²²"Seest thou how faith wrought with his works, and by works was faith made perfect?" ²³"And the scripture was fulfilled which saith, Abraham believed God, and it was imputed unto him for righteousness: and he was called the Friend of God." ²⁴"Ye see then how that by works a man is justified, and not by faith only." ²⁵"Likewise also was not Rahab the harlot justified by works, when she had received the messengers, and had sent them out another way?" ²⁶"For as the body without the spirit is dead, so faith without works is **dead**ᴳ³⁴⁹⁸ also." – James 2:15 - 26*

As we see, James is saying faith only has *profit*, Strong's G3786, (gain / benefits) when it is acted upon. If one does not act upon their faith, then it is *dead*, Strong's G3498, (like a corpse) / obsolete / null / empty / false / fruitless / not worth anything etc.

Faith needs active action to exist. One cannot have faith without action. Why is that one might ask? Good question. If we look back at our faith equation, there are parts that require action and parts that do not. For example, as James says we can believe that God exists, but that does not mean anything. Why? Because, whether you believe or not it does not change whether God exists or not. He does… even all the demonic powers know that. The same can be said for the chapters earlier explaining who God is, God's character, and God's character toward mankind. What we learned are facts about God which He gave us through His word. They are there, they do not change whether we "believe" or do not "believe" in what was said. What they do however is prompt us to make a conscious choice, to really believe in them (have confidence, trust, assurance in, and reliance on) or simply have what was stated as facts floating around in our minds not really meaning anything to us. You see, you can have read this book to this point nodding your head in agreement and yet not really have made a difference in you at all. Why, because you made a conscious choice to know the information, but not do anything with it. Let us put it this way, in modern terms; you found a lottery ticket and after some research you find out that it was the only winning ticket for a jackpot worth 500 million. You exclaim, I am RICH!!!!! Is this statement true or false? (ok for all you melancholy's – all lawsuits and contesting why it is yours aside is this a true or false statement?)… and the answer is… wait for it… It is a false statement. Why, because although you have the ticket, it is not worth anything until it is turned in and verified by the Lotto agency. If you never turn it in, you never get the money the ticket represents. You have all the knowledge and the facts in your head about the ticket, but unless you act and turn in the ticket, it is worthless / dead / obsolete / empty, and once it expires it no longer exists.

For this matter, one can read the whole Bible, over and over and over again, and if that person does not make a choice to receive what is said, as the Holy Spirit is convicting them, then the Bible is only a story to that person. It means nothing… it is no better or worse than any other book. It is just a bunch of information floating around in their mind.

The whole faith equation is predicated on the variable **F**. One must act on what has been stated in the Bible, in the scriptures listed in this book or else there is no real faith. Look at Chapter 2 which talked about thoughts and feelings. It was a call for each one of us to mind our thoughts and feelings and really understand where they are coming from. This requires action, one has to actively engage their mind and process through what they are thinking and feeling. If one is not doing that, then thoughts and feelings just course through them and they act and react based on them without regard to anything (sounds like the man of the tombs to us (Luke 8:26-39)).

The last chapter laid down the premise that as God speaks to us, we need to believe in what He is telling us. Again belief takes action... I have to consciously make a decision that I am going to believe what God tells me.

Then there is this chapter, which puts the rubber to the road if you will, do I have enough confidence in, trust, reliance on and assurance in God and what He spoke to me, to do it? Do I? Will I? All of what this book has stated so far rests on this point. It is like a tipping point, if you will, and your choice makes all of what was stated so far either fall into your mind's trashcan or it prompts your body to physically do something.

So what are we really talking about here? What does acting on it really mean? It can be summed up into one word **OBEDIENCE**. Oh man... we as mankind so hate that word. Even as children somehow we just hate that word. It is the exact opposite of every fiber of our being. At birth we are born into disobedience. It is part of our genetic, emotional, and spiritual makeup inherited from the Adamic fall. We still have not recovered from that fall, it still trips us up, it is still satan's greatest tool, it still leaves us hurting. And yet that is where God is and where He wants us to be... acting on what He says.

But what is obedience? Well that is another good question that deserves an answer. It is an attitude of the heart. It is saying "I want to do what God tells me to do, because I love Him". I love Him for who He is and then for what He has done for me. It is a way of showing God how much we honor Him, how we want to put Him first in our lives. When our children obey us and our commands, it honors us as parents and is one way they show us their love for us, it is the same with us toward God. God's very nature demands, it; however, just like children we can obey sullenly or we can obey with all the joy our relationship with God embodies and that is what honors Him. Jesus even touches on this subject in John 14:15 "If ye love me, keep my commandments.", He wants us to love Him, it is more than just knowing that He speaks to me through thoughts and feelings, it is more than knowing who He is, it is more than knowing His character, it is more than knowing His character toward me, it is more than believing what He says, it is keeping His commands. Doing what He tells me to do, what He reveals to me, what He speaks to me, what the testimony of the Holy Spirit gives me, it is *obedience* Strong's H8085 hearing God, understanding God, and in turn *choosing* to obey God.

We want our actions to continually show God that we love Him and that is why we *choose* or desire to choose to obey Him. In that choosing, I have to act on what He tells me to do, the way He tells me to do it, and when He tells me to do it (we will cover more on this in Chapter 9). For anything less does not honor Him.

As a negative case in point let's look at King Saul:

> [17] *"And Samuel said, When thou wast little in thine own sight, wast thou not made the head of the tribes of Israel, and the LORD anointed thee king over Israel?"*
> [18] *"And the LORD sent thee on a journey, and said, Go and utterly destroy the sinners the Amalekites, and fight*

*against them until they be consumed." ¹⁹"Wherefore then
didst thou not obey the voice of the LORD, but didst fly
upon the spoil, and didst evil in the sight of the LORD?"
²⁰"And Saul said unto Samuel, Yea, I have obeyed the voice
of the LORD, and have gone the way which the LORD
sent me, and have brought Agag the king of Amalek, and
have utterly destroyed the Amalekites." ²¹"But the people
took of the spoil, sheep and oxen, the chief of the things
which should have been utterly destroyed, to sacrifice unto
the LORD thy God in Gilgal." ²²"And Samuel said, Hath
the LORD as great delight in burnt offerings and sacrifices,
as in **obeying**ᴴ⁸⁰⁸⁵ the voice of the LORD? Behold, **to
obey**ᴴ⁸⁰⁸⁵ is better than sacrifice, and to hearken than the
fat of rams." ²³"For **rebellion**ᴴ⁴⁸⁰⁵ is as the sin of witchcraft,
and **stubbornness**ᴴ⁶⁴⁸⁴ is as iniquity and **idolatry**.ᴴ⁸⁶⁵⁵
Because thou hast rejected the word of the LORD, he hath
also rejected thee from being king." – 1 Samuel 15:17 - 23*

God told Saul to do something, Saul went and did it, but he did it on
his own terms, in his own way. Saul chose to act on what God told him
to do, but he did not do it the way he was told, when he was told to do it,
and therefore his actions did not honor God. What are some of the words
Samuel used to describe the attitude of Saul's heart when doing what God
wanted done? They were *rebellion* (Strong's H4805), *stubbornness* (Strong's
H6484), and *idolatry* (Strong's H8655)... all of these put Saul before
God and God's reaction was that He rejected Saul as king. He rejected the
one He chose to be king. And He removed His spirit from Saul. When
this happened Saul was never the same after that. He suffered, his family
suffered, his kingship suffered, and his country, the people he was to care
for, suffered.

Think of it this way, if God was an investor, our obedience is God's
Return On Investment (ROI). When it is done in a way that honors God,
it returns to Him 100+ fold. But if it does not honor Him it is like a bad
investment, it costs Him. For you see God can do anything He wants, but
He chooses to use us, to work through us, to minister to each other… to
minister to our fellow mankind. This is why obedience done with a joyful
spirit, the way He tells me to do it, and when He tells me to do it is so
critically important. You see I can be saved, I can have assurance in the fact
that I am going to heaven. If I do nothing else in my life other than that,
then when God calls me home, I represent one. But, obedience is so much
more. It isn't buying my way into heaven with works, for we all know per
Ephesians 2:8 "For by grace are ye saved through faith; and that not of
yourselves: *it is* the gift of God:", that works alone do not do anything for
me. Rather it is working with God to reach every person (man, woman,
and child) for God so that none are left behind and all go into heaven with
us. It is taking the whole of our faith equation and giving it meat, giving it
traction, setting it free to work, allowing God to work and when we allow
God to work through us, GREAT things are done for His Glory.

Let us ask this question, why was Jesus able to do all the miracles
He did? Was it simply because He was God? We realize that this will be
controversial but we would submit that the answer is no. The answer is
a deeper understanding of the relationship between the trinity of God.
Most of the book of John deals with the relationship between Jesus and
God. When one really understands what Jesus is saying in many of His
statements, we find the key to why and how God ministered through Him.
For example:

> [19]*"Then answered Jesus and said unto them, Verily,
> verily, I say unto you, The Son can do nothing of himself,
> but what he seeth the Father do: for what things soever he*

doeth, these also doeth the Son likewise." [20] *"For the Father loveth the Son, and sheweth him all things that himself doeth: and he will shew him greater works than these, that ye may marvel." – John 5:19 – 20*

And then:

[8] *"Philip saith unto him, Lord, shew us the Father, and it sufficeth us."* [9] *"Jesus saith unto him, Have I been so long time with you, and yet hast thou not known me, Philip? he that hath seen me hath seen the Father; and how sayest thou then, Shew us the Father?"* [10] *"Believest thou not that I am in the Father, and the Father in me? the words that I speak unto you I speak not of myself: but the Father that dwelleth in me, he doeth the works."* [11] *"Believe me that I am in the Father, and the Father in me: or else believe me for the very works' sake."* [12] *"Verily, verily, I say unto you, He that believeth on me, the works that I do shall he do also; and greater works than these shall he do; because I go unto my Father."* [13] *"And whatsoever ye shall ask in my name, that will I do, that the Father may be glorified in the Son."* [14] *"If ye shall ask any thing in my name, I will do it." – John 14:8 - 14*

In John 5:19 – 20 above, Jesus says He sees what God has done and God shows Him what He wants done. God was communicating to Jesus what He wanted Jesus to do. John 14:9 – 11 reveals to us Jesus and God were in such close communion with each other, that they are one. Meaning they are one in thought and purpose. Jesus knew the exact thoughts of God and then HE DID THEM. He was obedient, even unto His brutal death. (Watch the Passion of Christ if you do not believe this) Even unto requiring His separation from God. This is obedience. BUT Jesus does not stop there… look at this again John 14:12 "Verily, verily, I say unto you, He that believeth on me, the works that I do shall he do also; and greater works than these shall he do;…", He says that because of HIS obedience, if we BELIEVE (remember last chapter) we will do the same works that He did and even greater. Why? Because if we believe and act to pray and do what God tells us, "will I [Jesus] do, that the Father may be glorified in the Son.".

Going further, God applies it to us even though Jesus has gone to heaven for the last 2,000 years. In John 16:13 – 15 Jesus states:

> [13] *"Howbeit when he, the Spirit of truth, is come, he will guide you into all truth: for he shall not **speak**[G2980] of himself; but whatsoever he shall hear, that shall he speak: and he will shew you things to come."* [14] *"He shall glorify me: for **he shall receive**[G2983] of mine, and **shall shew**[G312] it unto you."* [15] *"All things that the Father hath are mine: therefore said I, that he shall take of mine, and shall shew it unto you." – John 16:13 - 15*

Let's pull out the words here in a different order. All things that are God, have been given to Jesus v. 15. Jesus then takes all things given to Him and gives them to the Holy Spirit v14. The Holy Spirit receives, Strong's G2983, all the things that are Jesus v. 14 (that are spoken to Him v13 or received) and then speaks (v13) and/or shows (v14) these things to US. This is God speaking to us through the Holy Spirit in all the ways we already mentioned at the beginning of Chapter 6. We have two things to do, Believe and Act. It is a simple God said and I did in the way He said. That is obedience. No fanfare, no craziness, no nonsense, but a simple

He said and I did. As we do this, God is free to move bringing Glory and Honor to HIS NAME. The beauty of this is that when we are in alignment with God and doing exactly what He said, we cannot misuse what He gives us. It is a protection which we get in being in alignment with Him.

In one of our review sessions, Walter asked the question "Knowing and living in God's character since Jesus died… how have we gotten so far away? We have no excuses." The answer is we as Christians continually fail in the area of acting on what God tells us (obedience) and therefore we are continually negating what He wants done because we do not allow Him to minister through us to this broken world.

In the next chapter we are going to do a FAITH recap with working biblical examples. But before we leave this chapter, we want to review one story between Jesus and Peter to show action in… well in action.

> [25] "And in the fourth watch of the night Jesus went unto them, walking on the sea." [26] "And when the disciples saw him walking on the sea, they were troubled, saying, It is a spirit; and they cried out for fear." [27] "But straightway Jesus spake unto them, saying, Be of good cheer; it is I; be not afraid." [28] "And Peter answered him and said, Lord, if it be thou, bid me come unto thee on the water." [29] "And he said, Come. And when Peter was come down out of the ship, he walked on the water, to go to Jesus." [30] "But when he saw the wind boisterous, he was afraid; and beginning to sink, he cried, saying, Lord, save me." [31] "And immediately Jesus stretched forth his hand, and caught him, and said unto him, O thou of little faith, wherefore didst thou doubt?" [32] "And when they were come into the ship, the wind ceased." [33] "Then they that were in the ship came and worshipped him, saying, Of a truth thou art the Son of God." – Matthew 14:25 - 33

Peter has gotten a lot of bad rap in many sermons, but this man was always at the forefront pushing the boundaries. Imagine the scene, the wind is howling, the waves are crashing, the boat is tossing, and all of a sudden the disciples see a figure walking on the water. Now we do not know about you, but we have never seen anyone walk on water, so if you did in even the calmest of situations, you would be in wonder, amazement and probably a little unnerved. Jesus calms them by letting them know who He is. And then Peter (you got to love Peter!), says almost as much as an amazing thing as experiencing Jesus walking on the water. He asks Jesus, if it is really Him, tell him to come to Him on the water. What we find interesting here is we are not sure that Peter fully believed that the figure on the water was Jesus at the point of his asking? We are also not going to debate his motivation either, but the point is he is the only one that even conceives the idea to ask to walk on the water. Now we would maintain that the thought came from God that he should ask. And it was probably so that later Peter would have this experience to draw on when the bottom fell out for him at Jesus' death. (That it was not in Peter's strength that things would happen but rather his faith in Jesus providing) Jesus answers and says "Come". Now, again what is implied in that word? It is a promise and oath that Peter can get out of the boat and walk on the water to Jesus. Now Peter has a choice, he can either stay in the boat or he can get out of the boat. Stay in the boat and his faith in Jesus does not exist. Get out of the boat and his faith in Jesus exists. There is nothing else here just this choice with these two outcomes. Now let us ask, how many times have you asked for God to move on your behalf, He said He would and then you do not move on your part? Actually let's state it this way. Do courage and strength come when we ask the question like Peter did, or do they come when we move? We submit that there is no courage and strength in making the request; they only come when we take the first step, when we move. AND they only grow in us if we keep moving. Peter acts, Peter moves, Peter gets out of the boat, steps **onto** the water and starts walking toward Jesus. This is faith in its purest form, God said and Peter did. Then again satan comes in and starts to attack, because when we move in obedience, satan automatically starts losing. satan starts to distract Peter. Now we do not know if Peter stopped walking or not, but as these distractions take hold, we think he either slowed down or stopped and just like we stated a couple of sentences ago, when we stop, courage and strength diminish. Why? Because we are not being obedient. And just like Peter, we sink. Peter realizing the dire situation he is in, does the best thing he could do and calls for Jesus to save him. Then Jesus chastises him saying "Thou of little faith". But let us say, Peter at least had faith, he was the only one that got out of the boat. Was he the only one that received the thought to ask to walk on the water toward Jesus? We do not know, but if he wasn't, he was the only one in this situation that exhibited faith. The rest of the disciples were "safe" (We use this term loosely considering the storm they were in) inside the boat. Now the real question, which of the disciples brought Jesus more glory? Was it ones who stayed in the boat to observe or Peter who got out of the boat and "walked" with Jesus? Which brought Jesus a ROI in this situation? Which learned a valuable lesson to understand and increase their faith? Was it any wonder that Peter was one of 3 that Jesus was closest to?

So here is the point. Faith always calls us out of the boat. Just like money under a mattress (in most cases) does not increase, one has to invest it into something, which always requires risk, in order for it to grow. This is ROI in the financial world. God invests Himself in us, and just like one that has to let go of their money, we have to let go of ourselves and allow God to move in our lives for His Return on that investment. As He speaks to us, we need to act on it, obey Him, and allow Him to move so that His investment returns 100+ fold. It always requires us to be where Jesus is.

Where is Jesus? He is out on the waters, in the storm, in the worst of it, bringing all His character as God to the situation, and He chooses to help in the storm through you and us. It is our prayer that you will act and do what God has told you to do, and join He and us out on the waters of life ministering to our fellow man.

We would like to close this chapter with the song is **"Oceans (Where Feet May Fail)"**. We recommend that you go to *www.youtube.com* and in the YouTube search bar, search for *"Oceans (Where Feet May Fail) by Hillsong United"* minus the quotation marks.

IN SUMMARY

This is what we know about acting on what God says:

- Per James there is no faith without action.

- Action is really being obedient, doing what God tells us, how He tells us, and when He tells us.

- Obedience only counts when we do it with a joyful spirit.

- The closer we are to God, the more faith we have because we are in Him and He is in us. We understand what He is telling us.

- Faith always calls us out of the boat of life on to the waters where God is working.

Again this chapter described variable **F** acting on what God says in our basic faith equation **FAITH** = **A** and **B** and **C** and **D** and **E** and **F**.

In the next chapter we will look at biblical examples of faith lived out using our basic faith equation.

CHAPTER EIGHT

The Basics of Faith Recap

As we come to this chapter, we have learned so much about ourselves, God, and how God relates to us. We have gone on a journey of what faith is and how it basically operates. In this chapter we are going to do a recap of what we have learned so far, so we can take faith deeper. We want to walk through our equation through a number of biblical stories and show you the pattern God gave us to explain faith.

Let's quickly review our basic faith equation. Remember this is a computer Boolean Logic equation and it evaluates to either Exists (True/On) or Not Exists (False/Off). All variables must Exist (be present/in operation) for the equation to Exist. If one or more variables do Not Exist (are present/in operation) then the whole equation does Not Exist and one's faith is non-existent.

FAITH = **A** and **B** and **C** and **D** and **E** and **F**

Here are the variables in summary form:

A = minding and paying attention to your thoughts/feelings and purposefully making sure they are in line with God.

B = believing in God and who he is…our creator, our savior, the one and only God.

C = having confidence, assurance in, reliance on God's character.

D = having confidence, assurance in, reliance on God's character towards us (He has good planned for me).

E = understanding what God told me to do and believing it came from Him.

F = my action of acting on what God told me (obedience).

Before we do the stories, we want to make sure we are all on the same page as to what faith is and is not lest we somehow got off the same page. To do this we are going to look at a couple of scriptures that, I (Rich) have struggled with until Walter helped me understand what they mean. These scriptures have Jesus revealing to us what a small amount of faith can do. He stated that we only need faith as small as a mustard seed for things to happen…for God to move.

[20] "And Jesus said unto them, Because of your unbelief: for verily I say unto you, If ye have faith as a grain of mustard seed, ye shall say unto this mountain, Remove hence to yonder place; and it shall remove; and nothing shall be impossible unto you." [21] "Jesus answered and said unto them, Verily I say unto you, If ye have faith, and doubt not, ye shall not only do this which is done to the fig tree, but also if ye shall say unto this mountain, Be thou removed, and be thou cast into the sea; it shall be done." [23] "For verily I say unto you, That whosoever shall say unto this mountain, Be thou removed, and be thou cast into the sea; and shall not doubt in his heart, but shall believe that those things which he saith shall come

to pass; he shall have whatsoever he saith." [24] "Therefore I say unto you, What things soever ye desire, when ye pray, believe[G4100] *that ye receive them, and ye shall have them."*
– Matthew 17:20 - 24

[5] *"And the apostles said unto the Lord, Increase our faith."* [6] *"And the Lord said, If ye had faith as a grain of mustard seed, ye might say unto this sycamine tree, Be thou plucked up by the root, and be thou planted in the sea; and it should obey you." – Luke 17:5 - 6*

What I find so funny about these scriptures is Jesus states if we have faith as small as a mustard seed, which is one if not the smallest of seeds, that we can tell mountains to be moved and they will, or for trees to be uprooted and moved and they will. Now let's think about that. Jesus says just a tiny amount of faith, can do these things. So if that were the case, why did He only command a tree to wither? For that matter, why didn't one of the disciples "try this out" to see if it would work? Look over the centuries since Jesus' death and to my knowledge no one has ever commanded a tree to wither and it did, a tree to uproot itself and plant itself in the sea and it did, or command a mountain to move and have that actually happen. I would bet there have been some who have tried it with no results. The question then is why? Why has it never worked? Theoretically we as Christians should be doing this all over the world. It should be second nature, no big deal, a big sigh and command and then the mountain moves. Mountains and trees should be moving all over the earth. But no, this has never happened. So the question is, if it only takes a tiny amount of faith to do these things, why do we not see these things take place?

In Mark 11:24 Jesus gives a condition that we have *to believe*, Strong's G4100, which means to have faith and not doubt, but is that really it? Maybe we all have had so much doubt in the last 2,000 years that it has prevented us from doing these things? I would say that this is not true either. We have had great men and women of faith throughout the ages. I can't see where they would not have had enough belief, and no doubt, to command these things and have them happen. But this still doesn't answer the question.

Maybe it is more we have never really understood faith to begin with. As God was pressing upon me what faith is, I began to see that we approach what Jesus says from the wrong standpoint. Faith turning into belief needs to bring Glory and Honor to God. Remember in our last chapter, our Faith, the whole of the equation is God's investment into us, and it is His ROI. It is what shows the world He exists, it is what helps bring the world to Him, it is what reaches out and draws others in. I think this is such a key point we often miss when reading these verses. If you put what Jesus says into our faith equation, you will see it actually fails the very first variable...minding our thoughts and feelings and therefore the whole faith equation is negated to non-existence. For if God did not ask me to ask Him to remove the mountain so it is no more, if God did not ask me to ask Him to move the mountain into the sea, and if God did not ask me to ask Him to have the sycamore tree to uproot itself and plant itself into the sea, then what in the world would make *me* think God would answer those requests? For if God did not tell me, then the thoughts are either from my natural self, or from satan. We are told to ask for God to do things in accordance with His will (Romans 8:5 "For they that are after the flesh do mind the things of the flesh; but they that are after the Spirit the things of the Spirit.", and Romans 8:27 "...he that searcheth the hearts knoweth what *is* the mind of the Spirit, because he maketh intercession for the saints according to *the will of* God.") If God does not want the mountain moved, the tree withered, or the tree uprooted and planted into the sea, and I ask for that to happen, what would make me think that God would answer those requests?

Pause to let it sink in....

The answer is **He would not**.

This was such a light bulb moment for me when I grasped this. Faith isn't asking for wants, needs, or desires. Faith is asking God for what God tells me to ask for, **WHAT HE SPECIFICALLY TOLD ME**, just like we spoke of in Chapter 6. Oh this was such a liberating moment!!! If God tells you to ask Him to move a mountain into the sea and you know that thought is from God, not from satan, or from your natural self, *then and only then* the only thing left in the faith equation is your obedience to ask God to do it and wait on Him to fulfill it.

Faith is as simple as that— Faith is as small and tiny as that.

So here is a tag on question...why didn't Jesus command a mountain to be removed? Why didn't Jesus command a tree to uproot itself and plant itself into the sea? The answer... ***BECAUSE GOD NEVER TOLD HIM TOO***. If He would have, we are 100% certain it would be in the Bible.

For the last 20–30 years, many people have been saying that all one needs to do is think of what they want, ask God for it, and believe He will grant it. Complete hog wash with no scriptural basis. Their premise is *you* get what *you* believe. That thinking has nothing to do with God. Real faith is not believing in what you get, it is believing in what God promised. The problem we have is we pray / ask for this and for that with no thought of where the thought came from. Why would God honor any prayer which is not in accordance with what He wants? He wouldn't. God is only going to grant those things in which we ask for in accordance with His will whether it is for us, or for those we are interceding for.

Further, the only reason I would ask for a mountain to be removed/moved into the sea, if God didn't tell me to do so, is:

- to test God

- because I am arrogant

- to impress others

None of these things glorify, honor, or bring me closer to God, they only feed my own ego.

This again is why a tiny amount of faith can do great things, because we are not believing in the end result, but rather believing in God fulfilling His promises. We only do what He wants done. Therefore we can trust He will do what is asked because that is what He wants.

This verse sums up the point: Matthew 13:52 "Then said he unto them, Therefore every scribe *which is* instructed unto the kingdom of heaven is like unto a man *that is* an householder, which bringeth forth out of his treasure *things* new and old."

Or let us paraphrase here: therefore anyone who actively exercises faith is like an owner of a house which contains great wealth and treasure (the Holy Spirit who has been given all that Jesus has who has been given all that God has) and by the very exercise of faith sets the Holy Spirit free to move as God desires. This is another pause moment. Let this sink in. Think of the miracle that God allows to happen here. The Holy Spirit, *the very embodiment of God's power,* **LIVES IN US**, and to set Him free (saving a dying world) all we have to do is act on what God tells us. Then God moves. He Moves, HE does the MIRACLE, and we get the blessing of being part of it.

Don't believe us? Then how does one explain all the miracles that have been done since Jesus' ascension? How does one explain this one from scripture ?

> [1]*"Now Peter and John went up together into the temple at the hour of prayer, being the ninth hour."* [2]*"And a certain man lame from his mother's womb was carried, whom they laid daily at the gate of the temple which is called Beautiful, to ask alms of them that entered into the temple;"* [3]*"Who seeing Peter and John about to go into the temple asked an alms."* [4]*"And Peter, fastening his eyes upon him with John, said, Look on us."* [5]*"And he gave heed unto them, expecting to receive something of them."* [6]*"Then Peter said, Silver and gold have I none; but such as I have give I thee: In the name of Jesus Christ of Nazareth rise up and walk."* [7]*"And he took him by the right hand, and lifted him up: and immediately his feet and ankle bones received strength."* [8]*"And he leaping up stood, and walked, and entered with them into the temple, walking, and leaping, and praising God."* [9]*"And all the people saw him walking and praising God:"* - Acts 3:1 – 9*

And

> *"For the man was above forty years old, on whom this miracle of healing was shewed."* – Acts 4:22

So, first things first, why did we add Acts 4:22? We think that this verse is almost as much as a key point as the healing that took place. Let's make an assumption here per my (Rich) Zondervan study Bible, Peter was martyred sometime between 63 and 68 AD. We would submit then that

Peter was probably very close to the age of Jesus. If Jesus was killed in 30 AD (again per my Zondervan study Bible Jesus was born in 3–2 BC) he would have been around 33 which meant Peter was probably real close to that age. So you're saying ok what does this have to do with verse 4:22. It has everything to do with it. If Peter, from a Jewish religion tradition, became a man at age 13 then He would have been going to the temple on some regular basis for around 20 years. If not, then definitely while he was following Jesus around. Okay??? Well again it is very important… Let us ask you this question, if the man was over 40 years old and had this condition since birth, how many times in the 20 years prior to this day had Peter and John walked past this man? Think about that. They walked past this man let's say at least 20 times and never once *until this day* did they offer to heal this man. For that matter, how many times did Jesus walk past this same man, and never offer to heal him? Think about that? I would bet they had all given the man alms at some point through these 20 years, *but they never offered to heal.* WHY? What was so different on this day? If you apply the faith equation we have laid forth, the very first variable was all of a sudden made true. ***GOD TOLD THEM THAT THIS DAY THE MAN WAS TO BE HEALED AND THEY WERE THE ONES TO START IT TO HAPPEN.*** What else would have changed? There is nothing else. And what did they do? They stopped, they focused (assuming that they were confirming that God had told them to do this), they believed, and in front of everyone present, they acted doing what God told them to do. They reached out the hand to help the man up (a promise and oath if you will). The man receiving what they were saying was of God, believed and taking the hand (believing the promise) started to stand. THEN GOD AS JEHOVAH REPHEKA (healer), JEHOVAH JIREH (provider), JEHOVAH RACHUM (merciful), JEHOVAH CHANAN (gracious) ***MOVED*** AND HEALED THE MAN AT THAT MOMENT. And then what happened? The man "entered with them into the temple, walking, leaping, and praising God". Who got the glory and honor? God. Who received the blessing of helping, Peter and John. What was the impact of being obedient? People saw, listened to Peter and John, and at least another 2,000 people were saved (Acts 4:4). That is what God wants to do. That is 2,000+ return on investment... invest in one and 2,000 are saved. There is no reason why God should not be moving through you and us in the same way today. As Walter told us, "God orchestrated a sequence of events to affect many, but it all hinged on Peter and John to do what God asked them to do."

The question is why isn't God moving? And if we are real honest with ourselves, we will realize it is because we never do all of the faith equation. We either nix it in variable A, by not minding our thoughts and feelings, or we nix it on variable F and not acting on what God tells us to do. I know that I (Rich) am as guilty of this as anyone. But you know what, we can change. We can change and actively engage ourselves to understand what God is saying and what God wants,

Personal growth in Christ happens one thought at a time.

and then we can *CHOOSE* to act on that so that He can move through us, in all **HIS POWER**. We invite you to make the choice to change.

We would like to close this chapter with the song ***"Standing on the Promises of God"***. We recommend that you go to *www.youtube.com* and in the YouTube search bar, search for *"Standing on the Promises of God"* minus the quotation marks.

IN SUMMARY

Here is the faith recap:

- Make sure you are one with God. Do not try to feed your own ego.

- Make sure you listen to your thoughts and feelings.

- Understand that God wants to work through you.

- You may need to change. Change your lifestyle, change what media you are feeding your mind, change your heart if it is hard, and you must let God's word sink from your head to your heart so that you know, that you know Him.

- You must act and do what God tells you to do.

- You will receive a blessing by walking with God as you watch Him move through you.

FAITH = **A** and **B** and **C** and **D** and **E** and **F**

Here are the variables in summary form:

A = minding and paying attention to your thoughts/feelings and purposefully making sure they are in line with God.

B = believing in God and who he is…our creator, our savior, the one and only God.

C = having confidence, assurance in, reliance on God's character.

D = having confidence, assurance in, reliance on God's character towards us (He has good planned for me).

E = understanding what God told me to do, and believing it
came from Him.

F = my action of acting on what God told me (obedience).

In the next five chapters we are going to explain how to move your
faith from being simply in or not in existence, to return exponentially in
effectiveness.

SECTION II

Maturity: Taking Faith to the Next Level

The beauty of God and what He wants does not stop at faith either existing or not existing. He wants so much more for us, more than just sufficiency, more that we might willing to imagine, past our own strength, past our limits, way past abundance, way past the physical, past the emotional, into the realm of the spiritual only confined to how far we allow God to take us. Faith needs to grow, mature, to multiply, and move into the realm of the exponential.

To start moving past a simple existence faith, we as Christians need to MATURE. We need to grow up. We need to get off the "milk" as Paul says, and start chewing on some real "meat". One of the reasons we are so weak in our faith is that we have never studied what faith is or have never been properly taught what faith is. All the chapters previous to this have matured you if you have let them. We would view the prior chapters as stage 1 – 3 baby food. Babies go through a process to learn to eat and move away from only milk. First they have to learn to eat from a spoon and swallow stage one foods. Then with stage two foods, they start getting soft solids so that they now understand there are other textures to be aware of, and in stage three food the young baby/toddler has food they have to chew to swallow. All these are progressions for the baby so he/she can start eating "table food". The real stuff that will help them grow into adult hood. Christians need to mature the same way. In this book, the previous chapters have moved us from milk to stage 3 understandings of scripture. Now it is time to get table food if you will, the stuff that will help us grow and mature.

We do not just want our faith to be existing, or not existing, but we want our faith to multiply in its effectiveness. Effectiveness means the power to produce a result that is wanted.

So what are maturing factors that make our faith multiply in effectiveness? We are glad you asked that very insightful question!!! We believe there are three of them. The first one is called Clarity. We must be very clear in what God wants us to do, when He wants it done, and how He wants it done. We hit on this some in Chapter 7. The second one is called Forgiveness. We, like Jesus, must operate with the grace of forgiveness for those who hurt us in some way. To be blunt Jesus says that if we come to Him asking for something and we are not right with our brothers and sisters in Christ, He will not listen. The third one is Binding/Loosing. We have to learn to bind satan and his minions to thwart his operations in order to loosen the bondage the world is in submission to and allow God's power to move.

The next three chapters will be dealing with each of these aspects of maturity.

CHAPTER NINE

Aspect One of Maturity: Clarity

There are two parts of Clarity. One is understanding what God wants, how He wants it and when He wants. The other, which is a negative side of clarity or the absence of clarity, is doubt. Let's start with doubt first so that we understand the absence of clarity and then move into what clarity is.

Below are some good verses to read about doubt:

> ⁶*"But let him ask in faith, nothing **wavering**.^{G1252} For he that wavereth is like a wave of the sea driven with the wind and tossed."* ⁷*"For let not that man think that he shall receive any thing of the Lord."* ⁸*"A **double minded**^{G1374} man is **unstable**^{G182} in all his ways."* – James 1:6 - 8

and

> *"Jesus answered and said unto them, Verily I say unto you, If ye have faith, and **doubt**^{G1252} not, ye shall not only do this which is done to the fig tree, but also if ye shall say unto this mountain, Be thou removed, and be thou cast into the sea; it shall be done."* – Matthew 21:21

and

> *"For verily I say unto you, That whosoever shall say unto this mountain, Be thou removed, and be thou cast into the sea; and shall not* **doubt**[G1252] *in his heart, but shall believe that those things which he saith shall come to pass; he shall have whatsoever he saith." – Mark 11:23*

In the above verses *wavering/doubt* are defined in Strong's G1252 with the following words: to separate thoroughly, withdraw from, oppose, or hesitate. ***Doubt then is taking something that you know to be true and withdrawing from/opposing/deciding against/hesitating in that truth***. Further James says that a person who does this becomes *double minded*, Strong's G1374, which means two spirited, that is, vacillating (in opinion or purpose) and therefore is *unstable* which in Strong's G182 is defined as inconstant. Per *www.merriam-webster.com* inconstant means "likely to change frequently without apparent or cogent reason". Doubt and wavering leads a person to become someone who vacillates in what they know to be true and then due to that, become inconstant or inconsistent as a synonym.

So why is doubt so bad?... because it opens the door for satan to influence our thoughts. Ah you say...we are all the way back to Chapter 2? Well... yes, we are back at Chapter 2 and Chapter 6. Let me (Rich) explain vacillating using a funny real example. Sometimes when my wife and I are hungry and we are tired of our own cooking, we go out to eat. However, then we are confronted with the fact of the plethora of restaurants to choose from. Do we want fast food or sit down? What type of food do we want (American, Italian, French, Mexican, Chinese, Turkish, Thai, etc.) Then how much are we willing to spend, how much time are we willing to commit to this endeavor... and then our minds start vacillating with all the options and we become overwhelmed and just go back home and either skip the meal or make something simple like peanut butter and jelly. We are not in charge of our thoughts. We are not in control of our feelings. We are hungry and the mere chaos in our minds negates the hunger, because of all the rampant thoughts going through our head of what to eat. This is a form of doubt... wavering to the point of vacillating to the point of no consistency... we just shut down.

Now this is a funny true example. But when it comes to doing this with God's Word it can become seriously tragic. Tragic you say? Yes tragic, with long reaching consequences that mankind can never recover from. Huh??? Yes... let's look at the doubt outcome which has affected every person in the human race. Now your saying yeah right, there hasn't been any such thing... but alas yes there has and it is in the Bible three chapters in.

> [1] *"Now the serpent was more subtil than any beast of the field which the LORD God had made. And he said unto the woman, Yea, hath God said, Ye shall not eat of every tree of the garden?"* [2] *"And the woman said unto the serpent, We may eat of the fruit of the trees of the garden:"* [3] *"But of the fruit of the tree which is in the midst of the garden, God hath said, Ye shall not eat of it, neither shall ye touch it, lest ye die."* [4] *"And the serpent said unto the woman, Ye shall not surely die:"* [5] *"For God doth know that in the day ye eat thereof, then your eyes shall be opened, and ye shall be as gods, knowing good and evil."* [6] *"And when the woman saw that the tree was good for food, and that it was pleasant to the eyes, and a tree to be desired to make one wise, she took of the fruit thereof, and did eat,*

and gave also unto her husband with her; and he did eat."
[7]"And the eyes of them both were opened, and they knew
that they were naked; and they sewed fig leaves together,
and made themselves aprons." – Genesis 3:1 - 7

I (Rich) love and hate this story. I love it because the pure evilness of satan and how he so subtly just nails us is more evident here than anywhere else. (Well the temptation of Jesus would be a good one to look at too, but that would be from a different standpoint) I hate this story because it affects me in ways I really would rather not be affected. It has affected me from birth before I could even make choices. It has condemned me and has separated me from God. From a spousal standpoint it broke my heart watching my wife go through 3 pregnancies, with all the things it did to her body and the pain she was in. All the way to never having gotten to experience earth the way God intended. But I digress from the point.

So there is a lot of information between the lines of this story that we need to pull out of these 7 scriptures and we will start in the form of questions:

- Why was Eve talking to a snake? (This is just a funny one which always makes me chuckle. Your discoursing with an animal, that right there should have raised red flags. Same with Balaam when he talks with his donkey.)

- Why would satan approach Eve asking her about one of the two trees they were not allowed to eat the fruit of?

- Why did he pick the tree of good and evil over the tree of life?

- Why did satan approach Eve rather than Adam?

- Where were Eve and Adam when this discourse took place?

- What was really said by all parties?

- Did satan lie in what he told Eve?

So let's go through this step by step. Where were Adam and Eve when this took place? They were by the tree that had the fruit which would reveal to them the difference between good and evil. Now why? Of all the places they could be in the garden, why would they be there? Eve said that God had told them they should not touch that tree or eat that tree's fruit. So why would they be anywhere near that tree? And in the answer to that question, we learn lesson one about doubt… if we are not minding our thoughts/feelings, then we will be drawn to places we should not be. Places God does not want us to go because He is protecting us. Second doubt lesson… once we open our minds and go near the places we are not to go, wavering starts to take place. We would submit that satan chose Eve and chose this tree because Eve was already there and her thoughts were already looking at the tree, looking at the fruit, lingering on those thoughts of what would really happen, how would that fruit really taste, how exquisitely would it flow over the tongue and into the stomach, what would she really get to know and how powerful would that be to her. Third doubt lesson… then the pulling away from/withdrawing from/opposing/hesitating, comes into play. Here is where satan enters and starts questioning. Oh the subtle line of questions he starts with. He starts with such innocent ones: Did God say you should not eat of the trees of the garden? And the answer is no we can eat of any tree but two. Now again, Eve and Adam are already at one of the trees they are not allowed to eat of and Eve is eyeing the tree and not taking captive every thought. *satan already sees there is conflict in Eve over this tree because of where she is and what she is doing.* Then Eve tips her hand with satan and this is where he hooks her. She stayed a little too long on these thoughts and feelings for this tree and it led her to the fourth doubt lesson… staying too long where you should not be leads to vacillating. It leads to being double-minded. How do we know this? Look at what Eve said about the tree and the fruit: Genesis 3:3 "But of the fruit of the tree which *is* in the midst of the garden, God hath said, Ye shall not eat of it, neither shall ye touch it, lest ye die."

Compare that with what God actually said:

> [16]*"And the LORD God commanded the man, saying, Of every tree of the garden thou mayest freely eat:"* [17]*"But of the tree of the knowledge of good and evil, thou shalt not eat of it: for in the day that thou eatest thereof thou shalt surely die." – Genesis 2:16 - 17*

Now to Eve's credit here, I am not sure if God told her she was not to eat of the tree or not, or if she got that information from Adam (since she had not been created yet). However, remember Adam is with her listening to this discourse. But the vacillating takes place when Eve did not tell satan exactly what God had said. The words were twisted. Where? God never said not to touch it, He said not to eat it. And at this point, satan knew he had Eve. Double-mindedness leads to doubt lesson five… twisting God's words, or not keeping what was originally said. This opens the door for satan to do his greatest game plan, the one he uses every time with man and the one he wins most often. In fact, he is so successful at it, that he even used it on Jesus with his temptation (Matthew 4:1–11). He twists God's words just ever so slightly at our weakest moments and we being double-minded, listen. At this point doubt has fully taken control and the chances of pulling ourselves back to where we should be is very, very difficult. And the rest of the story is tragic… Eve is so unstable that satan is able to give her, or have her pick one of the fruits, she takes it and does not die, like *she* thought, again because that is not what God said, and because she does not die, she takes a bite. This doubt is so out of control, that she hands the same to Adam, and he also takes a bite. Now here is another good question that we asked… Did satan lie to them with what would happen? The answer is no he didn't. Genesis 3:4 - 5 [4]"And the serpent said unto the woman, Ye shall not surely die:" [5]"For God doth know that in the day ye eat thereof, then your eyes shall be opened, and ye shall be as gods, knowing good and evil.", which is lesson six of doubt… when we choose the path that satan gives us, we might get what he promised, but it is never what we expected to get. They did not die a physical death like they expected, they died one much worse… they died a spiritual death… and in that death they received exactly what satan promised, they now know good and evil, but with it came everything satan had: evil, separation from God, no purity, no power, curses, etc. At this very moment, mankind was affected from then until God brings the new heaven and earth and we are all condemned at the moment of conception because of these tragic choices.

The danger of doubt is that it kills any hope of faith. They cannot co-exist. Why, because doubt makes us question what God told us (Chapter 6). Whether it is not trusting, to outright opposition, to the worst of changing course and following satan rather than God, no matter the depth of doubt, it negates our faith. It stands in opposition to what God tells us and makes us question God and His plans towards us. To the point we twist what God tells us or tell ourselves that God did not really tell us that, or maybe it is not as important that I do that now and I'll just sit on it. It separates us from God, creates a crack that satan can start to pound a wedge through until we are completely separated from God. Just like splitting wood with a wedge, when it gets to the end it becomes pieces that are separated from each other. That is the danger of doubt. As we can see a person may ask or petition God for many things but if they are wavering or are double minded then God will not answer the request.

As mature Christians we MUST keep a constant guard up from satan and the thoughts and feelings he attempts to put into us. We MUST take captive every thought/feeling and subjugate it to Jesus: 2 Corinthians 10:5 "Casting down imaginations, and every high thing that exalteth itself against the knowledge of God, and bringing into captivity every thought to the obedience of Christ;"

Let's look at the temptation of Jesus.

> [1] *"Then was Jesus led up of the Spirit into the wilderness to be tempted of the devil."* [2] *"And when he had fasted forty days and forty nights, he was afterward an hungred."* [3] *"And when the tempter came to him, he said, If thou be the Son of God, command that these stones be made bread."* [4] *"But he answered and said, It is written, Man shall not live by bread alone, but by every word that proceedeth out of the mouth of God."* [5] *"Then the devil taketh him up into the holy city, and setteth him on a pinnacle of the temple,"* [6] *"And saith unto him, If thou be the Son of God, cast thyself down: for it is written, He shall give his angels charge concerning thee: and in their hands they shall bear thee up, lest at any time thou dash thy foot against a stone."* [7] *"Jesus said unto him, It is written again, Thou shalt not tempt the Lord thy God."* [8] *"Again, the devil taketh him up into an exceeding high mountain, and sheweth him all the kingdoms of the world, and the glory of them;"* [9] *"And saith unto him, All these things will I give thee, if thou wilt fall down and worship me."* [10] *"Then saith Jesus unto him, Get thee hence, Satan: for it is written, Thou shalt worship the Lord thy God, and him only shalt thou serve."* [11] *"Then the devil leaveth him, and, behold, angels came and ministered unto him."* - Matthew 4:1 - 11*

How did Jesus defeat satan's temptations? By speaking to satan the accurate words of God… exactly as they were spoken and in the right context. Jesus had the knowledge of the Word. By doing this, satan was not able to gain entry into Jesus' mind because Jesus, even at a very physically weak moment, was on guard and taking captive all His thoughts and feelings subjecting them to His knowledge of God.

Remember the question I (Rich) struggled with in Chapter 5, "I know God can, my question is will He?" One statement is a faith statement. It is concrete it is full belief it is a stake in the ground I know God can. However, the second statement is all doubt. It is a question Will He? There is no stake in the ground here, no concrete. It is two thoughts in my mind contending with each other negating each other, and thus becoming double minded. Therefore, according to James, when I am in this attitude, whatever I am praying for will not come to pass because I am not trusting, believing, having confidence in, or assurance in God working on behalf of my request.

Another example we see in the Bible is when Jesus himself was not able to perform miracles because of the lack of belief from those He was trying to minister to.

> 4 "But Jesus said unto them, A prophet is not without honour, but in his own country, and among his own kin, and in his own house." 5 "And he could there do no mighty work, save that he laid his hands upon a few sick folk, and healed them." 6 "And he marvelled because of their **unbelief**.G570 And he went round about the villages, teaching." – Mark 6:4 - 6

Here we see the word *unbelief*, Strong's G570, which is the opposite of *belief* (believe), Strong's G4100. What is interesting here is unbelief can be translated as unfaithfulness or disobedience (faithlessness). What Mark appears to be telling us is that the people actively did not believe in Jesus, and what He was willing to do for them. Even though He healed some, they actively did not believe/put their trust in Him. So then the question becomes, how could this be translated as disobedience? Ah that is a great question and it has a very simple answer. If God was telling those that they needed to go to Jesus to be healed/delivered/saved/etc. and those people actively did not believe and allow Jesus to act on their behalf, then they were being disobedient to what God was telling them to do. We can picture Him standing there in the middle of the crowd beckoning them to come to Him and instead of coming, they argued with Him about who He was and why they had to come to Him to be set free. It is like a person freely giving away (no strings attached) a million dollars to anyone who wants it and instead of going up and asking for the million dollars we think of all the things the person might be trying to do to own us. We never ask for the million dollars and we go away mad rather than receiving the gift. We are like Naaman and his attitude:

> [10] "And Elisha sent a messenger unto him, saying, Go and wash in Jordan seven times, and thy flesh shall come again to thee, and thou shalt be clean." [11] "But Naaman was wroth, and went away, and said, Behold, I thought, He will surely come out to me, and stand, and call on the name of the LORD his God, and strike his hand over the place, and recover the leper." [12] "Are not Abana and Pharpar, rivers of Damascus, better than all the waters of Israel? may I not wash in them, and be clean? So he turned and went away in a rage." [13] "And his servants came near, and spake unto him, and said, My father, if the prophet had bid thee do some great thing, wouldest

thou not have done it? how much rather then, when he saith to thee, Wash, and be clean?" [14] *"Then went he down, and dipped himself seven times in Jordan, according to the saying of the man of God: and his flesh came again like unto the flesh of a little child, and he was clean."*
– 2 Kings 5:10 - 14

Again this is why it is critical to be mindful of the thoughts in our head… where are they coming from and why. This cannot be stressed enough that the thoughts we listen to make or break us when it comes to faith.

How do you remove doubt from your prayers? We have to recognize the strength of God's promises. Knowledge of His promises what we studied in Chapters 3, 4, and 5 removes all doubt because we can ask forgiveness and cleansing thus giving us the assurance we are in right standing with God and can approach Him boldly. 1 John 1:9 "If we confess our sins, he is faithful and just to forgive us *our* sins, and to cleanse us from all unrighteousness." This will help make sure we are coming before God doubt free. However the best way is to have an absence of doubt. The absence of doubt is clarity.

What then is clarity? Going back to Chapter 6, clarity begins when God tells us something… when He makes a promise and an oath to do something, either for us or for someone else and WE believe. Further, it is to clearly know beyond any shadow of doubt that you understand what God told you to do, when He told you to do it, and how He told you to do it. When one knows the answers to these items, it prevents doubt because one knows all the facts. Another clarity item might be your position in the church. If you are an elder then by definition in the Bible, this position carries promises of God when it comes to healing and sins.

[14]"Is any sick among you? let him call for the elders of the church; and let them pray over him, anointing him with oil in the name of the Lord:" [15]"And the prayer of faith shall save the sick, and the Lord shall raise him up; and if he have committed sins, they shall be forgiven him."
– James 5:14 - 15

When you do what God tells you to do, then the doubt is completely removed because God has now made a promise that He will work and do what you are acting on/praying for. You have full confidence. All you need to do is have assurance in God's promise then pray and ask. God will take care of the rest.

Let's study an example of clarity, say someone is sick and God says pray for that person, we assume that the prayer is for healing. So we pray for the person to be physically healed of the sickness. At this point the question becomes did we act with clarity? We would say no. Why? Well, did we ask God specifically how He wanted us to pray? Or did we just go off and pray for the sickness to be removed and expect God to answer the prayer? Hmmm… never thought of it that way before. Neither had we.

We need to first pray for clarification with how God wants us to pray or we need the testimony of the Holy Spirit to bear witness this is of God. Then, when we have that answer, we can pray in confidence for the request and specifically for that request. We may come to find out, what God wanted us to pray for might not even be for the sick person; maybe it is for someone to be saved who knows the sick person. But we wouldn't know to pray that way if God didn't give the thought to us about that sick person, and we would be praying for the wrong thing if we don't ask for clarification. Further, we would be disappointed if healing didn't take place because we made an assumption. Assumptions hurt our faith and create doubt when God doesn't answer the prayer.

A good example of clarity from scripture is Philip:

> [26]*"And the angel of the Lord spake unto Philip, saying, Arise, and go toward the south unto the way that goeth down from Jerusalem unto Gaza, which is desert."* [27]*"And he arose and went: and, behold, a man of Ethiopia, an eunuch of great authority under Candace queen of the Ethiopians, who had the charge of all her treasure, and had come to Jerusalem for to worship,"* [28]*"Was returning, and sitting in his chariot read Esaias the prophet."* [29]*"Then the Spirit said unto Philip, Go near, and join thyself to this chariot."* [30]*"And Philip ran thither to him, and heard him read the prophet Esaias, and said, Understandest thou what thou readest?"* [31]*"And he said, How can I, except some man should guide me? And he desired Philip that he would come up and sit with him."* [32]*"The place of the scripture which he read was this, He was led as a sheep to the slaughter; and like a lamb dumb before his shearer, so opened he not his mouth:"* [33]*"In his humiliation his judgment was taken away: and who shall declare his generation? for his life is taken from the earth."* [34]*"And the eunuch answered Philip, and said, I pray thee, of whom speaketh the prophet this? of himself, or of some other man?"* [35]*"Then Philip opened his mouth, and began at the same scripture, and preached unto him Jesus."* [36]*"And as they went on their way, they came unto a certain water: and the eunuch said, See, here is water; what doth hinder me to be baptized?"* [37]*"And Philip said, If thou believest with all thine heart, thou mayest. And he answered and said, I believe that Jesus Christ is the Son of God."* [38]*"And*

*he commanded the chariot to stand still: and they went
down both into the water, both Philip and the eunuch;
and he baptized him." [39]"And when they were come up
out of the water, the Spirit of the Lord caught away Philip,
that the eunuch saw him no more: and he went on his way
rejoicing." – Acts 8:26 - 39*

This is a wonderful example of a person acting in faith. Philip was an evangelist and God was using him to proclaim the scriptures of the Good News to others, to tell them about Jesus. We say that to lay some ground work: Philip knew what God wanted him to do and was actively doing it in the scriptures prior to this snippet.

So the angel spoke to Philip and told him to go to a certain place. Since God spoke through the angel, Philip knew he was God's messenger and Philip believing God's words/thoughts went.

Now comes the question... when Philip got to the location, did he stand up and start evangelizing? No he didn't. Well why not? He knew his gifting, he knew how God was using him, and we are 99% sure that anyone there besides Philip was not a Christian. So why didn't he just do something? Even on the way, how many people did he pass by? Did he evangelize to any of them? Should he have? Ahh... here we see clarity in action. Philip recognized that this was a special occasion from God and God had specific intent on why He brought Philip to this place.

So what did Philip do? He waited. He waited for more direction. He quickly and obediently did what the angel said, but he did not make assumptions and he didn't just start doing something. He waited for more direction. We don't know for sure, but in our opinion, we believe while he was waiting he was asking God... okay God, I did what you asked, now how do You want to use me right now?

Then God answered him in Acts 8:29. The Holy Spirit told Philip to approach the Eunuch's chariot. The Holy Spirit *put* the thought into Philip's mind to do the next step. Go next to the chariot.

So when Philip got there he started evangelizing to the Eunuch telling him that he needed to be saved and the Eunuch said yes you are right, accepts Jesus and there is a big celebration….right? Umm… No.

Philip again shows clarity in action. He only does the next step. He goes up to the chariot and he *observes* what is going on. He *LISTENS* to what the Eunuch is reading.

So then Philip starts evangelizing and telling the Eunuch he needs to be saved and the Eunuch says you are right and does it… we are on the same page now? Ummmm…. Again No.

Philip, we are sure, was excited that the Eunuch was reading the scriptures, but he didn't force anything on the Eunuch. He simply asked him a question. Do you understand? He felt the Eunuch out to see where he was spiritually and if he was ready to receive. In our opinion, we are sure Philip was praying that God would grant him an opening to share the gospel with the Eunuch. God answered the prayer because it is why He *sent* Philip to that place. It was in accordance with what God wanted Philip to do. The Eunuch says he doesn't understand and wishes Philip to explain it to him. Philip now in in full clarity can exercise faith that this man was to be saved, and ministers to the Eunuch explaining all from the beginning and ends with the Eunuch being saved and baptized.

This is showing maturity by using clarity… making sure we are doing exactly what God wants done. God spoke through an angel and through the Holy Spirit to Philip. God allowed the Eunuch not to be at peace with understanding the scriptures, putting the thought into his mind that he needed help. Philip looking for an opportunity asked a question and the Eunuch thought no I do not understand maybe this guy can help me. What a beautiful interplay to show us how to move in maturity of clarity.

Because everyone was minding their thoughts, the Eunuch is saved and baptized. And now he became a light unto the darkness of the country he was returning to. As a side note, there is much Christian tradition about Simeon Bachos the Eunuch. He went back to his country and introduced Christianity. This started the Ethiopian church which was produced many of the early fathers and was the second largest church governing body, if you will, outside of the church at Constantinople. (This goes to prove you may never know who God may bring across your path. Who will take the message to millions of others.)

As we see through this example, clarity removes doubt, and allows God to move in the spirit of men so that they can come to a saving knowledge of His son Jesus. If Phillip would have done anything else, he would have either missed the opportunity, or offended the Eunuch and not had been able to minister to him.

As maturing Christians, we need to start learning how to be clear with the things God tells us. It is a humble attitude of asking God what He wants done. It is not a rebellious attitude of "I am not doing anything until you do such and such". It is knowing that sometimes God only reveals to us pieces. We need to act in faith with each piece so that God can continue to move. It is a step by step process and we only need to know the step we are currently in. We have to learn to be content and trust God knows the whole plan, because after all it is His plan not ours. Clarity is getting to where God wants us in this step and then asking Him what He wants us to do next. Sometimes this will come right away and sometimes we may have to wait. Sometimes when we wait we may be able to do other things, and sometimes we may need to do nothing but dig deep into prayer, His Word, and oneness with God so that when He says Go we are filled to overflowing with His presence.

We would like to end this chapter with the song, **"You're already there"**. We recommend that you go to *www.youtube.com* and in the YouTube search bar, search for *"You're Already There by Casting Crowns"* minus the quotation marks.

IN SUMMARY

We learned the following about clarity:

- Doubt is the absence of clarity.

- Clarity is the absence of doubt.

- To prevent doubt, we need to clearly understand what God tells us with the when, how and what.

- Clarity isn't always given as a whole, sometimes we only get what we need to know one step at a time.

- God knows the whole and we just need to do the steps He wants.

- You will receive a blessing and have a great ministry when you learn to clarify what God wants you to do.

Clarity is the first aspect of maturity. The next aspect of maturity is forgiveness.

CHAPTER TEN

Aspect Two of Maturity: Forgiveness

In this chapter we will discuss forgiveness the second aspect of Maturity. One of the biggest hindrances to our faith is unforgiveness and/or bitterness towards others. This undermines any prayers or requests we make to God. But don't take our word for it, let's look at scripture.

> [9]"*After this manner therefore pray ye: Our Father which art in heaven, Hallowed be thy name.*" [10]"*Thy kingdom come. Thy will be done in earth, as it is in heaven.*" [11]"*Give us this day our daily bread.*" [12]"*And forgive us our debts, as we forgive our debtors.*" [13]"*And lead us not into temptation, but deliver us from evil: For thine is the kingdom, and the power, and the glory, for ever. Amen.*" [14]"*For if ye forgive men their trespasses, your heavenly Father will also forgive you:*" [15]"*But if ye forgive not men their trespasses, neither will your Father forgive your trespasses.*" – Matthew 6:9 - 15*

These are familiar scriptures but what are they really saying? Let's investigate this together.

Jesus' disciples asked Him how they should pray. Prayer is a natural outflow of our faith. It is taking all we know about God and desiring to be in relationship with Him. Jesus said the words above to give them an example. We are going to focus on the forgiveness words. Matthew 6:12 shows Jesus said we need to ask God to forgive us of our sins. Why, because we commit them all the time either knowingly or not knowingly. These sins are anything which is contrary to God and usually show up in our attitudes, thinking, desires, etc. Is the attitude of our heart humbleness and reverence or something else toward God? So we always need, as part of praying, ask forgiveness. However, Jesus doesn't end there, He also says that we need to forgive those that have done wrong to us.

Sounds simple enough, maybe we can sneak by and not do the second half. But no, Jesus continues in 6:15 saying that if we do not forgive our fellow man of the wrongs they do toward us, neither will God forgive us of the wrongs we have done toward Him. Wow that is a stop and backup the train statement.

You mean that God will not forgive me? That is what the scriptures say, He will not forgive you.

Jesus even goes further than this. He says in the following:

> *23"Therefore if thou bring thy gift to the altar, and there rememberest that thy brother hath ought against thee;" 24"Leave there thy gift before the altar, and go thy way; first be reconciled to thy brother, and then come and offer thy gift." – Matthew 5:23 - 24*

If we are aware (usually through conviction of the Holy Spirit) that a brother or sister in Christ has an issue with us, *whether our fault or theirs,* **WE** are to go and reconcile with them before we offer anything to God and we would add before we ask Him for anything.

As we really stop and look at what we are being told through Jesus, God takes this subject very seriously because it has a direct effect on our faith. How does this effect faith you might say? Let's look at our faith equation again:

A Minding my thoughts and understanding those from God;

and

B My total belief in God;

and

C My total confidence and reliance on God's character;

and

D My assurance that He has good planned for me;

and

E Belief in what God told me to do;

and

F My action of acting on those thoughts (obedience);

= Faith

According to Matthew 6:15, God will not forgive us. We can hit that in a couple different parts of our equation here. It could be A, if God is telling us that we need to forgive someone, yes you know exactly when He is doing it, and we consciously ignore those thoughts are we really minding our thoughts and feelings? No we are not. We have already stated that the equation must be there in its entirety to work. If A is missing then we cannot pray in faith for anything because we are not minding our thoughts.

But it doesn't just stop at **A**. It also affects **B**. How can I have total belief in God if I don't listen to him?

Or **C**, I can't have total reliance on God's character if I am not willing to do what is listed in scripture ?

Or even **D**, not forgiving people is saying that God does not have good planned for me but only evil.

Or **E**, I don't believe in what God is telling me to do... Forgive.

And finally **F**, because if I don't act and forgive, then I do not have faith.

There are men and women who pray for their unsaved spouse's salvation, but yet they harbor bitterness and unforgiveness in their hearts for what the spouse has done to them. Why would they think their prayers will be answered? Where is the faith? Why are they even praying? Are they really praying for the spouse's salvation, or are they really praying that spouse will change and treat them the way they want to be treated? What is the underlying thought here? Isn't that what these scriptures are saying?

> ³*"And why beholdest thou the mote that is in thy brother's eye, but considerest not the beam that is in thine own eye?"* ⁴*"Or how wilt thou say to thy brother, Let me pull out the mote out of thine eye; and, behold, a beam is in thine own eye?"* ⁵*"Thou hypocrite, first cast out the beam out of thine own eye; and then shalt thou see clearly to cast out the mote out of thy brother's eye."*
> *– Matthew 7:3 - 5*

If the person praying is not in right standing with God, or more to the point they are in direct conflict with God, why would God answer? Especially if they are praying for someone else to treat them better. Why would God grant that when they are not treating God in the right way.

As part of growing and maturing we have to learn to forgive and not harbor bitterness towards others. I (Rich) have been dealing with this very thing. Over the course of 5 years, God has been putting thoughts in my mind of all the bitterness that was in my heart. I was quite surprised and taken aback at first. After all I felt I had dealt with all this "stuff". But I realized, *burying it and trying not to think about it*, is not the same thing as having dealt with the feelings and thoughts and most definitely not the same thing as having asked God to forgive me of this bitterness, hatred and unforgiveness I have carried around for so many years.

I had to let go. As God put thoughts in my head of all the things I was bitter about. I had the choice to ask forgiveness and forgive or to walk away. God had brought me to a point of decision. Do you know what motivated me to forgive? I was stuck in my Christian walk and realized if I wanted to move forward to where God wanted me, I had to deal with this first. Does satan still try to sucker me into these bitter thoughts? Yes, but I now catch them faster and see what they really are and then pray that God will forgive the bitterness and then I rebuke the thoughts in Jesus Christ's name.

This is a great lesson for us, God wants us in a pure state so that we can minister in His name to others. Hurting people, hurts other people. We don't want to hurt others but help them to a saving knowledge of Jesus. We cannot do that from a hurt state and must deal with any bitterness, hatred, or unforgiveness that is in our hearts.

If we do not then we end up like the servant in Matthew 18. He was forgiven of a great debt but would not do in kind. Let's see what happens:

> [31] *"So when his fellowservants saw what was done, they were very sorry, and came and told unto their lord all that was done."* [32] *"Then his lord, after that he had called him, said unto him, O thou wicked servant, I forgave thee all that debt, because thou desiredst me:"* [33] *"Shouldest not thou also have had compassion on thy fellowservant, even as I had pity on thee?"* [34] *"And his lord*

was wroth, and delivered him to the tormentors, till he should pay all that was due unto him." ³⁵"So likewise shall my heavenly Father do also unto you, if ye from your hearts forgive not every one his brother their trespasses."
– Matthew 18:31 -35

Here we see that the man's bitterness and unforgiveness led him to be put into prison to be tormented. Then Jesus says the most amazing thing, "so likewise shall my heavenly Father do also unto you". Whoa.

Jesus is very serious on this subject and it is time we as Christians take Him seriously on this subject. There are dire consequences here. When a person in that time was put in prison to work off a debt, all they owned was sold and they stayed in prison working for a pittance of what they could make. They were not treated well, not fed well, and left to die if they didn't perform.

So likewise what is Jesus saying here? We believe that the same thing happens to us today. It may not be a physical prison but it is most certainly an emotional and spiritual one. We put our relationship with God on the line. We put our emotions on the line, often letting them eat away at our being, we become outwardly bitter and spiteful. We isolate ourselves from people and we withdraw from everything. We are tormented by the thoughts of the wrongs which were done to us and think of ways to get back at those people. The thoughts are constant and never stop. Sounds like a prison to us.

What does God do, He gives us over to these things thus allowing us to be put in this prison. Until we start to forgive and ask forgiveness we are stuck there.

Not only that, we put ourselves in prison from being used by God. If He can't trust what we will do, why would He put us in front of people to help lead them to salvation? Especially since we are not dealing with the people themselves but satan and his minions master puppeteering these people. satan already knows all our hurts so who do you think he uses to have those hurts deepened, the very ones that God wants us to minister to. So now we have also put ourselves in jail spiritually, and when one is not doing what one was created to do, well they are just a miserable wretch. (We don't say this lightly. We have been there)

Bottom line, we have to leave the responsibility to God for the other person who hurt us. We have to trust that God will take care of the hurt that was done to us. We need to move on. We need to mature. Is it going to be easy? No. Is it going to be painful? Yes. Is it critical? Yes. Why? Think of it this way, how many people are you willing to watch walk into hell on the final judgment day because you did not let go and forgive? Are you willing to watch strangers you'll never get to meet? Are you willing to watch friends? Family? Your children?

Will forgiveness heal us and make us whole? Yes. Think of what great things God could do through you if you were free of the bitterness you have been harboring all your life.

So are you truly minding your thoughts?

Do you truly believe in God?

Do you believe in God's character?

Do you believe in God's character towards you?

Do you believe that God has a good plan for your life?

Do you believe in what God promises you?

Are you willing to take the first steps and act on it?

Now is the time!

God is standing right next to you waiting for you to take his hand.

Will you take it? WILL YOU?

We pray that you do and that God may bless you with the freedom you deserve and that He wants to give you.

We would like to close this chapter with the song *"Forgiveness"*. We recommend that you go to *www.youtube.com* and in the YouTube search bar, search for *"Forgiveness by Matthew West"* minus the quotation marks. After you listen to the song, we would also recommend searching for a live concert version which has the full story behind the song "Matthew West-*"Forgiveness"* Story LIVE with Surprise Guest Renee & Eric- Bradenton, FL 10-24-12". Keep the inner quotation marks.

IN SUMMARY

We learned the following about forgiveness:

- Forgiving others is a very maturing thing. It is necessary for one to multiply their faith and to see great things happen.

- God commands us to forgive others.

- We do not truly have faith if we harbor unforgiveness and bitterness toward others.

- We are in prison until we start to forgive others.

- We can be free!!!!

As we start to deal with forgiveness, we can then move to binding and loosening, our last maturity topic.

CHAPTER ELEVEN

Aspect Three of Maturity: Binding and Loosening

This is the third and last aspect of our Maturity variable in the faith equation. This chapter deals with understanding binding and loosening and how to use that information in regards to our faith.

As a lead in to this chapter, let's look at the verse Matthew 18:18 "Verily I say unto you, Whatsoever **ye shall bind**[G1210] on earth shall be **bound**[G1210] in heaven: and whatsoever **ye shall loose**[G3089] on earth shall be **loosed**[G3089] in heaven."

Quickly looking at two key words bind and loose let's look at their meanings... *bind*, Strong's G1210, means exactly how we use the word today: to bind, be in bonds, knit, tie, wind. *Loosed*, Strong's G3089, means break (up), destroy, dissolve, melt, put off. So when we talk about binding we want to put something into bindings (rope, shackles, zip ties, etc.) so that it cannot move or have freedom to move. Loosen is a little more abstract, when we speak of loosening something we want what is loosened to be destroyed, dissolved, melted off so that it is no more.

Having introduced our main words, we would be remiss with not taking some time to digress and discuss what and who we are binding and what is to be loosened. Hopefully without taking this book sideways too much, we will have an explanation of both. There are obviously two sides at work in our world and they are good and evil and the Holy Spirit and satan. When we speak of binding, we want to bind satan and those who serve him so that they stop spreading evil in this world. At the same time, we want to open the doors for the Holy Spirit to move in this world (in men, women and children's hearts) to loosen the bondage satan and evil has put on them. We are not loosening the Holy Spirit because that would mean we are destroying the Holy Spirit, but rather we are releasing the Holy Spirit to move destroying, dissolving, melting the bondage of evil. Let's look at good, evil, satan and the Holy Spirit.

Good is a little difficult to interpret mainly because God himself has declared Himself as good. However, when we say God is good, it is a deeper meaning than what we would translate that word to be from the current English language. When we say God is good we have to look at His names we discussed in Chapter 4. Two of them in particular describe Him as good, Yahweh (Jehovah) and Jehovah-Qâdôsh. Remember Yahweh means God has always existed, He was not created. One way we looked at this name is to say that He is absolute… He is free from anything and everything. He is not a mixture of anything but pure in His being (substance). This would describe God from a natural standpoint. Then from a moral standpoint He is Jehovah-Qâdôsh. He is clean… morally pure, morally right and is the only being, if you will, that is or another word is Holy. So as we define good, we need to look at good from the standpoint in speaking of God and that God is naturally and morally pure in the purest sense we can understand. This is a key point because God's creation is either good or evil based on *what they are doing in relation to God*. Let's dive into good and evil to hopefully make this clearer.

The word good is first found in Genesis 1:4 "And God saw the light, that *it was* good:[H2896] and God divided the light from the darkness.", per Strong's H2896 good means to be good (not spoiled). Other words used to describe this word are: beautiful; best; better; bountiful; cheerful; in favour; fine; glad; graciously; joyful; kindly; kindness; loving; merry; most; pleasant; pleasure; precious; prosperity; ready; sweet; wealth; and welfare. We believe these words are used to describe the outflow of God, but they do not necessarily describe God. We would then submit that when something God creates is being good (doing what God created it to do, the way He wants it done, when He wants it done), then at that point it is: beautiful; best; better; bountiful; cheerful; in favor; fine; glad; graciously; joyful; kindly; kindness; loving; merry; most; pleasant; pleasure; precious; prosperity; ready; sweet; wealth; and welfare *in relationship to God*, and everything else in creation. When something God created is doing what God created it to do, then and only then is it all the words listed previously. Why?... *because it is in right relationship to God*. When something is in right relationship with God, then the outflow of it will be all the words we listed previously. When a rock is being a rock, then it is doing all that God created it to do and therefore it can be described as good[H2896].

Then what is evil? Good (no pun intended) question which deserves an answer and as most of our questions we have, the answer is found in the Bible. Evil is first mentioned in the Bible in Genesis 2:17 "But of the tree of the knowledge of good and **evil,**[H7451] thou shalt not eat of it: for in the day that thou eatest thereof thou shalt surely die." Per Strong's H7451 *evil* (natural or moral) can be translated into the following words: adversity, affliction, bad, calamity, distress, grief, harm, heavy, hurt, ill favoured, mischief, misery, sore, sorrow, trouble, vex, wicked, wretchedness, wrong. As you can see, it is pretty much the opposite of good. None of these words really sound like much fun alone, but when one puts them altogether, one can really see how bad the word evil really is. Or maybe a better way of saying it, these show us what the word evil does... what it causes, or what happens when what God creates, is not doing what God created it to do. When what God created is not doing what it was created to do, it is *separated from God* and that separation causes the created to spoil in itself due to its relationship to God. The outflow of the created then is all the words above. When a rock is not being a rock, then the above words would describe what happens to it as *it is separated from God*, and everything else in creation that is good. Again good and evil are judged against God and what is being judged, is judged on relationship… is it in right relationship to God.

Where did evil come from? Another excellent question and that answer is found in Isaiah 45:7 "I [God] form the light, and create darkness: I make peace, and create **evil**:[H7451] I the LORD do all these *things.*"

God created evil? Yes that is what the Bible says: God created evil. If that sounds strange or not believable, then we humbly offer this human "logical" argument of what the Bible says… If God did not create evil, then either evil created itself or another being created evil. In either case, creating something out of nothing is only something God can do. That is what we as Christians believe and what the Bible teaches. It is also shown in the names of God that we covered in Chapter 4. But continuing the argument, if God did not create evil, then either evil is equal to God or there is another being that is equal to God. We know per the Bible that God is the I am who I am and there are none besides Him. Therefore we can deduce that God created evil at some point. The fact that God created evil is a very comforting thought. Why? Because if God did not create evil, He would not have power over evil. He at best would be able to cancel out evil or neutralize it, but not have complete power over it.

Again when we look at something God created and view its outflow against God then it is viewed as either good (doing what God created it to do) or it is evil (doing anything other than what God created it to do). Evil is what we want to bind (to tie up and prevent from doing any more damage) and then also what we want to loosen (to melt off, put off, dissolve, destroy) the bondage it puts on mankind… more on that coming up. Now let's look at the Holy Spirit.

The Spirit of God (Holy Spirit) is first described in the Bible in Genesis 1:2 "And the earth was without form, and void; and darkness *was* upon the face of the deep. And **the Spirit**[H7307] of God moved upon the face of the waters.". Per Strong's, *Spirit* H7307 is translated as, wind with the root word of blowing (like a breath when one speaks). We could literally translate it as the breath of God. When God speaks, He is breathing out His Spirit if you will.

In the new testament it is first described in Matthew 3:16 "And Jesus, when he was baptized, went up straightway out of the water: and, lo, the heavens were opened unto him, and he saw **the**[G3588] **Spirit**[G4151] **of God**[G2316] descending like a dove, and lighting upon him" the *Spirit* Strong's G4151 is translated as breath, but goes deeper referring to God's spirit, Jesus' spirit or the Holy Spirit. Since we know that God, Jesus and the Holy Spirit are one, but in different forms, and from the scriptures John 16:13 – 15 we studied in Chapter 7, we know God has revealed everything to Jesus and Jesus has revealed everything to the Holy Spirit. The Holy Spirit is God. To understand this, let's see what the Holy Spirit's role is.

What does the Holy Spirit do? Good question and again for that answer we need to look at some verses in the Bible:

1 God gives life through the Holy Spirit physically to Man and to all creatures:

> *"And the LORD God formed man of the dust of the ground, and breathed into his nostrils the breath of life; and man became a living soul." – Genesis 2:7*

> [29]*"Thou hidest thy face, they are troubled: thou takest away their breath, they die, and return to their dust."* [30]*"Thou sendest forth thy spirit, they are created: and thou renewest the face of the earth."* – Psalms 104:29 - 30

… and to man spiritually:

> *"It is the spirit that quickeneth; the flesh profiteth nothing: the words that I speak unto you, they are spirit, and they are life."* – John 6:63

2 The Holy Spirit lives in those who have accepted Jesus as their savior:

> [16]*"And I will pray the Father, and he shall give you another Comforter, that he may abide with you for ever;"* [17]*"Even the Spirit of truth; whom the world cannot receive, because it seeth him not, neither knoweth him: but ye know him; for he dwelleth with you, and shall be in you."* – John 14:16 - 17

3 The Holy Spirit imparts extra supernatural (not of ourselves but from God) wisdom, understanding and knowledge in areas needed for God's will to be done:

> *"And I have filled him with the spirit of God, in wisdom, and in understanding, and in knowledge, and in all manner of workmanship,"* – Exodus 31:3

4 The Holy Spirit allows people to prophesize. We see this in King Saul when he was anointed to be king:

"And when they came thither to the hill, behold, a company of prophets met him; and the Spirit of God came upon him, and he prophesied among them."
– 1 Samuel 10:10

We also know that toward the end of days when God pours out the Holy Spirit on His people, our sons and daughters will prophesize:

[16]"But this is that which was spoken by the prophet Joel;" [17]"And it shall come to pass in the last days, saith God, I will pour out of my Spirit upon all flesh: and your sons and your daughters shall prophesy, and your young men shall see visions, and your old men shall dream dreams:" – Acts 2:16 - 17

What are they prophesizing about? About God, who He is, His goodness, what He is doing and what He is going to do, to proclaim Him to everyone.

5 The Holy Spirit convicts us in righteous anger to fight the social injustice of this world (to help those who need our help):

"And the Spirit of God came upon Saul when he heard those tidings, and his anger was kindled greatly."
– 1 Samuel 11:6

6 The Holy Spirit gives us visions for things God wants us to know so that we can share them with others:

[24]"Afterwards the spirit took me up, and brought me in a vision by the Spirit of God into Chaldea, to them of the captivity. So the vision that I had seen

went up from me." [25] *"Then I spake unto them of the captivity all the things that the LORD had shewed me."*
– Ezekiel 11:24 - 24

7 The Holy Spirit comforts us (advocates to us and for us on our behalf unto God):

"But the Comforter, which is the Holy Ghost, whom the Father will send in my name, he shall teach you all things, and bring all things to your remembrance, whatsoever I have said unto you." – John 14:26

8 The Holy Spirit embodies truth (who God is, what God wants):

[25] *"But this cometh to pass, that the word might be fulfilled that is written in their law, They hated me without a cause."* [26] *"But when the Comforter is come, whom I will send unto you from the Father, even the Spirit of truth, which proceedeth from the Father, he shall testify of me:"*
– John 15:25 - 26

9 The Holy Spirit shows us how to live by revealing to us all that Jesus embodies (God's Word, the Bible):

[13] *"Howbeit when he, the Spirit of truth, is come, he will guide you into all truth: for he shall not speak of himself; but whatsoever he shall hear, that shall he speak: and he will shew you things to come."* [14] *"He shall glorify me: for he shall receive of mine, and shall shew it unto you."* [15] *"All things that the Father hath are mine: therefore said I, that he shall take of mine, and shall shew it unto you." – John 16:13 - 15*

10 The Holy Spirit convicts (reproves) us of our sins to guide us in right living:

> ⁷*"Nevertheless I tell you the truth; It is expedient for you that I go away: for if I go not away, the Comforter will not come unto you; but if I depart, I will send him unto you."* ⁸*"And when he is come, he will reprove the world of sin, and of righteousness, and of judgment:"* ⁹*"Of sin, because they believe not on me;"* ¹⁰*"Of righteousness, because I go to my Father, and ye see me no more;"* ¹¹*"Of judgment, because the prince of this world is judged."*
> *– John 16:7 - 11*

11 The Holy Spirit, as truth, uses that truth to set us free from evil and satan's bondage:

> ³¹*"Then said Jesus to those Jews which believed on him, If ye continue in my word, then are ye my disciples indeed;"* ³²*"And ye shall know the truth, and the truth shall make you free."* *– John 8:31 - 32*

12 The Holy Spirit gives us the boldness to proclaim Jesus to the world:

> *"And when they had prayed, the place was shaken where they were assembled together; and they were all filled with the Holy Ghost, and they spake the word of God with boldness."* *– Acts 4:31*

Finally as a side note, we know Jesus was full of the Holy Spirit and through that power He was to do the following:

> *[1] "The Spirit of the Lord GOD is upon me; because the LORD hath anointed me to preach good tidings unto the meek; he hath sent me to bind up the brokenhearted, to proclaim liberty to the captives, and the opening of the prison to them that are bound;" [2] "To proclaim the acceptable year of the LORD, and the day of vengeance of our God; to comfort all that mourn;" [3] "To appoint unto them that mourn in Zion, to give unto them beauty for ashes, the oil of joy for mourning, the garment of praise for the spirit of heaviness; that they might be called trees of righteousness, the planting of the LORD, that he might be glorified." – Isaiah 61:1 -3*

The Holy Spirit then shows us and teaches us God's goodness and works to bring us into a right relationship with God.

Who is the main proponent then who works to bring evil throughout Gods creation? That would be satan. So that begs the question who is satan and again the answer to that is found in the Bible in the following verses:

> *[12] "Son of man, take up a lamentation upon the king of Tyrus, and say unto him, Thus saith the Lord GOD; Thou sealest up the sum, full of wisdom, and perfect in beauty." [13] "Thou hast been in Eden the garden of God; every precious stone was thy covering, the sardius, topaz, and the diamond, the beryl, the onyx, and the jasper, the sapphire, the emerald, and the carbuncle, and gold: the workmanship of thy tabrets and of thy pipes was prepared in thee in the day that thou wast created." [14] "Thou art the anointed cherub that covereth; and I have set thee*

so: thou wast upon the holy mountain of God; thou hast walked up and down in the midst of the stones of fire." ¹⁵"Thou wast perfect in thy ways from the day that thou wast created, till iniquity was found in thee." ¹⁶"By the multitude of thy merchandise they have filled the midst of thee with violence, and thou hast sinned: therefore I will cast thee as profane out of the mountain of God: and I will destroy thee, O covering cherub, from the midst of the stones of fire." ¹⁷"Thine heart was lifted up because of thy beauty, thou hast corrupted thy wisdom by reason of thy brightness: I will cast thee to the ground, I will lay thee before kings, that they may behold thee." ¹⁸"Thou hast defiled thy sanctuaries by the multitude of thine iniquities, by the iniquity of thy traffick; therefore will I bring forth a fire from the midst of thee, it shall devour thee, and I will bring thee to ashes upon the earth in the sight of all them that behold thee." – Ezekiel 28:12 - 18

Most Biblical scholars have noted that God is not really talking about a king of the city Tyrus… He is really talking about satan in the verses above. Here are some points to note from the above scriptures:

1   satan is a ***created*** being and from our studies we believe he was either the highest created being or real close to the highest. (Wisdom would be right up there at the top too)

2   he was very beautiful and many believe from verse 13 he was made with instruments either in him or on him to lead the heavens in praise of God and God's goodness. (Praising God for all the names we discussed in Chapter 4)

3 he was a part of the cherub angelic hierarchy. From the various cherubim scriptures in the Bible, cherubim were created to protect something… to cover something if you will as a protectant. Look at the two cherubim in Genesis that protected the Garden of Eden, the two that were on the top of the ark of the covenant, and others mentioned in the Bible.

Just a pause here in our numbering explanation of satan, a question: how did satan succumb to evil (verse 15)? Succumb means to give into something. For example, if I am resisting eating a piece of cake and then eventually giving in and eating the cake I could say I succumbed to the desire having the cake. We know from Genesis Chapter 1, God declares that He created everything and everything He created (outside of evil) was declared good. So satan was created as good. Now let's ask this question, since God is the absence of evil, why would God need a being to lead the heavens in worship of His goodness? Was satan created to remind the heavens and spiritual realms of God's goodness so that they would not succumb to evil? The reason we ask these questions is to bring us back to why satan was created. We would submit, without trying to be too controversial here, satan was created to cover evil… his covering cherub role was to protect all of creation from evil, to hold it at bay if you will and because of that, his secondary role would be to show all of creation/lead all of creation in praise of God's goodness. However, rather than covering and protecting, at some point, he succumbed to evil and became the main proponent of it throughout creation.

4 he succumbed to the evil he was to protect creation from and when iniquity (sin/unrighteousness) was found in him God cast him out of his spiritual realms position to earth. Look at verse 15 – 17 above and

*⁷"And there was war in heaven: Michael and his angels fought against the dragon; and the dragon fought and his angels," ⁸"And prevailed not; neither was their place found any more in heaven." ⁹"And the great dragon was cast out, that old serpent, called the Devil, and Satan, which deceiveth the whole world: he was cast out into the earth, and his angels were cast out with him."
– Revelation 12:7 - 9*

and

⁶"Now there was a day when the sons of God came to present themselves before the LORD, and Satan came also among them." ⁷"And the LORD said unto Satan, Whence comest thou? Then Satan answered the LORD, and said, From going to and fro in the earth, and from walking up and down in it." – Job 1:6 – 7

and

"And the LORD said unto Satan, Behold, all that he hath is in thy power; only upon himself put not forth thine hand. So Satan went forth from the presence of the LORD." – Job 1:12

Looking at these verses it does not mean satan cannot access God or the spiritual realms, it just means he lost his position and authority in the spiritual realms.

5 this casting to the ground (earth) (verse 17) gave him dominion if you will over the earth. Jesus refers to him as "prince of this world"…

> *"Hereafter I will not talk much with you: for the* **prince**[G758] *of this world cometh, and hath nothing in me."*
> *— John 14:30*

and as the "strong man"…

> *"Or else how can one enter into a* **strong man's**[G2478] **house,**[G3614] *and spoil his goods, except he first bind the strong man? and then he will spoil his house."*
> *— Matthew 12:29*

> *"No man can enter into a strong man's house, and spoil his goods, except he will first bind the strong man; and then he will spoil his house." — Mark 3:27*

> *"When a strong man armed keepeth his* **palace,**[G833] *his goods are in peace:" — Luke 11:21*

and in the temptation of Jesus, Jesus never corrects satan with his claims of being able to give Jesus authority over the earth

> [8] *"Again, the devil taketh him up into an exceeding high mountain, and sheweth him all the kingdoms of the world, and the glory of them;"* [9] *"And saith unto him, All these things will I give thee, if thou wilt fall down and worship me."* [10] *"Then saith Jesus unto him, Get thee hence, Satan: for it is written, Thou shalt worship the Lord thy God, and him only shalt thou serve."* [11] *"Then the devil leaveth him, and, behold, angels came and ministered unto him." — Matthew 4:8 - 11*

which again by default shows that satan has authority over the earth and all that are in it.

6 in Matt 12:29 and Mark 3:27 (listed above) the strong man has a *house*, Strong's G3614 or an *abode* and in Luke 11:21 (listed above) the strong man lives in a *palace*, Strong's G833 or *mansion* again referring to where satan abides (the earth)

7 it does not sound good for us, but don't fear because satan's authority has been broken through Jesus' death and resurrection

> *"And Jesus came and spake unto them, saying, All power is given unto me in heaven and in earth."*
> *– Matthew 28:18*

As a side note we find it interesting that satan was replaced by 4 cherubim and 24 elders to lead all of creation in praise and worship of God and His goodness

> *[8] "And the four beasts had each of them six wings about him; and they were full of eyes within: and they rest not day and night, saying, Holy, holy, holy, Lord God Almighty, which was, and is, and is to come." [9] "And when those beasts give glory and honour and thanks to him that sat on the throne, who liveth for ever and ever," [10] "The four and twenty elders fall down before him that sat on the throne, and worship him that liveth for ever and ever, and cast their crowns before the throne, saying," [11] "Thou art worthy, O Lord, to receive glory and honour and power: for thou hast created all things, and for thy pleasure they are and were created." – Revelation 4:8 - 11*

Above we stated earth has been given to satan, and from the time he was cast out of heaven till he is bound for 1,000 years, while Jesus has His millennial reign, satan has prince/strong man authority in and on earth. Let's look at some of the verses that describe the prince/strongman:

> *"Now is the judgment of this world: now shall the* **prince**[G758] *of this world be cast out." – John 12:31*

> *"Hereafter I will not talk much with you: for the prince of this world cometh, and hath nothing in me."* *– John 14:30*

> *"Or else how can one enter into* **a strong man's**[G2478] **house,**[G3614] *and spoil his goods, except he first bind the strong man? and then he will spoil his house."* *– Matthew 12:29*

> *"No man can enter into a strong man's house, and spoil his goods, except he will first bind the strong man; and then he will spoil his house." – Mark 3:27*

> *"When a strong man armed keepeth his* **palace,**[G833] *his goods are in peace:" – Luke 11:21*

What do these scriptures mean? First Strong's G2478 for *strongman* is defined as someone who is forcible (mighty, powerful) with the root meaning to hold... so someone that has the strength/power to hold something... for example to keep in submission. Not only is satan a strongman, but he is the *prince* of this world, Strong's G758 means satan is chief of this world or first in order of this world. He has setup residence here on earth as his dominion and his number one priority can be found in the verses 1 Peter 5:8 "Be sober, be vigilant; because your adversary the devil, as a roaring lion, walketh about, seeking whom **he may devour**:"[G2666] with *devour* meaning to swallow up/to drown. satan's number one goal is to destroy all mankind and he continually searches over the earth to see who he can destroy. His number one way of doing this is by drowning us, any form of suffocation, from our spiritual life breath of God. satan attempts to cut us off from God and by doing so we are suffocated because we are not being nourished by God. This usually happens by satan getting us to withdrawal from God. We will discuss more in Chapter 18, but we wanted to introduce the concept of drowning.

We have talked about good, evil, the Holy Spirit and satan, now let's get into deeper discussion on binding and loosening. We started with the premise that we want to bind satan and then allow the Holy Spirit freedom to work to loosen (destroy, dissolve, melt off) evil. When we think of binding, it can be done in numerous ways. One of the ways involves a mechanism that has a way of locking a portion/all of a person's body so that they cannot escape. For example, a leg shackle, handcuffs, stocks, jail cell, etc… these are all contraptions that have a lock and a key, the lock holds the bindings in place and one cannot be free then until it is unlocked with a key that matches the binding. Having stated this, it is interesting that the Bible talks about keys in the following scriptures:

> "And the **key**[H4668] of the house of David will I lay upon his [Jesus] shoulder; so he shall open, and none shall shut; and he shall shut, and none shall open." – Isaiah 22:22

> "I am he [Jesus] that liveth, and was dead; and, behold, I am alive for evermore, Amen; and have the **keys**[G2807] of hell and of death." – Revelation 1:18

*"And to the angel of the church in Philadelphia write; These things saith he [Jesus] that is holy, he that is true, he that hath the **key**^{G2807} of David, he that openeth, and no man shutteth; and shutteth, and no man openeth;"* – Revelation 3:7

*"And the fifth angel sounded, and I saw a star fall from heaven unto the earth: and to him [Jesus] was given the **key**^{G2807} of the bottomlesspit."* – Revelation 9:1

*"And I [Jesus] will give unto thee [Peter] the **keys**^{G2807} of the kingdom of heaven: and whatsoever thou shalt bind on earth shall be bound in heaven: and whatsoever thou shalt **loose**^{G3089} on earth shall be **loosed**^{G3089} in heaven."* – Matthew 16:19

Strong's H4668 and G2807 define a *key* just like we think of a key today. It is an item that is specially crafted to fit into a lock and to turn in such a way as to lock it (bind) or unlock it. What is interesting here is that all these verses speak directly of Jesus and that He has been given the keys to hell (also the bottomless pit), to death, to heaven and finally to earth. He has been given the keys to every realm: physical, emotional, and spiritual. How did Jesus get the keys to these things? Very good question and the answer is found in the following verses:

^{14}"And as Moses lifted up the serpent in the wilderness, even so must the Son of man be lifted up:" ^{15}"That whosoever believeth in him should not perish, but have eternal life." ^{16}"For God so loved the world, that he gave his only begotten Son, that whosoever believeth in him should not perish, but have everlasting life." ^{17}"For

God sent not his Son into the world to condemn the world; but that the world through him might be saved."
— John 3:14 - 17

and

"Who is he that condemneth? It is Christ that died, yea rather, that is risen again, who is even at the right hand of God, who also **maketh intercession**^{G1793} *for us. "*
— Romans 8:34

You see, Jesus received the keys because He did what God sent Him to do. He proclaimed, showed, and demonstrated to us who God is, how much God cares, and being obedient, He took all our sins and covered them with His blood as a sacrifice to bring us into right relationship with God. However, it does not stop there, because of His obedience, God did not simply leave Him as a dead sacrifice, God raised Jesus from the dead and made Him a living sacrifice by seating Him at God's right hand to intercede for us (Romans 8:34). satan continually accuses us before God to condemn us (like a prosecuting attorney), but Jesus is seated at God's right hand and makes intercession on our behalf (like a defense attorney). What is *making intercession*, Strong's G1793? For those that have accepted Jesus into their hearts, it is Jesus reminding God that He died for our sins and that His blood cleanses us… it means we are in right standing with God and no matter what satan says to condemn (destroy us), his words fall like dead stones and never reach God's ears. Jesus' death removed the level of authority that satan has over his kingdom. Jesus came in and set us free from a spiritual standpoint to give us spiritual freedom from satan. Then He sent us the Holy Spirit to loosen us (destroy, dissolve, melt away to nothing) from bondage to evil satan and his followers have put on us. We can be completely free from an emotional, physical, spiritual standpoint as the Holy Spirit loosens this bondage of evil from us. It was a changing of the locks. When one changes a lock, the key that previously worked no longer works because the lock is

satan's keys no longer work.

new. What God did through Jesus was to change the lock. satan no longer controls the lock Jesus does.

Building on this by going back to Matthew 16:19 "And I [Jesus] will give unto thee [Peter] the keys of the kingdom of heaven: and whatsoever thou shalt bind on earth shall be bound in heaven: and whatsoever thou shalt loose on earth shall be loosed in heaven." the next important thing to note is who does Jesus give the keys to? He gave them to Peter. Why is that important? Because in the prior verse, Matthew 16:18 "And I say also unto thee, That thou art Peter, and upon this rock I will build my church; and the gates of hell shall not prevail against it." Jesus renames Peter from Simon to Peter. Peter is the Greek word for rock. So in effect Jesus is saying that Simon (Peter) is a rock and on/with that rock (Peter) Jesus will start His church. Do you see? The keys have been passed from Jesus to His church. Who is the church? It is all those that have and will accept Jesus Christ as their personal savior. We are the church and the very keys, which when used on earth to bind something, have the authority to bind it in heavenly realms or when loosens something on earth has the authority to, loosen it in the heavenly realms *have been given to us*. **TO US.** They were given to you, to me, to every brother and sister in Christ that has been, is now and will come. *We have the keys.*

Great you say… this is exciting you say, I am feeling it you say, but what are the keys? We would submit that the key(s) are **FAITH…** our whole faith equation :

A Minding my thoughts and understanding those from God

and

B My total belief in God

and

C My total confidence and reliance on God's character

and

D My assurance that He has good planned for me

and

E Belief in what God told me to do

and

F My action of acting on those thoughts (obedience)

= FAITH

…what we have learned so far and what we are continuing to learn through this book, we have been discovering the keys that God has given us to change this world. Faith is the key that turns the binding and loosening lock and allows us to request things to be bound and loosened on earth and ultimately in heaven. How exciting that God would allow us to have such a powerful tool in our Christian arsenal!!!!

Again it all hinges on obedience… doing what God has asked to be done. That is what turns the lock.

Now that we know what the key(s) are, let's go back and work through binding. Who/what are we binding? To answer that let's look at two scriptures we have already studied and finish them:

> *"Or else how can one enter into a strong man's house, and spoil his goods, except he first **bind**^{G1210} the strong man? and then he will **spoil**^{G1283} his house."*
> – Matthew 12:29

and

> *"No man can enter into a strong man's house, and **spoil**^{G1283} his goods, except he will first **bind**^{G1210} the strong man; and then he will **spoil**^{G1283} his house."*
> – Mark 3:27

Again satan (the strongman) has had the world locked down into the submission of evil since the fall of Adam and Eve till the death and resurrection of Jesus, and God has used the very few men/women who honored Him to bring about an underground movement to break the authority of satan. These folks were Noah and then Abram/Sari. Through Abram/Sari offspring, He attempted to have a people set aside who would follow Him and His commands to break/battle the authority that satan has had, to show their fellow man God and how to live for God. However, that was never enough because satan kept trying to take out the Jewish people either through physically killing them through others or spiritually killing them by making them impure due to morality issues. But with Jesus coming,

Praying out loud helps give testimony to the freedom which has been given. It is announcing it in force to the physical and spiritual realms.

dying, and raising from the dead, that all changed. Now we live in satan's kingdom but we have an authority greater than satan, we have the key(s) (FAITH) that Jesus has given us, we are like a covert ops team who go in and destroy the power of the enemy and liberate others. How do we destroy the enemy? We bind him. We bind the strongman and all those who serve the strongman.

How do we bind the strongman? Oh my friends, this is so neat. I (Rich) have not studied the Greek language and have not done a deep dive in how the Strong's referencing was put together, but if I understand this, it is beyond cool! *Binding*, Strong's G1210, means to bind, be in bonds, knit, tie, wind up. However, it does not stop there, it uses G1189 to explain it further and G1189 means petition: - beseech, pray, make request. Did you catch that? To bind the strongman and those that serve him, we ask God (beseech, pray, make request) for the very thing(s) which God told us to ask (beseech, pray, make request) for. Sounds like part of our FAITH equation. Sounds like what we discussed in chapter 7. And it gets even better, when we move in obedience and ask, the strongman and his servants are bound by the promise of Jesus Christ and the power of His Name, and we can then go in and spoil his house. *Spoil*, Strong's G1283 means to seize (take by force) something from someone else… to plunder their goods. We get to take from satan, by force, that which was his and MAKE IT GOD'S. What is the "it"? "It" can be people: every man, woman, and child that we have influence with or into or come in contact with, whether by person or by hearing about them, those people we are to take by force from satan and

> You have the ability and capability through Jesus to make war against satan.

to make them God's. To lead them to a safe environment prepped where they can drop their guard and allow the Holy Spirit to minister to them, reveal to them who God is, convict them of their sin and prompt them to accept Jesus as their personal savior. Then to fill them, anoint them and baptize them with the Holy Spirit and God's presence. Another "It" can be the joy and peace satan stole from us. Another "It" can be any hurts, pain, sorrow, brokenness, fears, etc., and separation from God satan put on us.

When we open the doors to let the Holy Spirit work (invite Him in to what we are doing as part of our asking), then comes the loosening. *Loosen*, in Strong's G3089, means break (up), destroy, dissolve, melt, and/or put off. What are we loosening? The bondage of evil that satan has the world under. By allowing the Holy Spirit to be free to move in and out of hearts as He sees necessary, the bondage that satan has people under is broken up, destroyed, dissolved, melted, and put off of them. We are set free and given freedom from satan's condemnation for John 8:36 says "If the Son therefore shall make you **free**,[G1659] [G5209] ye shall be **free**[G1658] indeed." Or to paraphrase using Strong's, if Jesus (in conjunction with the Holy Spirit) sets you *free*, Strong's G1659 (liberated), you are *free*, Strong's G1658 (free like a son or daughter of a King). When we are set free from the bondage are no longer a slave to satan, but liberated to be free in all we do as a prince or princess would be in relation to a King (God). We are free like part of the ruling family. How is the bondage broken? Through the Holy Spirit who does all the things we mentioned earlier in the chapter. He: gives life physically/spiritually; lives in us if we have accepted Jesus; imparts God's wisdom, understanding and knowledge; prophesizes through us; helps us

> When Jesus sets you free, you are free indeed.

to fight the social injustice of this world; gives us visions (and dreams) for things God wants us to know; advocates to us and for us on our behalf unto God; embodies truth and uses that truth to set us free from evil and satan's bondage; shows us how to live by revealing to us God's Word; and gives us boldness to proclaim Jesus to the world. We can even ask God for more of the Holy Spirt as we see in Luke 11:13 "If ye then, being evil, know how to give good gifts unto your children: how much more shall your heavenly Father give the Holy Spirit to them that ask him?" As our faith grows, we are more sensitive to the Holy Spirit and what God is saying to us through him. As we do what we hear, our actions give the Holy Spirit freedom to move with us and to destroy satan and his bondage on this world. As we grow, we ask for more of the Holy Spirit, or for deeper revealing's of what the Spirit is telling us. We listen better and learn to tune out all the other noise and distractions that drag us down and away from God so that we can act in clarity and full assurance of what He is telling us to do.

Now as we have been progressing through this we realize we have not asked a critical question… **HOW DO WE TURN THE KEY**… ahh… and that my friends is what we are going to discuss next. I (Rich) was researching how to bind and loosen by searching through different internet search engines. I saw many blogs/commentaries online for and against this concept of binding and loosening. I realized that both sides really have it wrong. I realized that I myself did not understand it as the Strong's definition of loosen really threw me for a loop. Those that are for binding and loosening quote basically the scriptures we listed above and those that do not go along with that thinking, point out that those are the only scriptures. But as I researched more sites, I started to see I was expecting some supernatural phrase/formula to follow and was missing the whole point of how our very living for Jesus and becoming more like Him (so much like him, in fact that people do not even see us but they rather see Jesus shining through us) automatically binds satan so we can go in and plunder that which is his. The simple beauty of this is what both sides miss because they are too busy refuting each other. So here is our team's humble view of how to bind satan so we can go in and plunder him and melt away/destroy the submission to evil he has on this world.

We bind satan and those that follow him:

1 By always acknowledging Jesus is God's son... the Christ... the Messiah

Binds satan from having access to us through his lies denying: the Deity of Christ, atonement, Christ and His teachings, and protecting us from heresies and anti-Christians.

Reference:

> *"And Simon Peter answered and said, Thou art the Christ, the Son of the living God."* – *Matthew 16:16*

2 By understanding where the Bible came from and what it is to be used for.

Binds satan from having access to us through: fully knowing God's truth, not paraphrase scripture, not twisting scripture to fit our desires, and not allowing false prophecy/false teachings.

Reference:

> *[16]"All scripture is given by inspiration of God, and is profitable for doctrine, for reproof, for correction, for instruction in righteousness:" [17]"That the man of God may be perfect, throughly furnished unto all good works."* – *2 Timothy 3:16 - 17*

Dr. Larry Gilbert expresses this best in his book, How to Find Meaning and Fulfillment through Understanding the Spiritual Gift Within You. On page 155 he states that, "The Scriptures are to be used for doctrine (what to believe), reproof (what not to do, pointing out sin), correction (how to change) and instruction in righteousness (how to live right). In other words, the Bible is for *reaching* a lost person, then *teaching* him or her into full maturity."

3 By understanding the authority God has given to Jesus, the Christ and through His authority and power we have the freedom to bind and plunder satan and his kingdom.

Binds satan from having access to us through: his lies that he is the ultimate authority, fear of death, fear of hell, fear of man, hopelessness, despair/dejection, depression, torn spirit, and self-pity. He no longer has any right to any person saved or unsaved. Jesus has paid that price.

Reference:

> [19]*"And what is the exceeding greatness of his power to us-ward who believe, according to the working of his mighty power,"* [20]*"Which he wrought in Christ, when he raised him from the dead, and set him at his own right hand in the heavenly places,"* [21]*"Far above all principality, and power, and might, and dominion, and every name that is named, not only in this world, but also in that which is to come:"* [22]*"And hath put all things under his feet, and gave him to be the head over all things to the church,"* [23]*"Which is his body, the fulness of him that filleth all in all." – Ephesians 1:19 - 23*

4 By understanding that satan has a hierarchy of powers who are at work against God and us in all we do.

Binds satan from having access to us through: understanding that what we see in the physical realm is a small sliver to what is going on in the spiritual realm. When we realize a person is acting against us because they are under satan's control, we can extend grace/mercy to them, pray for them, pray that God will forgive their sins, and that the Holy Spirit will lead them to salvation. By praying in such a way we are asking that the person's thought patterns are changed. Understanding that satan is controlling others, helps us to realize that we are in a constant spiritual battle that is always raging around us. The power of God through the Word and faith is what calms the spiritual storm which swirls around us.

Then recognizing the fact that those who oppose us are under satan's influence, it is not them opposing us but satan.

Reference:

> *"For we wrestle not against flesh and blood, but against principalities, against powers, against the rulers of the darkness of this world, against spiritual wickedness in high places."* – Ephesians 6:12

5 By testing the spirits, the things we hear, see, do, experience, etc. to ensure they are from God based on His word.

This testing includes this book we have written. Although we have extensively quoted the Bible, we want you to understand anything that is not scripture ***is not*** the authoritive word of God. What we have written we believe the Holy Spirit has revealed and what should be shared. Our goal is that as it is read, the Holy Spirit has been giving testimony in agreement with what has been stated here. It should have been building you up and helping you to mature in Christ. Even if you have not agreed with the entirety, what has been written should make you research against scripture what is not agreed with and why. But we want to make sure we state, what we have stated in this book does not replace anything from scripture, but intended to help explain it so we understand it better.

Binds satan from having access to us through: strong deceptions; flattery; lies; false prophecy; superstitions; gossip; slander; false teachings; and items mentioned in number 1.

Reference:

> *[1] "Beloved, believe not every spirit, but try the spirits whether they are of God: because many false prophets are gone out into the world." [2] "Hereby know ye the Spirit of God: Every spirit that confesseth that Jesus Christ is come in the flesh is of God:" [3] "And every spirit that confesseth not that Jesus Christ is come in the flesh is not of God: and this is that spirit of antichrist, whereof ye have heard that it should come; and even now already is it in the world."*
> *– 1 John 4:1 -3*

6 By being very careful who we are listening to, taking counsel from, and who we discuss things of God with.

So many young people go to college and end up taking a philosophy course that blows their faith out of the water. Just because someone teaches a course, has a masters, or a PhD does not give them more authority than God. Any idiot can write and publish a book (I won't speak for Walter, but this includes me (Rich)). Publishing a book does not make you more authoritive than the word of God. It simply means the publisher felt the book was good enough to generate more money than expenses.

*** Be careful of what you are reading, and always make sure you weigh it against God's Word. If it does not line up, throw it into the trash and flush your brain to remove what you read.

Binds satan from having access to us through: rebellion; pride; anything used to predict the future; self-deception; strife; self-righteousness; magic; contentious; obstinate; scornful; seducers/enticers and rejection of God.

Reference:

> [6]*"As ye have therefore received Christ Jesus the Lord, so walk ye in him:"* [7]*"Rooted and built up in him, and stablished in the faith, as ye have been taught, abounding therein with thanksgiving."* [8]*"Beware lest any man spoil you through philosophy and vain deceit, after the tradition of men, after the rudiments of the world, and not after Christ."* – Colossians 2:6 -8

7 By not falling victim to loving the things of this world more than doing the calling God has placed on our lives.

We have needs: food, shelter, protection, some stability, but where we start to go astray is when we make our life passion accumulating stuff. I (Rich) have fallen victim to this at times until God shakes me up to help me realize I am going off course. What we need to really pursue with all our hearts is pursuing God (through studying scripture and prayer). Doing this will help us from falling victim, or satan flashing something in our face and we go off chasing it.

Binds satan from having access to us through: envy; extreme competition; jealousy; covetiness; love of money; idolatry; excessive appetites; chronic dissatisfaction; and chronic worrying (about losing stuff).

Reference:

> [15]*"Love not the world, neither the things that are in the world. If any man love the world, the love of the Father is not in him."* [16]*"For all that is in the world, the lust of the flesh, and the lust of the eyes, and the pride of life, is not of the Father, but is of the world."* – 1 John 2:15 - 16

8 By denying ungodliness and worldly lusts.

Binds satan from having access to us through: keeping our hearts and minds off wickedness, corruptions, and starting to want to do things that are contrary to the Bible

Reference:

> [11]*"For the grace of God that bringeth salvation hath appeared to all men,"* [12]*"Teaching us that, denying **ungodliness**[G763] **and worldly**[G2886] **lusts,**[G1939] we should live soberly, righteously, and godly, in this present world;"* – Titus 2:11 - 12

So a couple of words here, *ungodliness* Strong's G763 means wickedness. *Worldly* Strong's G2886 means corrupt things of this world. *Lusts* Strong's G1939 means a longing for something forbidden (contrary to the laws and precepts the Bible has).

9 By being fruitful, growing in our knowledge of God, and giving thanks to Him.

Binds satan from having access to us through: laziness; idle thoughts; complaining; entitlement; stife; self-righteousness; and arrogance/ smugness.

Reference:

> [10]*"That ye might walk worthy of the Lord unto all pleasing, being fruitful in every good work, and increasing in the knowledge of God;"* [11]*"Strengthened with all might, according to his glorious power, unto all patience and longsuffering with joyfulness;"* [12]***"Giving thanks***[G2168] *unto the Father, which hath made us meet to be partakers of -the inheritance of the saints in light:"* [13]*"Who hath delivered us from the power of darkness, and hath translated us into the kingdom of his dear Son:" – Colossians 1:10 - 13*

Being fruitful, doing what we know God wants us to do, our Faith statement, and at the same time always *Giving Thanks*, Strong's G2168, (expressing gratitude) for WHO God IS and then for what He has done.

10 Walking in the spirit, not allowing the sins of the flesh to manifest themselves in us (remember what Jesus said it is more than not doing the acts it is not even thinking about wanting to do these acts).

Binds satan from having access to us through: acts of the flesh, using our bodies (God's temple) for what God never intended our bodies to be used for… keeping our physical bodies pure, clean, and holy to Him. Living a life of Holiness and Sanctification (in a right standing with God separated from the sin of the world; we are in the world but not of the world). This holy living, gives us a testimony to others about God and his greatness. Keeps our faith in God.

Reference:

> [16]*"This I say then, Walk in the Spirit, and ye shall not fulfil the lust of the flesh."* [17]*"For the flesh lusteth against the Spirit, and the Spirit against the flesh: and*

these are contrary the one to the other: so that ye cannot do the things that ye would." [18]"But if ye be led of the Spirit, ye are not under the law." [19]"Now the works of the flesh are manifest, which are these; Adultery, fornication, uncleanness, lasciviousness," [20]"Idolatry, witchcraft, hatred, variance, emulations, wrath, strife, seditions, heresies," [21]"Envyings, murders, drunkenness, revellings, and such like: of the which I tell you before, as I have also told you in time past, that they which do such things shall not inherit the kingdom of God." [22]"But the fruit of the Spirit is love, joy, peace, longsuffering, gentleness, goodness, faith," [23]"Meekness, temperance: against such there is no law." – Galatians 5:16 - 23

11 By forgiving each other, especially when repentance has taken place. *Binds satan* from having access to us through: bitterness; resentment; revenge; murder; hatred; causing divisions; cruelty; anger/rage, etc.

Reference:

[10]"To whom ye forgive any thing, I [Paul] forgive also: for if I forgave any thing, to whom I forgave it, for your sakes forgave I it in the person of Christ;" [11]"Lest Satan should get an advantage of us: for we are not ignorant of his devices." – 2 Corinthians 2:10 - 11

12 By believing that what we ask of God, He will do … why, because we are only asking for the things He told us to ask for. For example, consider forgiveness. When we pray for forgiveness, we know we are in God's will and can trust we are forgiven.

Binds satan from having access to *us* through: pride, haughtiness, and asking for things that are outside of God's will (which causes doubt when not answered).

Reference:

> *"And all things, whatsoever ye shall ask in prayer, believing, ye shall receive." – Matthew 21:22*

13 By praying in agreement with each other.

Binds satan from having access to *us* through: pride, haughtiness, and asking for things that are outside of God's will (causes doubt when not answered), not only that, but Jesus joins us in our prayers and we know that satan has no power against anything Jesus asks for.

Reference:

> *"Again I say unto you, That if two of you shall agree on earth as touching any thing that they shall ask, it shall be done for them of my Father which is in heaven." [20]"For where two or three are gathered together in my name, there am I in the midst of them." – Matthew 18:19 - 20*

There is power in agreement/unity. There is power in numbers. This is a law which does not change. When we pray in like mind for the same thing, it gives more petition than when one person is praying. We know it is not about us but about what God can do.

[Reference Chapter 13 to understand the power of being in unity]

> **Note:** *What is interesting about this list is that it is progressive, it starts with God's power, then how to undergird ourselves and protect ourselves, and starting*

with helping others (number 14), we start to get into plundering satan and helping others recognize that they are no longer in bondage to satan. From this point forward, it is reaching into this world and setting others free. Praise God!!!!

14 By helping others.

Binds satan from having access to *us* through: pride; haughtiness; self-delusions; thinking that all one has is because of what they have done rather than from God; love of money; excessive appetites; worldliness; fear; lack of trust; anxiety/stress, etc.

Binds satan from having access to *others* through: fear, lack of trust, anxiety/stress, doubt, envy, covetousness, hatred, inner hurts, heaviness, hopelessness, despair, self-pity, etc.

Reference:

> [1] *"There was a certain man in Caesarea called Cornelius, a centurion of the band called the Italian band,"* [2] *"A devout man, and one that feared God with all his house, which gave much **alms**[G1654] to the people, and prayed to God alway."* [3] *"He saw in a vision evidently about the ninth hour of the day an angel of God coming in to him, and saying unto him, Cornelius."* [4] *"And when he looked on him, he was afraid, and said, What is it, Lord? And he said unto him, Thy prayers and thine alms are come up for a memorial before God." – Acts 10:1 - 4*

Alms were given to the poor who begged at the temple gates. *Alms*, Strong's G1654, was giving money to these people to help them. It was a commandment of God in the Old Testament. It was to recognize our brothers and sisters need help and to invoke compassion in us to help them. When we give alms it shows our heart is near God's.

15 When we pray for our brothers and sisters who are sick.

Binds satan from having access to *others* through: bent body/spine; being frail; lame; weak; cancer; breathing issues; any physical oppression; mental illness; seizures; dumb/mute; deaf; forgiveness of sins, etc.

Reference:

> [14] *"Is any sick among you? let him call for the elders of the church; and let them pray over him, anointing him with oil in the name of the Lord:"* [15] *"And the prayer of faith shall save the sick, and the Lord shall raise him up; and if he have committed sins, they shall be forgiven him."* [16] *"Confess your faults one to another, and pray one for another, that ye may be healed. The **effectual fervent**[G1754] prayer of a **righteous man**[G1342] availeth much."*
> – James 5:14 - 16

Through doing all the things mentioned previously we can be the *righteous man*, Strong's G1342, who can offer an *effectual fervent*, Strong's G1754, (actively working) prayer on behalf of those who need our help even to forgiving any sins that have not been repented of. There is no doubt because we are doing the asking on their behalf and God heals the whole person. The Word of God states this and we should believe it. The only thing limiting this is our faith in God's Word.

16 By proclaiming the good news of Jesus: He has come to save our world, to help man know that we are sinful and need to repent. Then by listening to the Holy Spirit and being willing to: cast out demons, heal the sick, and raise people from the dead. We are praying on behalf of others who may or may not know how to pray or may not be able to pray.

Binds satan from having access to *others* through: denying Christ; denying atonement; heresies; false teaching; deceptions; rebellion; self-righteousness; all fears; religious bondage; and non-truth.

Reference:

> [5] *"These twelve Jesus sent forth, and commanded them, saying, Go not into the way of the Gentiles, and into any city of the Samaritans enter ye not:"* [6] *"But go rather to the lost sheep of the house of Israel."* [7] *"And as ye go, preach, saying, The kingdom of heaven is at hand."* [8] *"Heal the sick, cleanse the lepers, raise the dead, cast out devils: freely ye have received, freely give."* – Matthew 10:5 – 8

> [12] *"And they went out, and preached that men should repent."* [13] *"And they cast out many devils, and anointed with oil many that were sick, and healed them."* – Mark 6:12 -13

17 When we stand in opposition to satan and what he is trying to do.

Binds satan from having access to *others* through: everything we have mentioned previously.

Reference:

> [7]*"Submit yourselves therefore to God. Resist[G436] the devil, and he will flee from you."* [8]*"Draw nigh to God, and he will draw nigh to you. Cleanse your hands, ye sinners; and purify your hearts, ye double minded."* – James 4:7 -8

Resisting, Strong's G436 means to stand in opposition to, to stand firm like a door that someone is trying to break into, and no matter what they do to that door, it does not budge, after a while they give up and go away. We Christians, must do the same to prevent satan from coming back and plundering us from what we have taken from him. We must emphasis' truth and pray against deception.

18 By using the only offensive weapon God has given us… His word, actively swinging and striking to root out the lies we have been fed our whole lives and to cut into the soul to reveal truth.

Binds satan from having access to *others* through: again everything we have mentioned thus far setting us free from those things.

Reference:

> *"For the word of God is quick, and powerful, and sharper than any twoedged sword, piercing even to the dividing asunder of soul and spirit, and of the joints and marrow, and is a discerner of the thoughts and intents of the heart."* – Hebrews 4:12

satan can't handle the truth! God's Word… the truth, pierces all that is false; all that covers; all that binds; all that hides; all that keeps secret; all that is dark; all that is not of God, and brings light, life, freedom, liberation and destruction to satan and his bondage. Because, John 8:32 "And ye shall know the truth, and the truth shall make you free."

Jesus' very presence within us and us acting in Faith binds satan and loosens the submission to evil on this world. One of the things we find interesting in the stories about Jesus in Matthew, Mark, Luke and John, is that Jesus never picked a fight with satan, or one of his spirits (Outside of Him traveling to the Gadarenes Matthew 8:28 to save the man suffering from legion). Jesus picked fights with the Jewish leaders, but never with satan, or one of his demonic spirit followers. *They picked fights with Him.* Which raises an interesting question…. why? Why didn't Jesus go after satan? The answer is He didn't have to, His mere presence (His being righteous and full of the Holy Spirit) forced satan and the demons to go after Him. They could not sit back and

Knowing God's Word and applying it into our lives shall set us and others free.

be quiet, they had to confront, because His presence forced them to. Did they try to take Him out? Yes, but they failed at every attempt (temptation of Christ, when they went to the Gadarenes, even Jesus's death). His mere presence on this earth and the Holy Spirit working through Him, dissolved all submission to evil for those that were around Him and it forced those who were authoritively putting people under submission to stop and question Jesus. As we do the 18 things above, we allow Jesus to shine so brightly through us that it has the same effect on satan and his demonic spirits. They have to act to question the authority coming through us otherwise they lose the submitting force they were able to apply before. This is why we fight such battles and find things to be struggling against us, nothing likes being restrained, but we do not see what is going on in the spiritual realm, we only see and feel it in the physical and what we see and feel is not always the full truth of what is happening.

Another topic on binding and loosening that we need to mention. There are times when we have to be bolder in our Faith and take more action against satan or his followers when binding them. Sometimes we have to take more direct action against them to help ourselves and others. In this we have the authority and power through Jesus Christ to rebuke them. Examples of this and how to do it are found in the following verses:

> [1] *"And he shewed me Joshua the high priest standing before the angel of the LORD, and Satan standing at his right hand to resist him."* [2] *"And the LORD said unto Satan, The LORD **rebuke**[H1605] thee, O Satan; even the LORD that hath chosen Jerusalem **rebuke**[H1605] thee: is not this a brand plucked out of the fire?" – Zechariah 3:1 2*

and

> *"Yet Michael the archangel, when contending with the devil he disputed about the body of Moses, durst not bring against him a railing accusation, but said, The Lord **rebuke**[G2008] thee." – Jude 1:9*

When we find that what we are praying for seems to be thwarted and we are not making progress we can pray/ask Jesus to rebuke satan and his followers. *Rebuke*, Strong's H1605 and G2008 mean to chide, admonish, and/or forbid. When we tell satan and his followers the "LORD rebuke you" we are asking Jesus in all His authority and power to forbid satan and his followers from having access to that thing/person. It is in effect removing yourself from the situation and allowing Jesus to minister directly.

One final topic we need to discuss, some of the Gifts of the Spirit. Yes we have to go here, because Isaiah 61:1 "The Spirit of the Lord GOD *is* upon me [Jesus]; because the LORD hath anointed me to preach good tidings unto the meek; he hath sent me to bind up the brokenhearted, to proclaim[H7121] liberty to the captives, and the opening of the prison to *them that are* bound." Jesus was sent to earth to set people free from submission to satan and evil. Jesus passed that mission onto His disciples. His disciples represented the early church and they performed those miracles. We as the church today represent Jesus, and we should be working on His behalf to continue to do what He was sent to do to our peers. Let's look at what Jesus commanded them:

> *"And when he [Jesus] had called unto him his twelve disciples, he gave them* **power**[G1849] *against unclean spirits, to cast them out, and to heal all manner of sickness and all manner of disease." – Matthew 10:1*

> *"And he [Jesus] called unto him the twelve, and began to send them forth by two and two; and gave them* **power**[G1849] *over unclean spirits;" –Mark 6:7*

> [1]*"Then he [Jesus] called his twelve disciples together, and gave them* **power**[G1411] *and* **authority**[G1849] *over all devils, and to cure diseases."* [2]*"And he [Jesus] sent them to preach the kingdom of God, and to heal the sick."* *– Luk3 9:1 - 2*

What did Jesus give the disciples? He gave them *power/authority*, Strong's G1849 and *power/miracles*, Strong's G1411. *Power/authority*, Strong's G1849 means to give one delegated influence, i.e. delegated authority over something. In essence Jesus delegated His influence (authority) in this world (because He was crucified and risen (the keys)) to the disciples (His church). It would be similar to what Pharaoh did for Joseph (Jacob's son) back in Genesis. He put Joseph in authority of the country in his place. Jesus has extended His authority to us. The second set *power/miracles*, Strong's G1411 means they were given force (miraculous power) over this world. So we the church have been delegated Jesus' authority on earth and have been given His spiritual force to do the miraculous. So this begs the question, what authority should we have as part of the church. To answer that, we look at what the outflow was of the early church using the delegated authority and force to do the miraculous:

> *12 "And by the hands of the apostles were many signs and wonders wrought among the people; (and they were all with one accord in Solomon's porch." 13 "And of the rest durst no man join himself to them: but the people magnified them." 14 "And believers were the more added to the Lord, multitudes both of men and women.)" 15 "Insomuch that they brought forth the sick into the streets, and laid them on beds and couches, that at the least the shadow of Peter passing by might overshadow some of them." 16 "There came also a multitude out of the cities round about unto Jerusalem, bringing sick folks, and them which were vexed with unclean spirits: and they were healed every one."*
> *— Acts 5:12 - 16*

and then Paul who started the church in the Gentile area also did the same:

> *11 "And God wrought special miracles by the hands of Paul:" 12 "So that from his body were brought unto the sick*

*handkerchiefs or aprons, and the diseases departed from them, and the evil spirits went out of them." [13] "Then certain of the **vagabond**[G4022] **Jews,**[G2453] **exorcists,**[G1845] took upon them to call over them which had evil spirits the name of the Lord Jesus, saying, We adjure you by Jesus whom Paul preacheth." [14] "And there were seven sons of one Sceva, a Jew, and chief of the priests, which did so." [15] "And the evil spirit answered and said, Jesus I know, and Paul I know; but who are ye?" [16] "And the man in whom the evil spirit was leaped on them, and overcame them, and prevailed against them, so that they fled out of that house naked and wounded." – Acts 19:11 - 16*

The early church was doing these things and Paul admonished Timothy to do the same. They were doing what God told them to do in reaction to those who came to them seeking help. Those who came were healed... EVERY ONE of them. This only came through the early church spending time seeking God, proclaiming Jesus, living a holy life, and being obedient to what God wanted done. Something that we the church of today in the USA really need to stop and think through.

And with this comes a solemn warning. We cannot fake what God wants done without getting hurt in the process. We left Acts 19:13 – 16 here on purpose to demonstrate this. Doing some research through Strong's, Sceva and his sons were proclaimed *exorcists*. That word in Strong's G1845 means, conjurer. In the Old Testament, a conjurer was called a wizard (Leviticus 20:27 and Deuteronomy 18:11). God commanded the Jewish nation to stone people claiming to have these skills. What is interesting is, if one looks up the *www.merriam-webster.com's* meaning for conjurer, one definition means "one that performs feats of sleight of hand and illusion". Whoa. So, if we understand this correctly, Sceva and his sons were giving the illusion of setting people free from unclean spirits. However, when they actually encountered one, it recognized they were not acting in Jesus' power/authority, and/or the power/miraculous, that was given to the church. They were not part of the church. Technically by Jewish law they should not have even been alive and we now know why, one cannot exercise fake authority of Jesus without the enemy recognizing it and get away with it for long. satan will not allow it. The scriptures themselves state that a house divided will fall. satan will not allow his house to be divided. One cannot drive out satan and his followers unless they are operating in the power of the Holy Spirit, because then it is satan driving out satan. At some point they will be shown for the fakes they are. We would extend this even further. When people try to do things that God did not ask them to do, then they are not acting in Jesus' authority/miraculous power and will eventually be hurt by what they are doing. Just something to keep in mind as you walk the journey God has you on.

Having said this warning, we still need to do what God wants done and to wrap this chapter up, here is why:

> [17]"And the seventy returned again with joy, saying, Lord, even the devils are subject unto us through thy name." [18]"And he said unto them, I beheld Satan as lightning fall from heaven." [19]"Behold, I give unto you power to tread on serpents and scorpions, and over all the power of the enemy: and nothing shall by any means hurt you." [20]"Notwithstanding in this rejoice not, that the spirits are subject unto you; but rather rejoice, because your names are written in heaven." [21]"In that hour Jesus rejoiced in spirit, and said, I thank thee, O Father, Lord of heaven and earth, that thou hast hid these things

*from the wise and prudent, and hast revealed them unto
babes: even so, Father; for so it seemed good in thy sight."*
– Luke 10:17 -21

So why should we ask God to heal, cleanse, forgive sins, drive out
unclean spirits and devils, and heal all sicknesses and diseases? Because it
brings Glory and Honor to God, it allows His goodness to be seen in this
world and it releases the Holy Spirit to move. These things destroy, dissolve,
melt away satan's submission of this world and allow people to have some
moments to realize God cares. What I (Rich) find interesting from the
scriptures above is Luke 10:18 "And he said unto them, I beheld Satan as
lightning fall from heaven." Why? The phrase here just seems like such an
odd statement to me. Science, not that I hold much in science, has studied
lighting for years to understand it and how it forms. I am not a scientist so
I went looking for information about lighting and found this site:

http://science.howstuffworks.com/nature/natural-disasters/lightning.htm

I am not sure how accurate it is, but it sounded reasonable to me.
To paraphrase the article, all the water in the air, the dust particles, and
temperatures affect the electrons in the air and therefore they start to split off
to create positive and negative areas with the positive area being above the
negative area (*important - hold this thought number 1*). This positive/negative
play causes massive electrical fields to occur and to resolve themselves they
"seek out" something to bring the electrical field back into order (*important
thought number 2 to hold*). At the same time, due to this electrical field
disruption taking place, the earth or more specifically items on the earth
respond to this electrical field disruption and positive charges (streamers)
start to go up into the air to resolve the negative charge (*important thought
number 3 to hold*). When the two meet, a conductive path from the cloud

to the earth is formed. With this path complete, current flows between the earth and the cloud. This discharge of current is "nature's" way of trying to neutralize the charge separation (*important thought number 4 to hold*). When the current flows (the strike), the air around the strike becomes extremely hot... so hot that it actually ***explodes*** (which causes the light) because the heat causes the air to expand so rapidly (*important thought number 5 to hold* (sorry only one more)). The explosion is soon followed by what we all know as **thunder** (*important thought number 6 to hold*).

Ok, you are saying I do not get this at all. Oh man my friends, all I can say is that God is beyond amazing and what Jesus says here in this one verse is just crazy awesome!!!! Here is what the Holy Spirit revealed to me, think of what I just paraphrased from what we see in the physical, in terms of the spiritual realm. Important thought number 1: the separation of electrons which create the positive area above and negative area below in the spiritual realm would be like the separation between God/good above and satan/evil below. Important thought number 2: this separation has created a massive spiritual disruption in the spiritual realms which has to be resolved and therefore it "seeks out" a way to resolve; this "seeking out" would be God sending thoughts/feelings (what we discussed in Chapter 6) to earth, more specifically to us His church revealing to us what He wants done to resolve it. Are you catching this yet? Important thought number 3: as we pray, beseech, make request of God to do what God told us to ask for and we act on that, we, the church, create positive/good (streamers) to start up to the spiritual realms. Important thought number 4: when what God has sent down meets what we are praying / doing (streamers), a conductive path is formed; when it is formed God's power, the Holy Spirit, flows (the current) between the earth and the heavenly spiritual realms to neutralize satan/evil (the disruption). I so hope you have caught this and are rejoicing with me. Important thought number 5: when the Holy Spirit flows, something happens to the issue of bondage / submission causing it to explode; the explosion signifies that the bondage/submission issue was destroyed, dissolved, melted away; the light created signifies GOD's GLORY being displayed. Do you understand now? All I can say is WOW! This is an on your knees moment. Are you ready for the last one? Important thought number 6: the thunder… wait for it… it is the angels in heaven and the church below REJOICING AND PRAISING GOD for what He has done; hence Luke 10:21 where Jesus is rejoicing in the spirit praising God. When Jesus said He saw satan fall from heaven as is lightning He was seeing satan's bondage/submission being destroyed in the lower heavenly realms and earth. What an awesome picture in the physical God has given us to understand what is going on in the spiritual realms. What does one follow up with? I do not know because right now I am just speechless.

We would like to finish this chapter with the great hymn *"Battle Hymn of the Republic"*. We recommend that you go to *www.youtube.com* and in the YouTube search bar, search for *"Battle Hymn of the Republic"* minus the quotation marks.

IN SUMMARY

We learned the following about binding and loosening:

- God created good and evil.

- The Holy Spirit role is to give life and to teach us how to live out God's goodness.

- satan was created, and satan's mission is to get everyone and everything to be evil.

- satan's domain is the earth and he and his minions hold the earth in submission/bondage to evil.

- Jesus' shedding of blood, death, and resurrection broke satan's authority on earth.

- Jesus gave His keys of authority to the church… us… all who are living and have a relationship with Jesus Christ as our personal savior.

- We the church have the right to bind and to loosen satan, his minions, and the bondage to evil.

- Faith is the key that turns the binding/loosening lock.

- By living a Christ like life we bind satan and his minions from us and others to protect us from him subjecting us to the bondage of evil and allow the Holy Spirit to flow.

- We bind satan by asking Jesus to rebuke satan and his minions.

- We spoil and plunder satan's domain with each person we minister to.

- We plunder satan by invoking the power/authority, miraculous/ power delegated to us by Jesus.

- We cannot fake it without being called out by satan.

- We are to work so that satan falls like lighting from the spiritual realms.

Now that we have covered the 3 aspects of Maturity, let's have a discussion why Maturity is so important to our faith.

CHAPTER TWELVE

The Criticality of Maturity

Faith has been given to us by God and as we have seen in prior chapters, God intends for our faith to grow with our Christian walk. In the Christian community we speak a lot about wanting to become a "mature" Christian, one who is actively learning and growing to become more Christ like. The more Christ like we become and the more knowledge we gain through God's Word, then we begin to grow and mature. We begin to learn what God expects of us and as we become obedient and know God, we can see that He has good planned for us. The more we follow God's instruction the greater our faith becomes.

All this really leads though to the question, why is maturity so critical? This verse really puts it into a humbling perspective: James 2:19 "Thou believest that there is one God; thou doest well: the devils also believe, and tremble." To just believe in God is no different than the demons. They know God, they used to serve God, God cast them out of their authority in the spiritual realms. Our team would be so bold to state they fear God more than we do. A scary thought we will add. So what separates us from them? The answer would be acceptance of God's message, repentance, and asking Jesus and the Holy Spirit to come and live in us. However, if we simply stop there and do not release control over to Them, They cannot move in the power we were intended to have. Maturity is relinquishing control of ourselves and giving it to God. It is an act of submission. It is a conscious choice in which we choose to let God lead and we to follow. When we do this we learn to become Christ like. As be become Christ like, God can then start to put us into situations to show the world who He is and allow His miraculous power to grow. God wants to do miracles through us to show the world it is no longer subjected to satan's bondage. We can be free. As we grow in maturity it shows the world Christ shining through us because we are different than everyone else.

For example, showing forgiveness to someone who does not deserve it, that is not "normal" it is not a normal response. Everyone knows this is not a normal response. When we forgive, it shakes satan and his bondage to the core. It opens the eyes of those are seeking a way to get out of the bondage and lights the way to God. Another example, seeking clarity, or even if we just stopped with not having doubt. People take notice when you put a stake in the ground and state God has told me to do this and this is what I am going to do. I am going this way, I invite you to come with me, but as for me and my house we will serve the Lord. People rally to leaders, people respect leaders, people follow leaders, and we are each called to lead as we follow God. People can tell when you have a clear purpose and are following that. They rally to it because they are so full of doubt themselves. Want to be a leader, then do the basics, do and be the basics we listed in Chapter 11. We all want to be a hero, but exist because they are already doing the right things which are changing them into a hero. Another example, understanding good and evil and being willing to help those who are unable to help themselves. Coming to their aid in their battles and fighting with them on their behalf. Helping to rescue loved ones from satan's grip, helping strangers you have never met in their fight, and in the process winning families to Christ, saving them from the pits of hell. This is what our maturity does, this is how God uses us, but if we are content with only having a small seed of faith, we miss the point of what Christ called us as a church to do. When we do this faith becomes effective, it becomes real touching God's most precious part of creation, you, I, and everyone else.

The rest of this chapter discusses some math concepts which show us that if we grow in becoming Christ like (growing in maturity) it expands our faith to really make a difference in this world. We invite you to study the concept, but do not get too bogged down in the math. The main point is we need to grow and we only grow by doing the things we know we are supposed to be doing, reading/studying God's Word; meditating on His Word; an attitude of humbleness; reverence; obedience and in such worshipping God; praying to learn his voice, and taking action with what He reveals.

Let's recap all the variables we have discussed so far:

A = minding and paying attention to your thoughts/feelings and purposefully making sure they are in line with God.

B = believing in God and who he is… our creator, our savior, the one and only God.

C = having confidence, assurance in, reliance on God's character.

D = having confidence, assurance in, reliance on God's character towards us (He has good planned for me).

E = understanding what God told me to do and believing it came from Him.

F = my action of acting on what God told me (obedience).

Remember then that **FAITH** = **A** and **B** and **C** and **D** and **E** and **F** all have to exist for faith to be present. If any one of them does not exist then there is no faith.

We have been saying that **A**, **B**, **C**, **D**, **E**, and **F**, either exist or not exist. With a small tweak to make our faith equation mean more, we are going to say if a variable exists it equals 1 and if it does not exist, it equals 0 (zero). So if **A** = 1 and **B** = 1 and **C** = 1 and **D** = 1 and **E** = 1 and **F** = 1 then Faith = 1 (exists). However again if any one of the variables is a 0 (does not exist) then Faith = 0. This is an important transition we are making here and it needs to be understood because of how maturity is applied to the faith equation.

Next, we learned about maturity. Maturity is made up of the following aspects: Clarity, Forgiveness, and Binding & Loosening. To make this fit our faith equation, we are going to expand it by adding maturity as a variable and name it variable **M**. **M**, maturity, is made up of 3 variables: clarity (C), forgiveness (F), and Binding and Loosening (B and L). **M** then is equal to **C * F * B&L (M=C*F*B&L)**. As you will notice here we are multiplying the 3 aspects together rather than adding them. Because we are multiplying them **M** then becomes a multiplier. A good definition of a multiplier is from the site http://www.ask.com/question/what-is-a-multiplier-in-math "A multiplier in math refers to a factor or digit of proportionality that makes another number be additionally recounted a particular number of times. A multiplication sign is usually used to denote multiplying." Wow... what does that mean? For example, if I have an equation of 2*2 the first number two is multiplied by the second number 2 times to get 4 (or 2+2 = 4). If I have 2*3 then the two is multiplied 3 times (2+2+2) and get 6. If I have 2*10 then it would be 2+2+2+2+2+2+2+2+2 which equals 20. If I have 2*0 then I end up with zero as there is nothing to add together.

Now we will take our two equations and put them together… Faith *
Maturity. So if my **Faith** = 1 then we will multiply that by the value of our
maturity. Meaning our maturity multiplies our faith. It becomes more than
existing or not existing. It becomes effective, producing a desired result.
But, if our faith is zero, then no matter how high our maturity number is
our total effectiveness will be 0. The name of this chapter is "The Criticality
of Maturity". Maturity is critical because it gives our faith effectiveness.
Effectiveness means the power to produce a result that is wanted. Maturity
gives our faith power to be effective. Where does the power come from… it
comes from being "Christ Like". We cannot be Christ Like without being
obedient. We cannot be obedient without the Holy Spirit helping us. The
Holy Spirit only does what Jesus tells Him and Jesus only does what God
says. So the root of the power is God, but it only becomes power if it is
used by us. For Maturity, the power is coming from it being a multiplier to
our faith. The Holy Spirit brings the continuity of what God wants done
through us by giving us confirmation it is God speaking so we can trust
what we are being told.

Again our faith equation now looks like this (Faith = **A** (1 or 0) and **B**
(1 or 0) and **C** (1 or 0) and **D** (1 or 0) and **E** (1 or 0) and **F** (1 or 0))*M or
(Faith (1 or 0))*M. If the whole faith equation is a 1 then we have 1 times
(*) the value of **M**. However, if faith = 0 then 0 times (*) **M** is 0. This means
even if one has great maturity, there is no faith, their faith is empty, and
thus their maturity means very little in relation to faith.

Looking closer at the three aspects of maturity, they are multiplied by
each other for a reason. If you think of each aspect (clarity, forgiveness,
binding/loosening) being on a scale of 0 to 10 where 0 is the lowest and
10 is the highest, we see each has to at least be a 1 in order to have a
level one maturity. A 0 in any one of the 3 aspects (clarity, forgiveness,
binding/loosening) means you have a maturity level of zero. A 10 in all

three categories means you have a maturity level of 1,000. There is only one human that was ever a 1,000 and He is the only one that will ever be a 1,000. His name is Jesus Christ. However, since we are on a Christian walk and the very definition of being a Christian is to be "Christ Like" we are continually maturing to be more and more like Jesus. Putting this in a graph format we have: *(See Fig. 12.1)*

Fig. 12.1 - MATURITY LEVELS

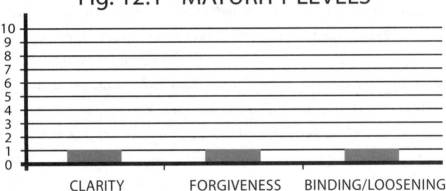

If we go back to our faith equation, if all variables **A** through **F** exist, then we said that would equal 1. When you look at the updated faith equation (Faith)*$\mathbf{M}$ we see that if a person has a maturity level of 0 it affects the whole faith equation, it makes it 0. One must be at least a level 1 in all three aspects to have effective faith or a faith that is working, to remain at a 1.

As one grows in God and in their Christian walk, hopefully they are also growing at some rate in clarity, forgiveness and binding/loosening. As they grow in each aspect of maturity, their overall maturity level changes.

For example, let's say a person is a Christian for a few years and has been reading the Bible and has been participating in discipleship classes and other classes to grow in their Christian walk. Let's say they have a Clarity of 1 and handle on Binding/Loosening as a 1 but they have some things that happened in their past which they are harboring bitterness for, so in forgiveness they are a zero. *(See Fig. 12.2)*

Fig. 12.2 - MATURITY LEVELS

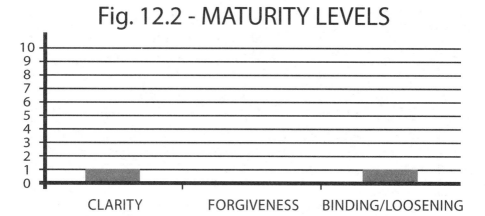

Looking at this in an equation, we have: Clarity (1) * Forgiveness (0) * Binding/Loosening (1) or 1*0*1. What is 1*0*1... it is 0. Therefore their overall maturity is zero. If they have faith (1) then 1*0 is 0 and therefore their total faith effectiveness is zero.

However due to some circumstances, which we are sure God orchestrated, this person starts to forgive those that have hurt them. Now they are at a forgiveness level of 2. So their overall Maturity level is 1*2*1 or 2. *(See Fig. 12.3)*

Fig. 12.3 - MATURITY LEVELS

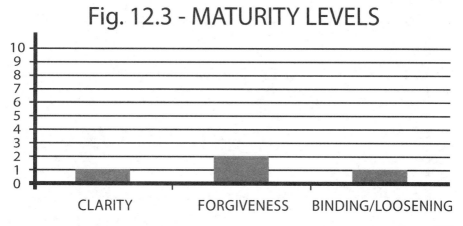

We already established they have faith (1), so now they have 1 *2 which equals 2 meaning their total faith effectiveness is 2.

Let's go further and say they have been in some training that taught them about Spiritual Gifts and they are working towards what God created them to do (Clarity). They are 2 in Clarity and 2 in Forgiveness and 1 in Binding/Loosening which gives them a maturity level of 4 (2*2*1). *(See Fig. 12.4)*

Fig. 12.4 - MATURITY LEVELS

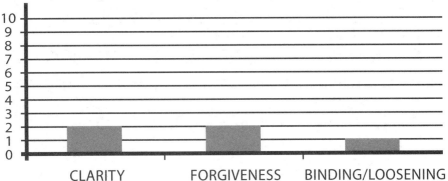

CLARITY   FORGIVENESS   BINDING/LOOSENING

If they have faith (1) then 1*4 is 4 and now their faith effectiveness has doubled. This is a huge improvement!

Now as they continue to grow throughout their life they will continue to rise into new maturity levels. Once a person is at a 5 in each aspect, they are at a maturity level of 125 (5*5*5) and a faith effectiveness of 1 * 125 or 125. *(See Fig. 12.5)*

Fig. 12.5 - MATURITY LEVELS

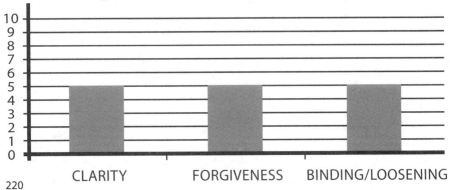

CLARITY   FORGIVENESS   BINDING/LOOSENING

Any improvements above this and the maturity levels really start to sky rocket.

For example a 6*5*6 is 180. If they have faith (1) then 1*180 is 180 and therefore their effectiveness is really soaring. *(See Fig. 12.6)*

Fig. 12.6 - MATURITY LEVELS

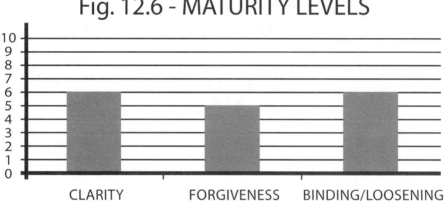

We hope you see how important it is that we continually mature in our Christian walk because of how our maturity affects our faith and how our faith affects our maturity. It is critically important that we grow in Faith and in Maturity so that we can become more Christ like. God has us here to reach a lost and hurting world and the only way that will take place is if we drop ourselves and grow to become like Christ.

To this point we have learned that Faith either exits or does not exist and that there are three areas in which we can multiply our faith's effectiveness. We have also seen that our faith equation is now (Faith)***M**. This chapter showed how we make our faith effective rather than simply existing or not. Multiplied effectiveness is good but not the best we can have. The best is our faith to have an exponential effectiveness. We can have exponential effectiveness? Yes we can and we'll explain how in the next chapter.

IN SUMMARY

We learned the following:

• We have tweaked our faith equation giving it a value of 1 if all the variables exist and a 0 if one, or more variables do not exist.

• Maturity equals Clarity times Forgiveness times Binding/Loosening.

• Maturity is a multiplier to our faith.

• Since Maturity is a multiplier it gives our faith effectiveness.

• Effectiveness produces the result of what we are being faithful about.

• Faith can have more than a multiplied effectiveness; it can have an exponential effectiveness.

Our faith equation now looks like the following:

Faith = **A** and **B** and **C** and **D** and **E** and **F** (1 or 0)
Maturity = Clarity*Forgiveness*Binding & Loosening
To the result of (Faith)*Maturity

CHAPTER THIRTEEN

^{N} the Final Variable

N is our final variable in the whole faith equation. Whew, we have covered a lot about faith to this point and we are almost done explaining what faith is. We hope that God has opened your heart and mind to what He is saying through this book.

^{N}. Don't you just love the variable ^{N} in math? We do. ^{N} is very exciting and we can't wait to explore it with you!!!

So what is ^{N}? Well by the very nature of its placement in an equation, we know ^{N} stands for the nth power. This nth power is also called an exponent and can allow an equation to increase exponentially. Wow… you mean our faith can have ^{N} number of powers? You bet it can!!!! Even more exciting this ^{N} number of powers exponentially increases our faith's effectiveness.

Before we go much farther let's talk about the definition of an exponent which is what ^{N} is. An Exponent is a mathematical notation that implies the number of times a number is to be multiplied by itself. For example, 2^2 or 2 to the second power is 4 (2*2). However, 2^3 or to the third power is 8 (2*2*2). We can start to see how quickly it grows hence the term exponential. Continuing 2^4 or 2 to the 4th power is 16 (2*2*2*2) and 2^5 or 2 to the fifth power is 32 (2*2*2*2*2). A final example, 2^{10} or 2 to the 10th

power is 1,024 (2*2*2*2*2*2*2*2*2*2), again see how quickly this grows when adding a simple power to an equation.

So in our faith model, what would ^{N} represent? Good question we must say… let's look at the following verses for the explanation:

> [19]"*Again I [Jesus] say unto you, That if two of you* **shall agree**^{G4856} *on earth as touching any thing that they shall ask, it shall be done for them of my Father which is in heaven.*" [20]"*For where two or three are **gathered together**^{G4863} in my name, there am I in the midst of them.*"
> – Matthew 18:19 - 20

Hopefully you see it. There are two types of ^{N} in these scriptures. The first type of ^{N} stands for the number of people praying in agreement on any one thing. *Agreement*, Strong's G4856, means to be harmonious. In today's terms we call this unity. For example, if you have 2 people then you have a power of 2. If you have 3, then you have the power of three. If you have 10, then you have the power of 10. And on and on it goes to infinity. Well actually no, it would be limited to the total number of people who understand faith and are applying it correctly based on the total number of people living at any given time on earth. But you have to admit that one million as an ^{N} power is pretty cool!!

The second type of ^{N} stands for Jesus. Jesus said where two or more are gathered together in His name, He is there also. *Gathered together*, Strong's G4863, means to lead together, that is, collect or convene. When we gather together, we are stepping out/leading/convening an environment in which

Jesus can come and join us because we are in union with each other. We know that Jesus sits at the right hand of God interceding on our behalf so he would be the second part of this.

Really if we could tweak the equation, it would be more of $N = {}_N N^N$ meaning the first N would be the number of people praying with the power of Jesus to exponentially increase that group of people's effectiveness. But that is confusing and we are not math majors so we are not sure that would be legal mathematically. But hey that is really what it should look like. However, to keep things simple will just say both types are represented as ^{N} which now makes our equation look like $((Faith)*Maturity)^N$.

Now to clarify some things... we need to make sure we are all on the same page. ^{N} is not the same thing as someone saying "Hey, I want a new house. So I talk to my spouse who is all over that idea and we start praying for a new house." Is this really two people praying in agreement as the scriptures say? We would contend no. By technical terms they are in agreement, but based on what we have learned about faith, they are not. If we go back to the beginning... where did the thought originate from? Did the spouse also have the thought from God or were they simply on board with the desire? What is God going to do with the new house? etc... where is the clarity here? There isn't any yet.

We are not saying you shouldn't pray for a new house. If God told you to pray for a new house, by all means do it. We are saying that we need to mind our thoughts and make sure we are totally clear on what God is asking.

Since we had graphs in the last chapter, let's show the representation of what exponentially increasing effectiveness looks like. (See Figure 13.1)

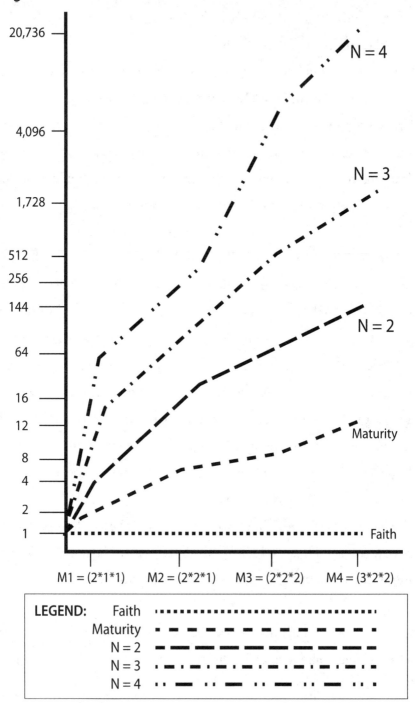

Fig. 13.1 - EXPONENTIAL EFFECTIVENESS GRAPH EXAMPLE

This graph is for example purposes only; it is not based on a study. We are going to first explain this graph in simple terms and then if you would like we have the entire detail to back up the lines.

There are 5 lines on this graph Faith, Maturity, N=2, N=3 and N=4. The first line, Faith, represents a person who has faith, meaning they have faith which exists. Each variable (**A, B, C, D, E, F**) exists for this person so they have faith. As we see this line remains constant as maturity is applied and as unity values are applied (N). The effectiveness of having faith remains 1. The next line up, Maturity, shows us what happens when we multiply Faith by 4 different maturity values (M1, M2, M3 and M4). We see that our faith effectiveness grows from 1 to a 12. This is huge, but is not exponential effectiveness. The next line up, N=2, shows what happens when we add two people praying in unity (faith*maturity)^2. As this line progresses to the right we see that when 2 people are praying in unity, faith goes from simply existing to an effectiveness of 144. This is

> There is power in prayer. The more people praying in unity, the larger the faith and the more effective the prayer becomes.

a very large jump from a faith simply existing. If we add one more person praying in unity to the mix, line N=3, we see that the total effectiveness rises to 1,728. Here we really start to see the power of maturity and faith coming into play as we join together asking God to move in the world as He directed. Finally, the last line at the top, N=4, details what happens when there are only 4 people praying in unity, having the same maturity, and having faith. The total effectiveness rises all the way to 20,736. This is absolutely amazing to us how much faith can mean when we all grow in maturity and bind together in unity praying, making request to God for the very thing(s) He wants us to do.

If you would like to look at the graph in detail then this section is for you. If you would rather not review the math, then go ahead and skip down a couple of paragraphs to the *(Skip to here)* section. The horizontal axis across the bottom represents different levels of maturity and shows how faith increases in effectiveness when a multiplier is applied. The first axis point M1 (2*1*1) represents a maturity of 2 which means our Faith equation is (Faith = 1)*(Maturity = 2) for a total effectiveness of 2. The next axis point, M2 (2*2*1), represents a maturity of 4 which means our Faith equation is (Faith = 1)*(Maturity = 4) for a total effectiveness of 4. Then next axis point, M3 (2*2*2), represents a maturity of 8 which means our Faith equation is (Faith = 1)*(Maturity = 8) for a total effectiveness of 8. Finally the last axis point, M4 (3*2*2), represents a maturity of 12 which means our Faith equation is (Faith = 1)*(Maturity = 12) for a total effectiveness of 12. The vertical axis represents the total effectiveness. Next, describing the lines, Faith is the dotted (▪▪▪▪▪▪) line that goes across the bottom. It does not change because it either exists/does not exit. For the all the examples, we will have it set to exists or the value of 1. The next line is the normal dashed (▬ ▬ ▬) line and this line shows what happens when we add maturity to faith. As we see the multiplier has an impact on our faith's effectiveness rather than a simple 1 in our example it went all the way up to 12. When we add in the exponent of N though, things really start to change.

The long dashed line (▬▬ ▬▬ ▬▬) shows how much faster our faith grows in effectiveness when N = 2 is included. Even with 2 people praying (representing the faith equation times itself twice), there is a big increase in effectiveness which starts at M1 $((Faith = 1)*(Maturity = 2))^2$

for a total effectiveness of 4, then M2 ((Faith = 1)*(Maturity = 4))^2 for a total effectiveness of 16, then M3 ((Faith = 1)*(Maturity = 8))^2 for a total effectiveness of 64 and finally M4 ((Faith = 1)*(Maturity = 12))^2 for a total effectiveness of 144. This is a major effective difference over a multiplier.

The normal dash dot (━ ▪ ━ ▪ ━) line N = 3 shows how exponentially effectiveness increases when we add just one additional person praying. Here with 3 people praying (representing the faith equation times itself three times), there is a much larger increase in effectiveness which starts at M1 ((Faith = 1)*(Maturity = 2))^3 for a total effectiveness of 8, then M2 ((Faith = 1)*(Maturity = 4))^3 for a total effectiveness of 64, then M3 ((Faith = 1)*(Maturity = 8))^3 for a total effectiveness of 512 and finally M4 ((Faith = 1)*(Maturity = 12))^3 for a total effectiveness of 1,728.

The last line the long dash two dotted (━━ ▪▪ ━━ ▪▪ ━━) line shows what happens if we add one more person praying with us N = 4. When we have 4 people praying (representing the faith equation times itself four times), there is a very large increase in effectiveness which starts at M1 ((Faith = 1)*(Maturity = 2))^4 for a total effectiveness of 16, then M2 ((Faith = 1)*(Maturity = 4))^4 for a total effectiveness of 256, then M3 ((Faith = 1)*(Maturity = 8))^4 for a total effectiveness of 4,096 and finally M4 ((Faith = 1)*(Maturity = 12))^4 for a total effectiveness of 20,736.

*(**Skip to here**)* Just think of this graph for a few minutes. When we have one person who has faith their faith effectiveness is 1, even with a small amount of maturity their effectiveness increases, but never by much. However, the power comes in with having other Christians, who understand faith, pray in unity, agreement, and like mind. For our example above, we are assuming the 2 to 4 others praying have the same maturity level. Even with keeping maturity constant, the max effectiveness becomes 20,736 rather than 12. That is absolutely incredible!!!! At our local church,

we have two forms of getting prayer requests announced to others. One form is an automated system in which one person puts through a prayer request and 46 people are called all given the same request. If all of us pray that is N = 46. If we assume we all have a maturity level of 12 then we have 12^{46} or twelve to the 46th power… the total effectiveness of that is 43 ,887,143,856,106,100,000,000,000,000,000,000,000,000, 000,000,000. That is a big number. The second form of announcing prayer for others is through Facebook, and there we have 230 members. Assuming they all had the same maturity level and they all prayed, then that would be 12^{230} or twelve to the two hundred and thirtieth power. Can you even image the effectiveness of this number? It would probably take up at least half a page to notate.

So as you can see ^N is very powerful and not to be ignored.

To be honest we see this as a rallying point with the church today. We are so disjointed! We are disjointed by physical countries, by cultures, by race, by denomination (meaning that we can't agree with each other on Biblical principles – some legitimate and some not), by time zones, and by a lot of other things that we can't think of off the top of our heads. We say this because we, as the church, really need to get on the same page. satan is killing us because we are not united, not in agreement and not of like mind. Even when we are physically in one place we are not united. We don't know what God has revealed as thoughts to each other because we do not share them. And if someone does, it is either shot down or comes in conflict with someone else's personal desires. So we never move forward. Is there any wonder why the world is in the shape it is today?

Well, we think NOW is a good time to move forward.

Gathering in unity gives us assurance that we are seeking God and what He wants done. Do we have any idea what would happen if we understood the thoughts that God was giving each of us, taking then the time to understand how they fit together, and then because of that understanding, being able to truly ask God to do what He wants done because we are in agreement? We see satan cowering in a corner at the very thought and that is exactly where he should be, not the other way around!

Why can't we do this? The answer is there IS NO REASON WHY WE CAN'T. We need to put down our pride, egos, ambitions, desires, personal agendas, and truly understand how God has gifted each of us, understand what God wants each of us to become, allow each other to become what God wants, and then we will see, that as long as we are Biblically sound, God wants us to work together to further His kingdom. Now there are a lot of "churches" that are not biblically sound and believe things contrary to the Bible, we are not speaking of them. We are speaking of the ones that are.

So what are we waiting for? Let's start gathering in groups and working towards this so that we can start now rather than it is too late! The following chapters show how we can do this through prayer.

We would like to end this chapter with a song called *"They'll Know We Are Christians By Our Love"*. We recommend that you go to *www. youtube.com* and in the YouTube search bar, search for *"They'll Know We Are Christians By Our Love"* minus the quotation marks.

IN SUMMARY

We learned the following about variable N:

- We hope you have seen the variable N stands for N, number of people praying in unity, agreement, and of like mind for anything.

- It also includes Jesus sitting at God's right hand interceding on behalf of all of us praying.

Now let's look at our final faith equation together

$$((A \text{ and } B \text{ and } C \text{ and } D \text{ and } E \text{ and } F)*(\text{Clarity}*\text{Forgiveness}*\text{Binding and Loosening}))^N$$

Or

FAITH = A and B and C and D and E and F (1 or 0)
Maturity = Clarity*Forgiveness*Binding and Loosening
To result of $((\text{Faith})*\text{Maturity})^N$

We have spent a very great amount of time defining and explaining faith and the aspects of faith. Now we are going to move to show how to apply faith in our daily living. The rest of this book will show how to exercise faith in prayer and ministering to God.

SECTION III

Applying Faith to Our Daily Living

We choose to divide this book up into three separate sections on purpose. First, we wanted to explain what faith is, the basics the foundations of faith, where it comes from and how it is composed. Without the foundations, one cannot move forward. If one does not understand the basics of something then, that person can never apply that something to their life and have meaning. It is not that the person is dumb, stupid, or ignorant, it simply means that we do not know what we do not know. If I do not know what faith is composed of, I can never properly apply faith inside of my relationship with God. If I do not apply right then, my relationship with God will never be right.

Second, we wanted to give a picture of maturing in Christ aspects and show the relation they have to faith. By maturing our faith, it can be more than just existent, it can be active, it can have power, and it can have an effect on the world around us. When we partner maturity with being in unity (with our brothers and sisters in Christ), faith can be exponential in effectiveness and God's power can truly flow unhindered, by us, into this world to make a difference.

You have probably heard this statement, "Knowledge is power". That is a good statement but not necessarily accurate. For example, I may possess knowledge of how to help someone stop choking by applying the Heim-lich maneuver, but if I do not apply that knowledge at the correct time, it will either hurt the person, or be too late and the person might still die of choking. A better statement then is "The proper knowledge applied at the correct time is power".

The first two sections of this book were to provide you with the knowledge of faith and how to make it effective. Now we come to the last section of this book and this section will show us how we apply all that we know about faith into our daily living. After all, what good is faith if we cannot properly apply it into our life and the lives of others to make a difference?

Our plan is to address what prayer is in relation to our faith so we may be the righteous person in James 5:16b "The effectual fervent prayer of a righteous man availeth much." prayer is effectual fervent and availeth much. Our whole life needs be effectual fervent and availeth in our sphere of influence, reaching out to a lost and dying world, showing them who God is and what God does. Reaching a world that desperately needs Jesus starts and ends with properly applying the knowledge of faith at the correct time. Our faith applied through our daily living is what changes us, those around us, and the world. When God shines through us, and people see Jesus rather than us, God's glory penetrates the protective shell around them and turns their hearts to seek Him. We get the privilege then of working with others to help them meet God and help them to grow/ mature into Christ likeness.

Let's start this section with a chapter which generally describes how we apply faith into our daily living.

CHAPTER FOURTEEN

How Do We Apply Faith?

Everything in the previous chapters defined faith and the aspects of faith. The rest of this book will explain how we apply faith in our everyday living.

The first application that we want to reiterate is we are on the winning side. Our very faith and applying it, as God directs, means we will win.

> "And I say also unto thee, That thou art Peter, and
> upon this rock I will build my church; and the gates of hell
> shall not prevail against it." – Matthew 16:18

As we discussed before, Jesus says His church is being built and hell shall not prevail against it. Hell here would include satan, all demonic forces, and the spiritual/physical boundaries of hell. In other words, nothing can come out of the gates of hell to take down the church as a whole. What does this mean to us today? *It means the church, every believer individually and collectively, has already won over satan and there is nothing he can do about it.* Does satan have power? Yes. Is it greater than God's? No. Jesus is telling us here that we are on the winning side. This is critical point that we need to make sure is firm in our minds.

The second area we apply our faith is by living a Christ like life. If one goes back to Chapter 12 and looks at the 18 ways to bind satan, the basics of living a Christ like life are the way we bind satan. We literally are doing two things at one time when we live out the basics of Christ.

The third way we apply faith is through receiving discipleship and giving discipleship. The church as a whole is made up of those who have accepted Jesus Christ as their personal savior. However, God never intended it to stop there, God intends that we continue to grow and mature to become "Christ Like". We are all disciples learning and growing in our Christian walk. As part of this walk Jesus commanded we do the following:

> [18] *"And Jesus came and spake unto them, saying, All power is given unto me in heaven and in earth."* [19] *"Go ye therefore, and* **teach**[G3100] *all nations, baptizing them in the name of the Father, and of the Son, and of the Holy Ghost:"* [20] *"Teaching them to observe all things whatsoever I have commanded you: and, lo, I am with you always, even unto the end of the world. Amen."*
> *– Matthew 28:18 - 20*

We are to go in the power of Jesus and *teach*, Strong's G3100, (disciple) others from all nations in the commands that Jesus explained and exemplified to us. We are to help others to grow and mature in their walk. We are to lead them from milk to meat as Paul states in...

> [12] *"For when for the time ye ought to be teachers, ye have need that one teach you again which be the first principles of the oracles of God; and are become such as have need of milk, and not of strong meat."* [13] *"For every one that useth milk is unskilful in the word of righteousness:*

for he is a babe." [14]*"But strong meat belongeth to them that are of full age, even those who by reason of use have their senses exercised to discern both good and evil."*
– *Hebrews 5:12 - 14*

Why should we and others grow from milk to meat? To understand what Christ Like living is and is not so we can properly handle the "word of righteousness" i.e. the Bible which is two things: our firm foundation that we stand on (the peace of the gospel) and also our sword, our offensive weapon, to bind the enemy and loosen the bondage the enemy has put on mankind. By the way Jesus says we are to **GO** and do this not sit back and wait for others to come to us. We all fall into this trap because it is so much easier to sit back and have others come to us. However Jesus says we need to **GO,** to actively get out of our comfort zone and reach out to those who want/need discipleship. To journey with them or maybe better yet, to invite them into the journey we are on, helping them along the way behind us or on their parallel path. We teach what we have learned all the while continually growing deeper ourselves… never stopping always pushing always learning through the revelation of the Holy Spirit.

How do we do this teaching? Great question, and the best answer is to do it through the Spiritual Gift mix that we are given when we accept Jesus as our savior. Spiritual Gifts are the nine basic task oriented gifts to serve mankind. These gifts are: Evangelist; Prophet; Teaching; Exhortation; Pastor/Shepherd; Mercy Showing; Serving (Helps); Giving, and Administration. Through the divine supernatural power of the Holy Spirit, we use the gift mix we are given to lead others to grow in their Christian Walk. From showing they need Jesus as their Savior, leading them to salvation, or ministering to them in one of the other 7 gifts, we help others mature in their Christian walk. A good study on this is the book TEAM

Ministry *"How to Find Meaning and Fulfillment through Understanding the Spiritual Gift within You"* by Dr. Larry Gilbert.

The fourth way we are going to discuss applying our faith is prayer. Prayer starts with realizing we have the answers our brothers/sisters and the world need to know to help them live. Part of prayer is realizing God is wanting us to be the following:

> *"And I [God] sought for a man among them, that should make up the hedge, and stand in the* **gap**[H6556] *before me for the land, that I should not destroy it: but I found none."* – Ezekiel 22:30

Here God is saying He continually looks for those who will be willing to stand between Him and those who do not know Him. He wants us to stand in the *gap*, Strong's H6556, (the break) between the living and the dead from a spiritual standpoint. The basis of this comes from something Moses and Aaron did for the Israelites.

> [44]*"And the LORD spake unto Moses, saying,"* [45]*"Get you up from among this congregation, that I may consume them as in a moment. And they fell upon their faces."* [46]*"And Moses said unto Aaron, Take a censer, and put fire therein from off the altar, and put on incense, and go quickly unto the congregation, and make an atonement for them: for there is wrath gone out from the LORD; the plague is begun."* [47]*"And Aaron took as Moses commanded, and ran into the midst of the congregation; and, behold, the plague was begun among the people: and he put on incense, and made an atonement for the people."* [48]*"And he stood between the dead and the living; and the plague was stayed."* – Numbers 16:44 - 47

We need to be aware that those who do not know God are dying both physically and spiritually. They are dying because they either do not know Jesus or they do and consciously turn away from Him. This choice they make puts judgment on themselves and separates them from God. If they physically die, they go to Hell. God is looking for us to stand in the gap on their behalf. How do we do that? Great question we would say. Actually the answer is pretty neat when you look at the example of what Moses and Aaron did on behalf of the people. While Moses prayed, Aaron offered incense. If we jump to Revelation we see

> "And when he [Jesus] had taken the book, the four beasts and four and twenty elders fell down before the Lamb, having every one of them harps, and golden vials full **of odours,**[G2368] which are the prayers of saints."
> – Revelation 5:8

Per Strong's, *odours* G2368 means incense. We stand in the gap by praying for those that do not know God: our nations, the world, and our brothers and sisters in Christ who are hurting and need help. Our prayers are like incense which go up to God. They are stored in vials and they are offered on the altar in heaven. God then recognizes the prayers as a pleasing offering and answers them. We say offering, because they are an offering, they take time to think through, apply faith, make/request, and hope for. It is a sacrifice of ourselves from our time and therefore it is an offering of our time/talents to God. Prayers are defined as supplication or in modern day English praying to God asking earnestly and humbly. (In the following chapters about praying, we will cover what we are to ask for) As we stated this example of Moses and Aaron is a vivid example of the power we have to earnestly ask God to not destroy those who need to accept Him as their savior.

Why is prayer so important? That answer can be found here:

> *"Confess your faults one to another, and pray one for*
> *another, that ye may be healed. The **effectual fervent**[G1754]*
> ***prayer**[G1162] of a righteous man[G1342] availeth[G2480] **much**."[G4183]*
> *— James 5:16*

So some definitions, per Strong's G1754 *effectual fervent* means to be active, efficient, and/or mighty (powerful); *prayer* G1162 means request / petition; *righteous man* G1342 means holy (when we are holy we are living a right life for God and are in right standing with God); *availeth* G2480 means forceful; and *much* G4183 means abundantly. So the active (faith) petition/request from a person in right standing with God is abundantly forceful. Why? Because a person who is righteous is exercising all aspects of faith we have described to this point. Further, by praying, they are asking God to ask Him what He already told them to ask for. Therefore, because they are being active in their faith, God will answer the petition. From the names of God we studied in Chapter 4, we know when He answers, He answers with all the sufficiency and might of His being and character. The power of our prayer comes from God, because He is the one and only God the GREAT I AM. It is His power that answers simply because we are active in our faith.

Following on the thought of prayer, the final application of faith is in ministering unto God.

> *"My sons, be not now negligent: for the LORD hath*
> *chosen you to stand before him, to serve him, and that ye*
> *should **minister**[H1961 H8334] unto him, and burn incense."*
> *— 2 Chronicles 29:11*

Here King Hezekiah calls out the Levites to sanctify or purify themselves so that they can perform their duties before God. As we know the Levites were not the priests but were the ones who took care of the priests, the temple, helped with the sacrifices and did other things before God. We can apply this to us, the majority of Christians are not of the line of Aaron (the priesthood) or of the line from Levi, but as Christians we are called out to be pure before God. We are called to purify His temple, which now resides in each one of us, so we can minister to Him and burn incense to Him. We already have seen how to "burn incense" (pray), but what does minister before God mean? Here *ministering*, Strong's H1961 H8334, means we exist to serve (wait on) God. How do we wait on God? By doing what He tells us to do. What His good pleasure and good will toward mankind tells us to do for them.

What else does it mean to minister? We need to look at some other commandments that Jesus gave His disciples:

> [21] *"Then said Jesus to them again, Peace be unto you: as my Father hath sent me, even so send I you." * [22] *"And when he had said this, he breathed on them, and saith unto them, Receive ye the Holy Ghost:" – John 20:21 - 22*

In this scripture Jesus is anointing the disciples with the Holy Spirit. We know today that when we accept Jesus as our personal savior that we are also inviting the Holy Spirit to live in us and work in us. So we are already anointed like the disciples. Next Jesus says He is sending them. What is one of the things God sent Jesus to do? God sent Jesus to be a light to the dark world, to show the dark world who God is, God's character, and God's character towards them. Based on that, Jesus says as God hath sent me even though I send you. So Jesus is sending us to be the same light unto the dark world that He was. We are to show the dark world who God is, God's character, and God's character towards them. How do we get other's attention to who God is and His character? We do this by following what Jesus told the disciples:

> *⁵ "These twelve Jesus sent forth, and commanded them, saying, Go not into the way of the Gentiles, and into any city of the Samaritans enter ye not:" ⁶ "But go rather to the lost sheep of the house of Israel." ⁷ "And as ye go, preach, saying, The kingdom of heaven is at hand." ⁸ "Heal the sick, cleanse the lepers, raise the dead, cast out devils: freely ye have received, freely give." – Matthew 10:5 - 8*

What is interesting here is God did not tell His disciples to go out to the world do the things listed in Matthew 10:8, He told them to go to the Jewish people (who were already supposed to have a relationship with God) and do these things. The Jewish people were to be the example. From them, God through Peter and Paul, extended the same to the Christian community. We are to help our brothers and sisters in Christ who are suffering from the things in Matthew 10:8 (the storms of life Chapter 18) and allow that to be the example shared with those who do not believe in God in order to draw them into relationship. We are Jesus' disciples as well, we are to be doing these things. We do not just go out and start healing those that don't want to first know God. What would be the point? Jesus said in Matthew do not throw your pearls to the pigs. We need to be a beacon to those that do not know Jesus and show them how we treat each other by our love. One of those aspects is freely giving of our faith by praying for the needs of our brothers and sisters in Christ. That isn't natural, but it so deeply desired and leads to others to be drawn to us.

We would like to close this chapter with the song, ***"Living by Faith"***. We recommend that you go to *www.youtube.com* and in the YouTube search bar, search for *"Living By Faith by Gaithers"* minus the quotation marks.

IN SUMMARY

To apply our faith we do it in a few ways:

- We realize and operate with the confidence we are on the winning side.

- We live out our daily lives applying faith as stated in Chapter 12, the 18 ways to bind satan.

- We apply our faith by receiving and giving discipleship.

- We apply our faith through prayer for ourselves and others.

- We apply our faith by ministering unto God.

Now that we have covered application of faith or some foundations of the application of faith let's look in the next chapter at basics of prayer.

CHAPTER FIFTEEN

The Basics of Praying: The Lord's Prayer

Praying in faith… what does that mean? As we go through life and go into different churches we hear so many different prayers, some flowing, some long, some short, some shouting, some whispering, some begging, some commanding, some simply asking, and we ask ourselves what is the right way to pray? We want God to hear what we are praying for. What do we need to do to get God's attention?

The best model we are given in the Bible is from Jesus Himself through two examples:

> [7]"*But when ye pray, use not vain repetitions, as the heathen do: for they think that they shall be heard for their much speaking.*" [8]"*Be not ye therefore like unto them: for your Father knoweth what things ye have need of, before ye ask him.*" [9]"*After this manner therefore pray ye: Our Father which art in heaven, Hallowed be thy name.*" [10]"*Thy kingdom come. Thy will be done in earth, as it is in heaven.*" [11]"*Give us this day our daily bread.*" [12]"*And forgive us our debts, as we forgive our debtors.*" [13]"*And lead us not into temptation, but deliver us from evil: For thine is the kingdom, and the power, and the glory, for ever. Amen.*" – Matthew 6:7 - 13

and

> [2] *"And he said unto them, When ye pray, say, Our*
> *Father which art in heaven, Hallowed be thy name. Thy*
> *kingdom come. Thy will be done, as in heaven, so in earth."*
> [3] *"Give us day by day our daily bread."* [4] *"And forgive us*
> *our sins; for we also forgive every one that is indebted to*
> *us. And lead us not into temptation; but deliver us from*
> *evil." – Luke 11:2 - 4*

There have been many interpretations of these scriptures so we do not want to belabor what others have spoken of. We want to focus more in a progression of how to prepare for prayer... how to enter into prayer. The first observation here and also based on preceding scriptures in Matthew, prayer does not have so much to do with the words said or how loud, soft, repetitive, chanted, thought, or anything other than the *attitude of one's heart.* For as we know from Matthew 15:19 "For out of the heart proceed evil thoughts, murders, adulteries, fornications, thefts, false witness, blasphemies:", the tongue is a tool to be used for good or evil and that is determined by one's heart or the attitude of one's heart. Realizing this, makes the examples of Jesus so much easier to understand. The common points from both scriptures are the following: 1) recognizing God's deity/ authority and holiness, not just in respect but in worship of who He is and what He is going to do when we ask; 2) asking that God's will (not our desires, thoughts, needs, wants, etc.) be done in both the earth and in heaven; 3) to ask Him to give us our daily sustenance; 4) to forgive us of our sins; 5) to help us forgive others for the things they have done against us; 6) asking to not be brought into temptation; and 7) asking to be rescued from evil. Again there are many others who have stated this prior to us so this is nothing really new. What we want to point out though is the progression of preparing ourselves to pray in faith. For example recognizing who God is, is critical for us to have a proper attitude in our heart as we come before Him praying. Again asking for God's will to be done, drives out of our heart all the selfish desires; needs; wants; ambitions, etc. We always need sustenance for our physical and spiritual existence and we recognize both come from God. We need to be forgiven of our sins so we can be in right standing before God. A repentative heart, which chooses to not sin, is another attitude we need to have. We need to have a heart of grace towards others who have wronged us in some way. We need God to tell satan no as he asks God to allow us to be "sifted as wheat", to make sure only the trials we need to help us grow closer to God are allowed. Finally, we need to be constantly rescued from the evil that satan tries to bring against us to destroy us. Each step here prepares our heart attitude, to put our heart in its proper place in relation to God and to what / who we are coming to pray for. We should feel like we are the only person who has been asked to pray for something and if we do not pray, we will have failed in our responsibility… we should take this seriously. We want our heart to reflect and be all that Christ embodies as we come before God as being covered in the blood of Jesus so we can come before God and stand before our accuser satan. We want God to recognize us, not hear satan, because of what Jesus has done. This is the point of the prayer examples Jesus gave us. So we can be prepared.

What is interesting in the examples above are the verses surrounding them. In Matthew, Jesus precedes the example with the following:

> [5]*"And when thou prayest, thou shalt not be as the hypocrites are: for they love to pray standing in the synagogues and in the corners of the streets, that they may be seen of men. Verily I say unto you, They have their reward."* [6]*"But thou, when thou prayest, enter into thy*

closet, and when thou hast shut thy door, pray to thy
Father which is in secret; and thy Father which seeth in
*secret **shall reward**G591 thee openly." – Matthew 6:5 - 6*

There are times we may be called upon to pray in public and when we do so, we must make sure our hearts are in the right attitude, meaning we are focusing on God and not the approval of others. However, Jesus is saying here, that most of our prayer time should be spent in private. It should be done where we are not distracted and where we can truly focus on the attitude of our heart in relation to who God is and what we are asking to be done. Jesus says a great way to do this is to go into a room and close the door. This is so we can pray freely minimizing distractions to us and to not cause distractions for others. We can be free to pray out loud instead of in silence. Praying out loud accomplishes a few things: it allows you to drown out other thoughts because you have to focus on what you are saying; it allows you to hear what is said so you have testimony of what you prayed for; and it keeps you focused. A main point here is that what we do when we pray by ourselves, will be *rewarded*, Strong's G591, to us openly. Or for a loose translation, what we pray for when we are by ourselves will be given away/up publicly. What are we to be praying for? We are to be praying for the things God asked us to ask of Him. Why does He ask us to ask Him for things? So that He may be glorified. How is God glorified? When others see/observe/experience who God is and what God does for them or for others they love. Therefore, when Jesus says we will be rewarded openly, it means we get to see God glorified publicly because we did what He asked us to do. Pretty neat we must say!!!

The verses directly following the example in Matthew state this:

[14]*"For if ye forgive men their **trespasses,**G3900 your*
heavenly Father will also forgive you:" [15]*"But if ye forgive*
*not men their **trespasses,**G3900 neither will your Father*
*forgive your **trespasses.**"G3900 – Matthew 6:14 -15*

We stated this earlier in Chapter 11. Again we have to be very careful of the attitude of our heart when we pray that we extend God's grace to others who have *trespassed*, Strong's G3900, against us (those who have fell, caused a fault, made an offence, and/or sinned against us). This is iterated in the prayer and Jesus gives clarification to us so we have to take this as another very important point He wants us to know.

Another item to note is in both prayers; Jesus says to ask for God to provide us our daily bread. We find this interesting because bread has two references in the Bible. One is for actual bread or a loaf of bread symbolizing our daily physical sustenance. However, bread is also used to refer to spiritual sustenance. That is found in the following scriptures:

> *"And Jesus said unto them, I am the* **bread**^(G740) *of life:*^(G2222) *he that cometh to me shall never hunger;³ and he that believeth on me shall never thirst." – John 6:35*

> ⁴⁷*"Verily, verily, I say unto you, He that believeth on me hath everlasting life."* ⁴⁸*"I am that* **bread**^(G740) *of life."*^(G2222) ⁵⁰*"This is the bread which cometh down from heaven, that a man may eat thereof, and not die."* ⁵¹*"I am the living bread which came down from heaven: if any man eat of this bread, he shall live for ever: and the bread that I will give is my flesh, which I will give for the life of the world."* ⁵²*"The Jews therefore strove among themselves, saying, How can this man give us his flesh to eat?"* ⁵³*"Then Jesus said unto them, Verily, verily, I say unto you, Except ye eat the flesh of the Son of man, and drink his blood, ye have no life in you."* ⁵⁴*"Whoso eateth my flesh, and drinketh my blood, hath eternal life; and I will raise him up at the last day."* ⁵⁵*"For my flesh is meat indeed, and my*

*blood is drink indeed." ⁵⁶"He that eateth my flesh, and
drinketh my blood, dwelleth in me, and I in him." ⁵⁷"As
the living Father hath sent me, and I live by the Father: so
he that eateth me, even he shall live by me." ⁵⁸"This is that
bread which came down from heaven: not as your fathers
did eat manna, and are dead: he that eateth of this bread
shall live for ever." – John 6:47 - 58*

These scriptures state that Jesus is the bread and the drink of life. Each use of *bread*, Strong's G740, represents a loaf of bread, but obviously Jesus is not talking about bread here, He is talking about Himself. The question then becomes how do we eat and drink Jesus? The following verse shows us how:

*"All scripture **is given by inspiration of God**,ᴳ²³¹⁵
and is profitable for doctrine, for reproof, for correction,
for instruction in righteousness:" – 2 Timothy 3:16*

We understand here that the phrase *given by inspiration of God*, Strong's G2315 means *"divinely breathed* in". God divinely breathed into man's mind His Word. Another way to put it is He spoke into man's minds His Word. They received it as audible thoughts if you will. Based on this passage, the Bible is God's *spoken* Word to man which man documented for all to read. Now that we understand the Bible is God's spoken Word, we then find the following in John:

*¹"In the beginning was the **Word**,ᴳ³⁰⁵⁶ and the
Wordᴳ³⁰⁵⁶ was with God, and the **Word**ᴳ³⁰⁵⁶ **was
God**."ᴳ²³¹⁶ ²"The same was in the beginning with God."
³"All things were made by him; and without him was not
any thing made that was made." ⁴"In him was **life**;ᴳ²²²²
and the **life**ᴳ²²²² was the light of men." – John 1:1 – 4*

250

*"And the **Word**^{G3056} **was made**^{G1096} **flesh,**^{G4561} and dwelt among us, (and we beheld his glory, the glory as of the only begotten of the Father,) full of grace and truth."*
— John 1:14

Here we understand that John is speaking about Jesus. In this passage and in many others in the Bible, Jesus is referred to as the Word of God with *Word* translated Strong's G3056 meaning something said. ***Jesus is the words that God has spoken.*** So back to our question, how do we eat Jesus and drink Jesus as to gain spiritual sustenance? We read (in mind and audible), study, learn, memorize, put into our hearts, the written Word of God. When we do this we are literally eating and drinking Jesus into ourselves from a spiritual standpoint. Our spiritual self is full and because God's Word never returns null, our hearts are put into a proper attitude when coming to God in prayer. So in essence the Word of God is essential to prayer. As prayer is an offensive weapon, if you look at a gun, you need bullets of the right caliber to shoot, or if a bow, an arrow made for it. If you look at prayer as the weapon, then the Word of God is bullets or arrows to fire. For it is not our words that carry power, but rather God's Word, Hebrews 4:12 "For the **word**^{G3056} **of God**^{G2316} *is* quick, and powerful, and sharper than any two edged sword, piercing even to the dividing asunder of soul and spirit, and of the joints and marrow, and *is* a discerner of the thoughts and intents of the heart."

To finish the Lord's prayer, then we need to look at the verses that follow the prayer in Luke:

⁵"And he said unto them, Which of you shall have a friend, and shall go unto him at midnight, and say unto him, Friend, lend me three loaves;" ⁶"For a friend of mine in his journey is come to me, and I have nothing to set *before him?" ⁷"And he from within shall answer and say, Trouble me not: the door is now shut, and my children are with me in bed; I cannot rise and give thee." ⁸"I say unto you, Though he will not rise and give him, because he is his friend, yet because of his **importunity**^G335 he will rise and give him as many as he needeth." ⁹"And I say unto you, Ask, and it shall be given you; seek, and ye shall find; knock, and it shall be opened unto you." ¹⁰"For every one that asketh receiveth; and he that seeketh findeth; and to him that knocketh it shall be opened." – Luke 11:5 - 10*

The main thrust of this scripture is to show that we are to be persistent in prayer. In Luke 11:8, the word *importunity*, (Strong's G335) per *www.merriam-webster.com* can be translated as *importunate* or overly persistent in request or demand. It is a persistence that has a negative connotation to the point of annoyance. It seems strange that Jesus would use a word that would have a negative connotation attached to it in reference to a relationship between us and God. We wonder though if it isn't so much as it is a negative between God and us as much as it would seem annoying to others. For example the passage above references one person who is asking another person to do something for them. The framing of it though is interesting. This isn't during normal hours; Jesus frames this to be in the middle of the night. One cannot wake someone shut behind doors and fast asleep from the outside without being loud, bold, brash, etc. The person seeking is shouting to the other person, asking them to do something. The person inside tries to have the seeker go away by shouting back with logic of why they do not want to get up and meet the need. However, the one seeking persists, and at this point it becomes an annoyance. Assuming that this person lives in a town, think of all the neighbors that are being woke up in the middle of the night due to this persistence. It becomes an annoyance to them as they are not even part of the situation but come dragged into it because it is inconveniencing them… they are losing sleep. The person inside is feeling reverse peer pressure and is compelled to answer the request simply to keep in the neighbor's good graces. We feel the seeker realizes this as well however their need is great enough that they are willing for others to be annoyed in order for the request to be met. To these others, they are being persistent to a negative point. What is interesting again, it isn't so much that Jesus is saying if we annoy God that He will answer as much as God wants to be known, pursued and recognized for what only He can do. The satisfaction of the fact that there is a need and the only way to fulfill it is going to God even if the need comes at an inopportune time and if it might inconvenience others, the need still is important and needs to be fulfilled. Think of it this way, how many times have you seen a young man pursue a young woman or vice versa, to the point that their persistence is annoying to watch/hear/see played out? They do crazy things, to show the other how much they want them and to be with them. They desire a relationship and are willing to do almost anything to have it. It becomes annoying to watch as a friend on either side, while the seeker blatantly becomes an annoyance to the point we start telling the one they are seeking, just go out with them already. The annoyance comes to the others who are around the situation but not necessarily main players involved. God wants us to want Him, to seek Him boldly even to the point that it may annoy others, to put Him above all else, even if it may inconvenience others and annoy others because of it. If you look at the scripture examples: woman with bleeding (Matthew 9:20–22), blind men (Matthew 20:29 – 34), Canaanite woman's daughter (Matthew 15:21 – 28), Widow's son (Luke 7:11 – 15), Demon possessed boy (Luke 9:38 – 43), Samaritan woman (John 4:7 – 42), feeding of the 5,000 and 4,000,

Jesus anointed (John 12:1 – 7), children coming to Jesus (Luke 18:15 – 17), the blind man being healed (Luke 18:35 – 42), the disciples were annoyed, and we believe this is what Jesus is describing. Jesus follows that story up with verse 9 reiterating that we must ask, seek and knock. The order here is impersonal to personal. Asking is impersonal; one can go around asking many people for something. However when we move from asking to seeking, we put effort into finding someone who specifically can do what needs to be done, or seeking to understand how to ask the right question, we are doing research to understand better what needs to happen so we can ask correctly. Knocking then represents, we know exactly where to go, and we personally knock on their door to involve them in regards to our request. Asking could be asking God to heal someone. Seeking would be to gain clarity of the situation and what the person is in need/healing of. While knocking is going into our prayer closet and specifically asking God to heal the person's artery where it has a blockage, dissolving the blockage to nothing so it will exit the body without causing any other issues and then to heal the artery walls so they are healthy where the blockage was so it does not burst. See we have moved from impersonal to personal. This only happens when we ask specific questions to have the right prayer to ask of God. We might have to become annoying in our questions to get the other person focused on what they are asking. We have to be persistent to make sure we are praying what God wants us to pray so that the request can be answered.

Jesus finishes the section with showing us not to be afraid to ask:

> [11] "If a son shall ask bread of any of you that is a father,
> will he give him a stone? or if he ask a fish, will he for a
> fish give him a serpent?" [12] "Or if he shall ask an egg, will
> he offer him a scorpion?" [13] "If ye then, being evil, know

how to give good gifts unto your children: how much more shall your heavenly Father give the Holy Spirit to them that ask him?" – Luke 11:11 - 13

We know from Chapters 4, and 5 Jesus deeply cares about us and He cares about what we care about. He knows what we need even when we do not, and the best gift He has to give us after salvation is another part of Himself... the Holy Spirit. As we ask for this and for that, He continually gives/fills us with the Holy Spirit so we can draw close to Him, hear Him, listen to Him, understand Him, and be one with Him. The Holy Spirit is what we need (what we are asking for) and that need leads us to be open to want to be filled with the Holy Spirit. The outside forces of this world continually reveal to us how much we need God and as situations arise in which we "have" to go to Him, it gives God one more way to draw close to us and fill us with His Spirit. No matter what the need we have might be, God uses that need to help us give all of ourselves to Him, so He can fill us completely with His Spirit. His very presence can live in us, if we allow Him there. Just like a parent who has a child that is asking for candy for lunch will give them food to nourish them properly, God wants to nourish us with His Spirit and presence.

I (Walter) have been processing through why so many of our prayers do not seem to be answered. We know God wants to answer our prayers, and we know we want our prayers answered, but when we are praying, do we really seek God? Are we just throwing up a few quick words and moving on through our day not giving them a second thought, or are we really seeking God? Are you being impersonal with God? Are you willing to move from impersonal to personal? Are you ready to move from just asking, to really seeking God and knocking at His door? Asking doesn't instill faith, faith comes as we seek and knock earnestly wanting to be in relationship with God. Romans 10:17 "So then faith *cometh* by hearing, and hearing by the word of God." Faith comes by hearing the word of God which means we need to be immersed in God's word through reading, hearing, meditation, prayer, etc. What is it going to take for you to get gut level intimate with God? Just some nuggets to start noodling as you read through the rest of this book.

As we bring this chapter to a close we would like to leave you with a great hymn called ***"Sweet Hour of Prayer"***. We recommend that you go to *www.youtube.com* and in the YouTube search bar, search for *"Sweet Hour of Prayer"* minus the quotation marks.

IN SUMMARY ———————————————

We looked at the two examples in the Bible to show some of the basics to praying. We learned praying has everything to do with the attitude of one's heart rather than what one says. To prepare our hearts the progression in the examples is to:

- recognize God's deity/authority/and holiness;

- ask God's will (not our desires, thoughts, needs, wants, etc.) be done in both the earth and in heaven;

- ask Him to give us our daily sustenance;

- forgive us of our sins;

- help us forgive others for the things they have done against us;

- ask to not be brought into temptation;

- ask to be rescued from evil.

In addition we learned:

- the majority of our prayers and time in prayer should be done in private between us and God,

- we need to have our hearts in a forgiven state between us and others,

- we need to be sustained physically,

- we need to be eating/drinking Jesus (God's Word),

- we need to be continually pursuing God even to the point it may annoy others by the amount of time we spend with Him and making requests of Him,

- we need to understand, that no matter what our need is, God uses it as a way to reach us and to give us the opportunity to be filled more with His Spirit. (Holy Spirit)

Now that we understand the examples Jesus gave us, we can move to prepare ourselves more specifically with what we have learned so far about faith.

CHAPTER SIXTEEN

The Basics of Praying: Preparing Yourself

The basics... we must always make sure we understand the basics before we move to the complex. This is how life is taught... this is how we experience life. As little children we know the world is around us but do not understand much about it other than it is there and it works. As we grow older we understand more and more of the basics. Then once we understand the basics we can apply the basics to many areas of life. So let's dive into the basics.

The first basic of praying, is to make sure we are grounded in who God is and who we are in relation to Him. We covered this in the Chapters 3, 4, and 5 (Who is God, God's Character and God's Character toward mankind). We need to be continually maturing in the knowledge of these three areas. This maturing comes through revelation of the Holy Spirit (for example the need to be saved), through experiences which God uses to teach us to rely on Him, and through studying the Bible, and how other people learned to trust God and take those facts and put them into our arsenal. In Eph 6:15 "...your feet shod with the preparation of the gospel of peace;", we see our feet need to be covered, or standing on the "gospel of peace. We have this peace, this firmness of footing if you will when we know beyond all other thoughts who God is, His Character, and His

Character towards us. How can we not be steadfastly rooted when we can fully and completely trust and rely on Him? Read, study and allow God and His presence to soak into you so you can KNOW Him.

The second basic of praying in faith, is to make sure your thoughts are of God. As we have discussed before, we need to ensure that what we are praying for is what God asked us to pray/ ask for. We need to make sure our thoughts are correct. A passage of scripture that God revealed to me (Rich) is the following from Zechariah:

> [4]"And said unto him, Run, speak to this young man, saying, Jerusalem shall be inhabited as towns without walls for the multitude of men and cattle therein:" [5]"For I, saith the LORD, will be unto her a wall of fire round about, and will be the glory in the midst of her."
> – Zechariah 2:4 - 5

Even though this scripture is applicable to the specific instance in time it was written, I think it has value for us today as well. God is saying that He will remove the physical walls of the city because He is going to put a spiritual wall of fire around the city to protect it. The spiritual realm trumps the physical realm… it is better or has more weight. God revealed to me a few years back that I should pray God would be a wall of fire around my heart and mind protecting me from thoughts and feelings which are not from Him. Further as this prayer is prayed, I am asking He would remove all thoughts and feelings not of Him from my heart and mind. I then ask God to fill me with thoughts and feelings from Him and the wisdom and discernment to know if they are from Him or not. I want all the thoughts and feelings filtered by and through God so they are purified and cleansed to bless me and those I am working with.

The third basic of praying in faith, is to know you are coming to God in a pure state. What does pure state mean you ask? Well we are glad you asked. Pure state means that you are coming to God guilt free to ask Him what He gave you the thought to ask for. It is a self-reflection, asking ourselves and God to reveal any and all sins so that we may repent and be forgiven of them, recognizing that satan may be running interference in our lives. For example, as we have discussed before, if you have unforgiveness and/or bitterness in your heart, why would you ask God for something other than to help remove that from your heart? We already know based on Chapter 11 that having not dealt with this, God is not going to answer you. So why would we ask for anything else? One of the very first things we need to do is pray that God would clear our heart/mind and reveal unforgiveness, and bitterness that may be in our hearts. If you are not aware of anything, then you should ask God to reveal to you if there is anything in your heart that you are harboring unconsciously. Following on this thought, maybe we are not the ones with unforgiveness, and bitterness issue, but we know someone who has something against us. If we know that they do, and we have not dealt with it, then Jesus says:

> ²³"Therefore if thou bring thy gift to the altar, and there rememberest that thy brother hath ought against thee;" ²⁴"Leave there thy gift before the altar, and go thy way; first be reconciled to thy brother, and then come and offer thy gift." – Matthew 5:23 – 24

If you know that there is an issue between another toward you, then you should first take the step and attempt to make things right. Then come back and offer God your gift i.e., asking God what He wants you to ask. Obviously this is only if you know. If you don't know then you are free until that is revealed to you.

The fourth basic of praying in faith we need to do, is to ask God to remove all doubt from our hearts and minds. This kind of relates to the second basic, but it is a little different. We need to make sure that we are coming to God with no doubt, or if we have doubt, we need to ask God to reveal to us what the doubt is so we can pray against it. For instance if we have doubt about a certain prayer we feel God is asking us to pray, maybe it isn't so much doubt as we are not clear on what He is asking. Maybe we need to ask more questions to ensure we ask specifically what He wants us to ask. We need to make sure we have asked all the right questions. Once we have asked all the right questions, then we should have the right answers and then we can pray in faith because we are praying in what God wants. Thoughts from God are not always answers in themselves. Sometimes they are to provoke our thinking to ask different questions which are the right questions we should be asking. Realize at times God will not take away the doubt because it is up to us to move forward in faith before He opens our minds more clearly. If we do not do what He asked us to do first, we cannot expect Him to reveal the next step. God rarely reveals the whole plan. He moves us one step at a time so we are not overwhelmed. All the great saints in the Bible, who were given big tasks, had them given in steps and only revealed what they needed to know at the time they needed to know it. They acted on what they knew, trusting God for the next step. This is moving without doubt. We want to make sure we do not have doubt because as we discussed earlier in James that a double minded man should not expect his request to be answered.

The fifth basic of praying in faith, is understanding what asking means. Jesus said:

> *"If ye abide in me, and my words abide in you, ye*
> *shall ask what ye will, and it shall be done unto you."*
> *– John 15:7*

Notice there are two conditions here: one we are abiding (staying, remaining, continuing) in God and two His words are abiding (staying, remaining, continuing) in us. We have to continually seek God's presence while keeping His words (the Bible, revelations of the Holy Spirit) in us. This means we need to start listening to the Holy Spirit, quit doing our fleshly desires, and do what the Holy Spirit is telling us to do. We cannot live in fleshy desires and do what God wants… sin will always prevent it. If our work lives are not holy then we are ignoring the spiritual truths and God will not be able to do what we ask.

When we are doing this, then we know we are ready to receive what God wants us to ask for and can ask for it with the knowledge He will do it. So then we can ask in complete confidence and God will answer it.

The sixth basic of praying in faith, is acting on the thoughts we have. If you get a thought to pray for someone or something, then you can pray in faith for that person or thing because that thought came from God. Actually here the faith question has already been answered, we need to be obedient and pray.

The seventh basic of praying in faith, is being aware of what is going on when God takes a long time to answer something. Are we praying for the right thing or is God just using that thing or thought to provoke us to go deeper into what he wants us to pray for. Again the faith isn't in the end result but in the promise of the end result. You may, or may not live to see the end result.

We would like to close this chapter with the song **"Pray"**. We recommend that you go to *www.youtube.com* and in the YouTube search bar, search for *"Pray by Sanctus Real"* minus the quotation marks.

IN SUMMARY

We learned there are seven main ways to prepare ourselves to pray:

- make sure you are grounded in who God is and who we are in relation to Him.

- make sure your thoughts are of God.

- know you are coming to God in a pure state.

- ask God to remove all doubt from our hearts and minds.

- understanding what asking means.

- acting on the thoughts we have.

- being aware of what is going on when God takes a long time to answer something.

Now that we are prepared to pray, if we are going to pray for something that involves other people, or if we are praying for another person, we need to prepare them.

CHAPTER SEVENTEEN

The Basics of Praying: Preparing Others

This is an interesting chapter title. Obviously we know we need to prepare ourselves for prayer, but have we ever stopped to think we are rarely only praying for ourselves. We were created to be relational beings and we live in relationship with others. Most of our prayers are for others not for us. Therefore we need to not only make sure we are prepared for prayer, but we also need to make sure those who we are praying for are also prepared for the prayers we offer on their behalf. For God declares that we need to be praying for each other: James 5:16 "Confess *your* faults one to another, and pray one for another, that ye may be healed. The effectual fervent prayer of a righteous man availeth much.", that we need to be praying for each other, holding each other up in prayer, undergirding (strengthening) each other, leveraging our faith into others so they can grow and mature in their own faith. Let's look into this at a deeper level.

First, we should really discuss who are the "others"… they can be a spouse; children; parents; other family; friends; members of one's church; co-workers; bosses; other people in other companies; those that who have been elected to govern over u;, those whose job it is to protect; those who are struggling; those who are not save;, those who we need favor with, etc. We live and breathe interacting with others constantly and we should pray for them.

So what is the process, how do we prepare them when there is such a wide array of people we interact with? We would like to submit these steps as a good starting point that you can tweak as you mature in your faith and prayer life. This will be very similar to preparing yourself, with some additional information to think through.

The first way to prepare the person is to pray satan would not have access to their thoughts and feelings. We need to ask that satan would not have access to those we are praying for in any way. We want God to rebuke him from having access. As we stated in Chapter 2, we are always under constant attack in our thoughts and feelings and we want them to be thinking clearly so that the Holy Spirit can move in their heart and minds. If we look at Jude 1:9 "Yet Michael the archangel, when contending with the devil he disputed about the body of Moses, durst not bring against him a railing accusation, but said, The Lord **rebuke**^{G2008} thee." Here the word *rebuke*, Strong's G2008, means to tax upon, censure or admonish, by implication forbid. Michael the archangel called upon the Lord (Jesus) to forbid satan from having access to the body of Moses. We need to do the same for those we are praying for. We need to ask Jesus to forbid satan and his minions from having access to the thought life/feeling life of those we are praying for so that God's truth can permeate into them and change their thinking. What happened when Jesus delivered the man of the Gerasenes? Mark 5:15 "And they [the towns people] come to Jesus, and see him that was possessed with the devil, and had the legion, sitting, and clothed, and in his right mind: and they were afraid." The man, when delivered, was quiet, complacent, clothed, and sane... sitting at Jesus feet no doubt with Jesus feeding Himself into the man. As a side note, I (Walter) want to point out when we say the man was delivered, it means satan was cast out of the man, he was no longer present in the man or around the man or having access to the man anymore. Because of this, the man was ready to receive because he was completely free, he was in a state where he could receive Jesus and what Jesus had to say. We want this same freedom for those we are praying for so that they will receive what we pray for them.

The second way to prepare the person, after they are ready to receive, is to ask God to forgive them of any sins they may have. Whoa... wait a minute here... you say, this is not Biblical. Just hold on and we will explain. This is asking **God** to forgive the person of their sins. It is not absolving them of their sins. No man has the right, or authority to forgive sins, this is reserved for God. However, we can ask God to forgive a person of their sins and as God answers this request, the person is free for a moment in time so the Holy Spirit can come into their life convicting them and leading them to a desire of accepting Jesus as their savior. We also want to make clear asking God to forgive a person of their sins is not the same thing as asking for salvation on their behalf. Each person must make this choice to repent of their sins, accept Jesus as their savior, and confessing Jesus as Lord of their life. If they do not then when they die they are going to hell. There is only one way to heaven and that is through Jesus Christ. Here are some scriptures that back our claim of asking God to forgive sins:

> [21] *"Then said Jesus to them again, Peace be unto you: as my Father hath sent me, even so send I you."* [22] *"And when he had said this, he breathed on them, and saith unto them, Receive ye the Holy Ghost:"* [23] *"Whose soever sins ye remit, they are remitted unto them; and whose soever sins ye retain, they are retained."* – John 20:21 -23

These scriptures go back to the idea of binding and loosening. If we pray that the person's sins are forgiven then this scripture says God will forgive them of their sins. We don't just want the person to have their mind's cleared, we also want to make sure the soul is clear/cleansed so the

Holy Spirit can move in their life. If they are God's, then they are no longer satan's and that is what we are ultimately commissioned to do, see every man, woman and child brought to God and His saving grace. God gave us this right and power through Jesus and then through the Holy Spirit. The Spirit dwells in us, just like it did for the 11 disciples and we are to stand in the gap for those we love and those we are in relationship with, to plead God's forgiveness on their behalf. Remember one of the reasons we are here is to loosen the bondage satan has on this world and the biggest way we can do that is if people are in right standing with God.

To further this thought, here is something very interesting that we stumbled onto while writing this book… look at:

> *"Jesus answered and said unto them, Verily I say unto you, If ye have faith, and doubt not, ye shall not only do this which is done to the fig tree, but also if ye shall say unto this mountain,* **Be thou removed,***[G142] and be thou cast into the sea; it shall be done." – Matthew 21:21*

and

> *"For verily I say unto you, That whosoever shall say unto this mountain,* **Be thou removed,***[G142] and be thou cast into the sea; and shall not doubt in his heart, but shall believe that those things which he saith shall come to pass; he shall have whatsoever he saith." – Mark 11:23*

and

> *"This [Jesus] is that* **bread***[G740] which came down from heaven: not as your fathers did eat manna, and are dead: he that eateth of this bread shall live for ever." – John 6:58*

We want to bring attention to *Be thou removed*, Strong's G142 and *bread*, Strong's G740 which has a root word of G142. G142 is a primary verb meaning to *lift* by implication to *take up* or *away* and/or by Hebraism to *expiate* sin. Expiate sin. What does that mean? We looked expiate up in *www.merriam-webster.com* and found something very interesting... the definitions mean "to do something as a way to show that you are sorry about doing something bad" or to make expiation - the act of making atonement. You see, in the western culture, we see commanding a fig tree to move or a mountain to move, but when Jesus used this phrase with the Jews, they knew he was talking about the fig tree (fruit of) or the mountain of sin being atoned for the person and therefore removed from them so they can be free. Following that with John 6:58, Jesus is speaking of people eating His bread which will expiate (atone) for their sins making them free. Free of what? Again the bondage of sin that satan keeps us under to separate us from God. Jesus is literally saying here, "You think these physical miracles I did are good? If you have faith you can even command that the sins of people be removed from them (expiated or atoned for) so they can be set free". For as Jesus said in the following:

> [2]*"And, behold, they brought to him a man sick of the palsy, lying on a bed: and Jesus seeing their faith said unto the sick of the palsy; Son, be of good cheer; thy sins be forgiven thee."* [3]*"And, behold, certain of the scribes said within themselves, This man blasphemeth."* [4]*"And Jesus knowing their thoughts said, Wherefore think ye evil in your hearts?"* [5]*"For whether is easier, to say, Thy sins be forgiven thee; or to say, Arise, and walk?"* [6]*"But that ye may know that the Son of man hath power on earth to forgive sins, (then saith he to the sick of the palsy,) Arise, take up thy bed, and go unto thine house."*
> – *Matthew 9:2 - 6*

Or, if you will "Hey guys, what do you think is more impossible... that I physically heal this man, or that I tell his sins to Be thou removed? What is done in the physical only gives testimony to what is done in the spiritual realm". For James says:

> *14 "Is any sick among you? let him call for the elders of the church; and let them pray over him, anointing him with oil in the name of the Lord:" 15 "And the prayer of faith shall save the sick, and the Lord shall raise him up; and if he have committed sins, they shall be forgiven him."*
> *– James 5:14 - 15*

James says we do not even have to ask for the person's sins to be forgiven. It happens as part of the anointing them in name of the Lord. The very anointing and praying over them will cause the Lord to forgive any sins they have committed. *We have the right and the responsibility to make request on behalf of those we are praying for that God forgive their sins so they can be in right standing with God and **have the opportunity to repent of their sins and accept Jesus as their savior.***

Following on this thought of forgiveness, the third way to prepare the person is to pray for a cleansing. We can pray for them to be purified and cleansed or another term would be sanctified. Think of them as a dirty dish. That dish will remain dirty till it is washed. After it is washed it is useful again for its intended purpose. But while it is dirty, the dirt could be fresh or rotten and stinking. We need them to be cleansed, head to toe so the Holy Spirit can come in and fill them with His presence, lead them to God and then fulfill their intended purpose.

The fourth way to prepare the person, is to ask that God would reveal Himself to them through the Holy Spirit. That He would change their heart and mind to seek Him and search for Him... to be aware of His existence and start to desire to have a relationship with Him. That God would then reveal all the things we discussed in Chapters 3, 4, and 5... for who He is, His character, and His character towards them specifically through the Holy Spirit. This will start to build their confidence and trust in Him so that they can listen and understand what God is telling them.

Once we have prayed for them in these steps making request of God that the Holy Spirit would open their hearts and minds to hear, listen, and start to obey God and what God wants done in their lives. We need to make sure we are praying what God wants for them not what we want. Our faith in our actions and in what we pray on their behalf, can be leveraged into their lives to strengthen them.

If we really stop and think what God wants to do, He wants us to intervene on behalf of others so He can show His might and His grace and mercy. Let's look at Abraham in Genesis 18:17 – 33. Here we understand that Jesus was sending His angels to determine how bad the people of Sodom were sinning with the implication that He was going to destroy them because of their wickedness. Abraham, knowing that Lot had moved to that area, makes request of Jesus proving Jesus' righteousness asking if He would destroy a city that may contain righteous people. Did you catch that Abraham did not ask for Lot and his family? He asked for all the righteous. He asked big, He asked what Jesus wanted, and because he asked what Jesus wanted, Jesus listened. Abraham starts with 50, and five times (50, 45, 30, 20, and 10) asks Jesus if the city will be destroyed if that number of righteous people are found and Jesus promises that even if He found only 10 people, He would spare the city. Think of that, Abraham made request of God to spare a city that was so full of wickedness that Jesus came to see if things were really as bad as the outcry against it. And for the sake of 10 people, He promised He would spare a city. We are not sure how many people were in Sodom and Gomorrah, but they were probably the leading cities of that time. Jesus was willing to spare a whole city based on the request of one man. He was willing to spare a whole city full of people who were not even part of this conversation between Abraham and Himself. Abraham was petitioning on their behalf. How true that "The effectual fervent prayer of a righteous man availeth much". Sadly the angels only found 4 people in the whole city who were righteous and only they were spared, they were brought out of the oncoming destruction before it took place. They were delivered and they were the only ones who were delivered. The interesting thought here though is Jesus expected Abraham to intercede on behalf of all the righteous people. Think about that, why else would He have taken the time to share with Abraham what was going to happen and then wait there with Abraham allowing him the time to ask for the righteous to be spared? We should really stop and re-evaluate who we are praying for and pray more like Abraham, think of all the people who could come to know Jesus as their personal savior if we did that.

We would like to end this chapter with the song *"Fix my Eyes"*. We recommend that you go to *www.youtube.com* and in the YouTube search bar, search for *"Fix my Eyes by King and Country"* minus the quotation marks.

IN SUMMARY

In this chapter we have learned that there are four steps we need to follow to prepare others for the prayers we are going to offer on their behalf:

- pray that their thoughts and feelings would be protected from satan's influence,

- ask God to forgive them of any sins they may have,

- ask that they would be purified and cleansed or another term would be sanctified,

- ask that God would reveal Himself to them,

Now that we and others are prepared let's talk faith in the midst of life's storms.

CHAPTER EIGHTEEN

Applying Faith in Life's Storms

We have covered a lot about faith… we defined it, laid the foundations of it, discussed how to make it multiply, even how to make faith be exponentially effective, and laid the foundations of applying it in daily living. We hope you have learned as much as we have as we wrote this book. Now we have come to where the tires meet the road if you will. This is the chapter we are sure you have been waiting to read and probably wanted to read first. However, we cannot have proper faith in the storms of life if we do not know what faith is. Not knowing how to use something can have very dire consequences and that is what we wanted to avoid as we walked you through faith. But we have now come to the question, how do we apply faith in the storms of life?

Before we tackle this question, we need to remind ourselves of what we have learned already. We need to take a few lines and make sure we understand God's intention toward us, His character toward us based on His names from Chapter 4. God is eternal, God is supreme, God dwells in us and has marked us as His, God is all sufficient, God sees our needs and provides, God heals us, God is right and holy, God is the leader of armies, God is our banner, God is our peace, God bends down to hold us (grace and mercy), God loves us. As a matter of fact per John 17:23 "I [Jesus] in them, and thou [God] in me, that they [All Christians] may be made perfect in one; and that the world may know that thou hast sent me, and hast loved them, as thou hast loved me." God loves us as much as he loves Jesus. There is no separation between His love for Jesus and His love for us. He loves us so much that:

> [11] *"For I know the thoughts that I think toward you, saith the LORD, thoughts of peace, and not of evil, to give you an expected end."* [12] *"Then shall ye call upon me, and ye shall go and pray unto me, and I will hearken unto you."* [13] *"And ye shall seek me, and find me, when ye shall search for me with all your heart."* [14] *"And I will be found of you, saith the LORD: and I will turn away your captivity, and I will gather you from all the nations, and from all the places whither I have driven you, saith the LORD; and I will bring you again into the place whence I caused you to be carried away captive." – Jeremiah 29:11 - 14*

He has plans for us of peace not evil... that we would grow to be Christ like so that He can put us into any situation and be a light to this dark world. If we pray, seek, and grow in Him, He will lead us through His plan to completion. For Romans 8:28 "And we know that all things work together for good to them that love God, to them who are the called according to *his* purpose." Following on this, we need to make sure we understand Numbers 23:19 "God *is* not a man, that he should lie; neither the son of man, that he should repent: hath he said, and shall he not do *it?* or hath he spoken, and shall he not make it good?" He never lies, He is truth, speaks truth and when He speaks, His Words (Jesus) are given power by His mere breath (Holy Spirit). For we read Joshua told the Israelites God has never failed, and what He says comes to pass: Joshua 23:14 "And, behold, this day I *am* going the way of all the earth: and ye know in all your hearts and in all your souls, that not one thing hath failed of all the good things which the LORD your God spake concerning you; all are come to pass unto you, *and* not one thing hath failed thereof." Not only do His words speak truth and always come to pass, but He also hears us when we call out to him.

> *"I sought the LORD, and he heard me, and delivered me from all my fears." – Psalms 34:4*

> *"This poor man cried, and the LORD heard him, and saved him out of all his troubles." – Psalms 34:6*

> *"The eyes of the LORD are upon the righteous, and his ears are open unto their cry." – Psalms 34:15*

> *"The righteous cry, and the LORD heareth, and delivereth them out of all their troubles." – Psalms 34:17*

> *"And it shall come to pass, that before they call, I will answer; and while they are yet speaking, I will hear." – Isaiah 65:24*

God loves us, wants fellowship with us, wants us to seek Him, wants us to call out to Him, wants to answer us, and wants to direct our lives to a Christ likeness which gives Him all the glory and honor due His name. His return on investment (ROI) is us becoming so much like Jesus, that people only see Jesus when they see us. When Jesus is shining through us, God can then put us into any situation, area, spot, purpose, and show this world that **HE LOVES IT AND ALL THAT IS IN IT**. He does this through you and us. "Hebrews 4:16 "Let us therefore come boldly unto the throne of grace, that we may obtain mercy, and find grace to help in time of need."

Now that we have reminded ourselves of God's character toward us, we can start to discuss the question: What are the storms of life? In basic terms, a storm is anything that has the potential to pull you away from your relationship with God / Jesus. Storms are very broad in scope but here are some things, or circumstances that could be a storm for you: a sickness; a disease; an addiction; a relationship loss; strife in a relationship; a divorce; death of a loved one; something evil happening to you, or a loved one (rape, molestation, verbal abuse, physical abuse, etc.); job loss; financial loss; an accident, or anything that makes you, or a loved one physically unable to do something you used to do; a still born child; child born with a birth defect, or disease/syndrome; church leadership moral failure; personal moral failure; church split; betrayal by a close friend; a child with a learning disability; a loved one not saved, and living a life apart from God; a child coming out as gay; becoming a victim of human trafficking, and the list goes on, and on, and on, fitting the unique individual and how satan might try to attack them. In very broad terms, the purpose of a storm is for satan to make you doubt God and pull you away from God even to the point where you may become angry/hate God. It is to knock you out of becoming Christ like and/or prevent you from being used to show the world God's presence. satan knows if you are free to become Christ like, he is going to lose territory (souls of lost men, women, and children) so his best option is to take you out of the fight and he uses storms to do it. If we look at John 17:15 "I pray not that thou shouldest take them out of the world, but that thou shouldest keep them from the evil.", Jesus prayed over the disciples present with Him and for all of us to come, that we would remain in the world to be a light unto the world. He prayed that we would be kept (guarded) from the things that are evil (hurtful). However, He also acknowledged that the world (satan's domain) would hate us as much as it hated Him. Storms in our lives, especially the ones that are not consequences from our bad decisions, are satan's domain resisting us, who we are, and Christ shining through us.

Many things discussed in the Bible have patterns related what we can see and observe on earth (the physical realm we have discussed before). Storms are one of these things we can use as a pattern to study so we can have a better understanding of what is going on and the purpose. Since none of us working on this book have had careers or education in studying Atmospheric storms the best place to get that information is from those who have. We are going to use the National Oceanic and Atmospheric Administration (NOAA) National Severe Storms Laboratory (NSSL) information found on the internet located at this link, https://www.nssl.noaa.gov/education/ svrwx101/thunderstorms

Let's look at how a storm forms. Thunderstorms have three stages in their life cycle: the developing stage, the mature stage, and the dissipating stage. The developing stage of a thunderstorm is marked by a cumulus cloud which is being pushed upward by a rising column of air (updraft). The updraft is created by the following process: the sun heats the surface of the earth, which warms the air above it causing warm moist air. If this warm moist surface air is forced to rise because of something resisting it (hills or mountains, or areas where warm/cold or wet/dry air bump together can cause rising motion), the warm air will continue to rise as long as it weighs less and stays warmer than the air around it. As the air rises, it transfers heat from the surface of the earth to the upper levels of the atmosphere (the process of convection). The water vapor it contains begins to cool, releases the heat, condenses and forms a cloud. The cloud eventually grows upward into areas where the temperature is below freezing. The cumulus cloud soon looks like a tower (called towering cumulus) as the updraft continues to develop. There is little to no rain during this stage but occasional lightning. However, this is a sign that a storm is brewing and about to become an issue that we need to be aware of for our safety.

The storm enters the mature stage when the updraft continues to feed the storm; precipitation begins to fall out of the storm, creating a downdraft (a column of air pushing downward). When the downdraft and rain-cooled air spreads out along the ground, it forms a gust front, or a line of gusty winds. The mature stage is the most likely time for hail, heavy rain, frequent lightning, strong winds, and tornadoes.

Eventually, a large amount of precipitation is produced and the updraft is overcome by the downdraft beginning the dissipating stage. At the ground, the gust front moves out a long distance from the storm and cuts off the warm moist air that was feeding the thunderstorm. Rainfall decreases in intensity, but lightning remains a danger.

One thing we noticed there are a lot of different storms:

Single-cell thunderstorms, are small, brief, weak storms that grow and die within an hour or so. They are typically driven by heating on a summer afternoon. Single-cell storms may produce brief heavy rain and lightning.

A **multi-cell storm**, is a common, garden-variety thunderstorm in which new updrafts form along the leading edge of rain-cooled air (the **gust front**). Individual cells usually last 30 to 60 minutes, while the system as a whole may last for many hours. Multi-cell storms may produce hail, strong winds, brief tornadoes, and/or flooding.

A **squall line** is a group of storms arranged in a line, often accompanied by "squalls" of high wind and heavy rain. Squall lines tend to pass quickly and are less prone to produce tornadoes than are supercells. They can be hundreds of miles long but are typically only 10 or 20 miles wide.

A **derecho** (pronounced similar to "deh-REY-cho" in English) is a widespread, long-lived wind storm that is associated with a band of rapidly moving showers or thunderstorms. Although a derecho can produce destruction similar to that of tornadoes, the damage typically is directed in one direction along a relatively straight swath. As a result, the term "straight-line wind damage" sometimes is used to describe derecho damage. By definition, if the wind damage swath extends more than 240 miles (about 400 kilometers) and includes wind gusts of at least 58 mph (93 km/h) or greater along most of its length, then the event may be classified as a derecho.

Wow this is great and interesting information you say but what does this have to do with faith. Well, it does not so much have to with faith as understanding what is going on with the storm and what the purpose of the storm is.

Let's back up and go back through the life cycle of a storm from a spiritual standpoint. The SON warms the earth… don't you just love it when science so easily explains what God does? As God moves on the earth, as He looks over the earth for needs to be met as (Jehovah-Jireh), His action starts to stir the spiritual realm and it becomes unstable. What becomes unstable though is important. It is satan and his domain which become unstable just like the warm moist air in the storm example. satan does not like the fact that God/Jesus/The Holy Spirit are moving in his domain and this causes the spiritual realm to become unstable. satan's unstableness is then pushed into something unmovable which would resist him and his action (we would submit this would be any Christian, or collection of Christians (church body, denomination, etc.)) and this resisting starts the updraft. This is a picture of what James is saying in James 4:7 "Submit yourselves therefore to God. Resist the devil, and he will flee from you."

The resisting of Christians causes satan to fight back and updraft is his fight into the spiritual realm. However, he cannot win there and his force of attempting to move his power upwards is stopped by God. satan's spiritual force then is pushed back down to the earthly domain and forms the spiritual wind/turmoil (the downdraft) that runs out in front of him as he tries to fight with God/devour those he is against. Just like what happens when the warm moist air rapidly cools and falls back to earth, causing the downdraft of wind to run in front of the storm. At this point the spiritual storm is matured and this is when we have all the different types of storms as noted above. As satan sees he is losing (whether being rebuked by God, rebuked by a Christian or collection of Christians, or by us simply resisting him and standing firm) God's love, mercy and compassion take over and absorb all the unstableness thus stopping/killing what is feeding the storm. Just like the wind cooling down all the warm air thus there is no warm air in front of the storm to continue to feed it.

We hope this is making sense. What another awesome example of how what we observe in the natural being a parallel to the spiritual.

What can feed the storm and make it continue is our reaction to what is going on during the storm. satan may throw at us a single cell storm and it either grows in progression to a derecho or stalls out depending on our response to it. For example, just this week, I (Rich) was called by one of my credit card companies with the report there seemed to be odd activity on my account. Now I could have reacted all crazy, like the world is falling apart, being mad at those who are causing disruption in my life, but I did not do that. I simply called the credit card company, worked through which charges were mine and which were fraudulent, had them cancel the card and send me a new one. That weekend we simply used our other card for our normal purchases and a few days later got the new cards in the mail to use. This is an example of a small single-cell storm that was quickly dissipated. Obviously the more people satan can get affected by the storm, the larger the storm is. If you have 10 people involved in the storm then you have 10 different temperaments, reactions, maturity, etc. and these factors may make the storm take longer to dissipate simply because it is harder to get everyone on the same page if they were not ahead of time.

Key Point: Always make sure you are on the same page (in unity), so a storm cannot grow into a derecho.

What we find interesting is the different types of storms and how they relate to what is going on spiritually in our lives. We talked with a brief example of the single-cell storm, and to follow on that, a **single-cell** storm is a testing of the enemy to see if you have any vulnerability's to exploit. These are usually anything from an annoyance, to a temptation that you thought of a little too long, to a minor sickness or minor accident, to something that makes you mad, which might progress to anger. These small storms are used to distract us from God and keep us busy with worry and fear. If we are mature and see what they are, with God's help we can dissipate them quickly by a proper reaction.

A **multi-cell** storm is when multiple single cell storms form together. Examples of these are more relationship in nature and are where satan is driving wedges between relationships. This could be simply being offended by someone saying something that is not received the way intended, all the way to outright hatred of another. It can be unforgiveness, bitterness, etc. Or it could be a disease that affects a family, a leadership disagreement in a church, etc. Again it is used to distract us from what we should be focused on and what we should be doing. What is also interesting here is the hail, intense rain and tornados. We feel these represent things in the spiritual realm as well. Hail hurts when you are hit with it. It can do damage to structures and even kill someone. We would submit that hail is equivalent of the words we speak in the heat of the moment which hurt others/ourselves. Intense rain could be brief feelings of hatred/anger at others which flood over the relationship *eroding* the base away. Tornados are normally very small and normally create small paths of destruction. This would equate to taking out a family, a parent to child relationship, a marriage, a friendship, etc. Just some thoughts to think about.

A **squall line** has one purpose only and that is to just plain knock you over and make you fall. This could be anything that makes you fall flat on your face. Maybe a moral failure, or job loss, financial loss, anything unexpected that hits out of no-where and knocks you to the ground.

Hopefully you get the idea. We would submit that there have been a very few derecho storms in the history of the world. The ones we can think of are: when satan and his followers were cast out of heaven to earth, the Adamic fall, the crucifixion of Jesus, Hitler with WWII, and when the anti-christ comes to power at the end times. These are storms that affect the whole earth and again are intended to knock man out of the picture.

Hopefully you have found this interesting and we did not digress too much from what we want to discuss. We have talked about storms from a macro standpoint but let's now move to a more micro discussion of what happens in a storm. As we have seen, a storm is meant to keep us off balance, off focus, off our mark, off of Jesus, off of becoming Christ like. I (Rich) grew up on a dairy farm in north central Ohio. I learned to read the signs nature was giving to alert a storm was brewing and coming our way. I am sure if you have spent any time outside you have been able to develop the same sense of what is going on. You start to sense that the air is changing, the sky starts to look different, the animals start to not behave normally, the trees/crops start to move differently, the wind starts to swirl, etc. Off to the horizon you see the line start to form and you can taste the rain in the air. The same happens from a spiritual standpoint. When we look back on the storms we have been through, we can see where things started to change and we started to become aware that something was brewing but we could not really put our finger on it. We just knew something was not right/normal. Maybe we started having different reactions than before, or started to see others having different reactions. Maybe in our bodies we just didn't feel right, or tight or cramped, etc. Maybe in the church we noticed the leadership started to act differently, or that friend that always called like clockwork didn't. If we are aware, we can usually sense something is up. Unless it is a squall line that is flying toward us so fast that we do not have time to really see what is coming, we usually are aware something is up. The storm itself has different components for us. First we have the wind. The wind, from a physical viewpoint, blinds and chokes us. It picks up dust, debris, leaves, sticks, etc. and hammers us with those items to make us avert our eyes to protect them. For some people like me (Rich) I have a difficult time breathing when the wind is in my face. I am not able to catch my breath without turning my head or covering my face. From a spiritual view, the wind represents the doubts satan throws at us. We are bombarded with doubt hitting us in the face, some smaller some bigger, but all used to blind us from the truth/choke us off from the truth, thus putting us into chaos. The chaos happens spiritually when we take our eyes off of Jesus. Just like Peter, when we notice the storm around us and look away or stop moving toward Jesus, we sink. The chaos from a spiritual standpoint is when things are not right, what we thought we knew we find out we didn't, reactions we are used to, do not happen, friends, family, seem distant, God seems to have left, no one seems to understand you and you can't seem to read the Bible or pray. You feel like you are choking from a spiritual standpoint and you try to protect yourself from the onslaught. We mentioned choking here on purpose to pull out what satan is doing to us during the storm and that is found in 1 Peter 5:8 "Be sober, be vigilant; because your adversary the devil, as a roaring lion, walketh about, seeking whom he may **devour**:"[G2666] The word *devour*, Strong's G2666 has an interesting meaning which is different than we might think in today's terms. The meaning is from G2596 and G4095; to *drink down*, that is, *gulp entire* (literally or figuratively), devour, ***drown***, swallow (up). The word that caught our eye here is drown. When satan walks through his domain seeking (plotting against) those to devour, his method of devouring is by drowning them. We typically think of drowning meaning when we go under water and never resurface. However, in broad terms drowning really would mean suffocation: any form of not allowing us to catch our breath or breathe air into our lungs. So choking on something blocking our airways, inhaling something that prevents air from getting in, being in a vacuum, being under water, etc. could all be forms of drowning... not getting air needed to sustain life. Now think about that from a spiritual realm. How does satan drown us... by pulling us away from our life source, God's Word and fellowship with God. Once he does this, he can flood us with doubts, with others who hurt us physically, verbally, emotionally, etc. With trying to shroud us in darkness, evil, evil influences, vexation, oppression, etc. These are ways we are choked, drowned out/away from God. Following on this thought, because you are feeling cutoff from God, you find getting direction on what to do seems almost impossible. The next component, rain, also feeds into part of the not being able to see, but it also makes our footing slippery. If we have to walk our footing becomes less sure and we watch to make sure we do not fall. It also drenches us making us cold, which in turn slows our body processes as it protects from the coolness and keeps heat to our vital organs. It also messes with our cognitive thinking and causes us to make bad decisions or slow to make decisions, we hesitate. The components: hail/lighting/super strong winds, are all meant to make us take shelter and hide from them. We know if we are hit with these things we can seriously get hurt. The same is true from a spiritual standpoint, we hide, however we do it wrong. We withdraw from family, friends, church, and even God. In seeking shelter, we go to the wrong place, ourselves, and cut ourselves off from those who can help us. Just like crawling into a small tornado shelter underground where no one can get to you and you cannot reach out… we cut ourselves off from those that can help us when we withdrawal and hide. Hopefully our analogies are making sense. Bet you never thought a physical storm had so many parallels to the spiritual realm.

Now that we have discussed storms from a physical and spiritual standpoint, we want to lead you through the question, how do I get out of the storm. Let's be honest, none of us like storms, they are not fun; they hurt; they leave wounds; scars; breaks; strains; on us physically; emotionally, and spiritually. None of us want to go through storms and you know what, that is ok. The desire to not go through a storm is not the issue, unless, that one desire becomes an idol in our lives replacing God. You see satan uses positive and negative motivations to pull us away from God. Positive ones would be seeking a new car, house, spouse, comfort, electronic device, etc. which we may want which again is ok, until it causes us to put that desire before God. Some fall for the positive motivation trap. Others fall for the negative motivation trap and the negative motivation comes in the form of life's storms. If satan can get us to focus on the storm and how it is affecting us, he may be able to cause us to make the desire to get out of a storm an idol. That desire replaces our desire to be a lump of clay in God's hands allowing Him to shape us the way He needs to in order to reach a lost and dying world. We need to be wary of falling into either trap because once trapped, it is very difficult to break the cycle of thinking and refocus on God.

The question we asked though still remains, how do I get out of this storm. The question is not necessarily a bad question, but it is not the best question. The problem with this question is it keeps us focused on the storm. There is no room to get a change of perspective and when we are in a storm of any kind, what we really need is perspective. When in a physical storm, we need to use wisdom and discernment to gain knowledge of what is happening. Think about that with us… in the USA we have the National Weather Service (NWS) and this governmental office monitors the weather across the globe to see how is it going to affect the citizens of this country. We have faith in the service this office offers and that they are constantly monitoring the weather so we can be safe. We put our trust, confidence in them and this system. The office is used to protect us by giving us guidance on what to do based on their expertise and to lead us into safety while the storm comes, rages, and moves on. They do not have the power to stop the storm, but their guidance is invaluable for those of us who do not have the personal resources to monitor the weather like they do. So what are some of the things they give us as knowledge? Well they have Storm Warning, Storm Watches, weather alerts, etc. They communicate in all forms through TV, radio, internet, mobile devices (both low and high tech), and if needed, they have the tornado sirens as warning devices. All these are to give us advanced warning and warning during the storm on what actions to take to protect us and guide us to safety. Now again let's use this analogy in the spiritual realms. Just like the NWS, we have God and since God is over

> **Getting our focus on God faster, is the key to getting through the storm and out of the storm faster.**

all in authority, He knows what is taking place in the spiritual realms. We put our faith then in God/Jesus/the Holy Spirit trusting they will give knowledge/wisdom, etc. when we need it to be/do what is needed. He uses His Word (the Bible) to communicate to us His plan and His warnings. He uses the Holy Spirit to impart guidance from Himself so He can instill wisdom and knowledge. Wisdom and knowledge come from discerning the following question while in the storm and that question is **WHAT DOES GOD WANT DONE?** Once we have direction with the answer to this question, we can move forward in full confidence where He wants us to go. The question again is for us to gain perspective in the storm to get our *focus off the storm and onto God*. We also want to be clear here, God at any time could choose to say to the spiritual storm howling around us TO BE STILL. Commanding that is a great miracle. However, the greater miracle is for Him to sustain us and take us through the storm, so that He can reveal Himself through us to a world which is desperate for His help and who do not know it.

Having stated this, what we would like to do now is lead you through some topics of perspective giving you the tools to work through a storm God may be leading you through so that you come out on the other side with Him rather than getting lost in the middle of it. These perspective items are to help us grow in our faith and maturity. I (Walter) believe that we cannot change if we do not know we need to change. The storms of life alert us to the needs and problems in this world so that we can become active agents sharing the *Good News* on God's behalf. It is very hard to relate to someone empathetically if we have never been in their shoes and have never gone through what they may be going through. We can be sympathetic, but if you really want to gain influence into someone's life to lead them to God, empathy is the only way to gain that influence and gain it incredibly fast. Real empathy only comes through experience. Experience can happen two ways. One is for God to put a supernatural (from Him) spiritual burden on your heart for those that may be affected by a specific storm… for example those who have been victimized by human trafficking. As God lays these victims on your heart and you respond and start to reach out to help them, God will instill empathy through their experiences into you so that you can reach them. Unfortunately the second one is only learned by, experiencing something for yourself… knowing, feeling, hurting, laughing, touching, sensing, it. These are the two ways to truly and empathetically reach our lost and dying world. Again we are laying the groundwork for perspective. If we understand the foundations of perspective, then when a storm of life hits, we can get our focus off the storm onto God faster (exhibiting faith and making it effective).

What is the number one perspective we can learn about when going through a storm? The answer is *what is the reason* for the storm? If we know the reason for the storm, it helps us keep our perspective or refocusing our perspective so we can face the storm doing what God wants done. Having said this, we want to again make sure we are on the same page. As we stated earlier in this chapter, we are not saying that God causes the storm in our lives. Storms come because of the choices we make and/or because satan asked God permission to "sift" us as wheat. How do we know this? Well it is in the Bible a few times… Job, for example and Peter for another. Here is Jesus telling Peter he is going to be sifted.

> [31]*"And the Lord said, Simon, Simon, behold, Satan hath desired to have you, that he may sift you as wheat:"*
> [32]*"But I have prayed for thee, that thy faith fail not: and when thou art converted, strengthen thy brethren."*
> *– Luke 22:31*

Now for those that did not grow up on a farm, sifting is a process of separating the grain from the stalk, chaff, hulls, etc. so only the wheat grain is left and all the other non-substance items, (stalk, hull, chaff) which was used in the growing process of the grain, are removed. Jesus is telling Peter he is going to go through a storm, one that because of his choices, he will create, and Jesus is letting him know when he gets to the other side of the storm, to go back and strengthen his brother's (the other disciples). Peter is to help lead them through their shame and grief. What is the storm here that takes place? Well they all told Jesus that they would never desert Him... no matter what. Yet in the garden when Jesus was arrested they ALL deserted Him. Then Peter ends up denying Jesus to the point of calling down curses on himself. We can only imagine the field day satan had with the remorse and shame the disciples had from the choices they made. This shame/remorse was so bad that Judas hung himself. The other example is Job. Job did everything right. He was the most righteous man on earth at the time. Then one day God wanted to show satan man was redeemable.

> [8]"And the LORD said unto Satan, Hast thou considered my servant Job, that there is none like him in the earth, a perfect and an upright man, one that feareth God, and escheweth evil?" [9]"Then Satan answered the LORD, and said, Doth Job fear God for nought?" [10]"Hast not thou made an hedge about him, and about his house, and about all that he hath on every side? thou hast blessed the work of his hands, and his substance is increased in the land." – Job 1:8 - 10

God touts Job's righteousness to satan and satan shoots right back saying Job has never been tested, he has always been protected and if satan could just have access to Job, he would prove Job only loves God because he has been blessed. satan had to ask for permission to attempt to devour Job. Oh and satan did not play nice either. satan attacked Job's family killing every one of them except his wife. satan stripped away all Job's finances, all his security, all his wealth, all his "friends", and wrapped Job in darkness to the point Job did not know if God was even there or even cared about him. Jobs wife grew bitter and lost her will to live. The "friends" Job did have left, ended up telling him what a horrible person he was… etc. You get the picture. *The point here is God never causes the storms in our lives. He permits them with limits (hedge - guarding us), but He does not cause them.* What God does do with the storms though is **redeem** them. He redeems them by going through the storm with us, helping us to learn more about God and to truly lean upon Him for our strength. Here are some verses to give you some perspective on how God redeems the storms in our lives.

> *⁶"Wherein ye greatly rejoice, though now for a season, if need be, ye are in heaviness through manifold temptations:" ⁷"That the **trial**ᴳ¹³⁸³ of your faith, being much more precious than of gold that perisheth, though it be tried with fire, might be found unto praise and honour and glory at the appearing of Jesus Christ:"*
> *– I Peter 1:6 - 7*

These verses are saying that the trial (trustworthiness), of our faith and the maturing of our faith is more precious that gold and it is purified by fire to be the purest faith possible. The storms are for a season to make our faith pure. Even though we are in and going through the heaviness (distress) of manifold (multiple) temptations (testing's), we can greatly rejoice, because when the temptations are over, the trustworthiness of our faith will bring glory and honor to God. Think about this, God is after our trustworthiness (do we really believe and act in faith) are we more than just flowing words, do we really trust in Him, does our faith exist, is it multiplying, is it exponential. Can God call you out upon the water, farther than your feet could ever wander, using you in the storm to minister to others who may never know or realize God wants to help them? (Refer to the song we ended chapter seven with and refresh yourself with why we want our faith to be exponential.) The one incident that sticks out to us is when God asked Abraham to sacrifice Isaac. That was a distressing temptation if there ever was one, and because of his faith and belief, God was given all the glory and honor.

> [71] *"It is good for me that I have been afflicted; that I might learn thy statutes." – Psalms 119:71*

Most of us come to God and start to seek Him because of a storm in our lives. We are being beat up by something and we realize there is something missing and we wish to fill it. Without the storm, we would never ask the question why do I feel this way and where do I turn for help. As we are afflicted (being beat up) we seek God and learn about Him through His statutes (His decrees, His Word).

> [26] *"Whose voice then shook the earth: but now he hath promised, saying, Yet once more I shake not the earth only, but also heaven."* [27] *"And this word, Yet once more, signifieth the removing of those things that are shaken, as of things that are made, that those things which cannot be shaken may remain."* [28] *"Wherefore we receiving a kingdom which cannot be moved, let us have grace, whereby we may serve God acceptably with reverence and godly fear:"* [29] *"For our God is a consuming fire." – Hebrews 12:26 - 29*

Another reason for storms is to shake us free from the things in our life which are not eternal. This can be anything we hold onto that may be competing with God. God does not need to or want to compete with anything and for us to realize we may have been holding to something else a little too tightly, He has to shake us free of that thing to show us what is temporal and what is eternal. It helps us to realize/refocus that we need to be seeking Jesus and the Kingdom of God (Matthew 6:33 "But seek ye first the kingdom of God, and his righteousness; and all these things shall be added unto you.") rather than anything else because ***everything*** else will be shaken away when Jesus comes back for us. We need to make sure our attitudes reflect a reverence and fear of God and that we are pressing toward the eternal glory He has promised us.

> *[1]"Therefore being justified by faith, we have peace with God through our Lord Jesus Christ:" [2]"By whom also we have access by faith into this grace wherein we stand, and rejoice in hope of the glory of God." [3]"And not only so, but we glory in tribulations also: knowing that **tribulation**[G2347] worketh patience;" [4]"And patience, experience; and experience, hope:" [5]"And hope maketh not ashamed; because the love of God is shed abroad in our hearts by the Holy Ghost which is given unto us."*
> *– Romans 5:1 - 5*

We reflect God's glory when we go through tribulations (pressure), and we know that these pressures worketh (accomplish) patience (endurance) and patience, experience (remember empathy this word means trustworthiness), and experience, hope (expectation). Our hope then does not disgrace us because as we mature, God's love and presence are reflected out of us through the Holy Spirit living in us. An interesting side word study is the word *tribulations*. Per Strong's G2347 tracing through the root words, it can be translated as a crowded (tight spaced) narrow path. If we look at, Matthew 7:13 "Enter ye in at the **strait**^G4728 gate: for wide *is* the gate, and broad *is* the way, that leadeth to destruction, and many there be which go in thereat:" The word strait is translated as narrow also. So Jesus spoke that to follow Him, we need to enter the narrow gate/path. We need to squeeze into that gate and onto that path and that squeezing causes pressure as we cannot take all the junk that is on us with us when following Him. Paul is saying that this squeezing process (which squeezes the junk in/on us, off), change us to be more Christ like. It is a process we all need to go through in order to allow God to grow us to become Christ like.

> *⁶"Surely he shall not be moved for ever: the righteous shall be in everlasting remembrance." ⁷"He shall not be afraid of evil tidings: his heart is fixed, trusting in the LORD." ⁸"His heart is established, he shall not be afraid, until he see his desire upon his enemies."*
> *– Psalms 112:6 - 8*

And

> *²"Looking unto Jesus the author and finisher of our faith; who for the joy that was set before him endured the cross, despising the shame, and is set down at the right hand of the throne of God." ³"For consider him that endured such contradiction of sinners against himself, lest ye be wearied and faint in your minds."*
> *– Hebrews 12:2 - 3*

These verses are to comfort us in the storm letting us know that the storm is perfecting our faith as long as we fix our eyes on Jesus. Our one and only focus while in a storm should be to turn back to Jesus and walk toward Him only. This was demonstrated by Jesus and Peter when Peter asked to get out of the boat and walk to Jesus during a storm. When he was fixed on Jesus, nothing else mattered and he walked right through the storm on the water even though all we have learned in our lives says that it is not possible. Jesus deals in the impossible and we can join Him in it if we focus only on Him and walk toward Him. Our faith becomes perfected simply because we are focused and walking to Him.

> ¹⁵*"For all things are for your sakes, that the abundant grace might through the thanksgiving of many redound to the glory of God."* ¹⁶*"For which cause we faint not; but though our outward man perish, yet the inward man is renewed day by day."* ¹⁷*"For our light affliction, which is but for a moment, worketh for us a far more exceeding and eternal weight of glory;* ¹⁸*"While we look not at the things which are seen, but at the things which are not seen: for the things which are seen are temporal; but the things which are not seen are eternal." – 2 Corinthians 4:15 - 18*

Here we see that the storms are for our sakes to help us understand God's grace. For what we normally focus on is only temporary but God wants us to be eternal and contain and show His eternal glory. Because of this, even though from outward appearances we may perish, inwardly God is renewing us day by day filling us with Himself… His presence. For Paul states, 2 Corinthians 12:9 "And he said unto me, My **grace**^{G5485} **is sufficient**^{G714} for thee: for my strength is made perfect in weakness." Most gladly therefore will I rather glory in my infirmities, that the power of Christ may rest upon me."

Again satan's purpose of the storm is to bring us to the lowest of lows. To make us weak, and when we are weak to turn away from God. That was his whole argument with God concerning Job. satan's premise was if Job was stripped of everything and tormented, then he would turn on God because God was no-longer blessing him. Just an FYI, satan does not change his tactics they are time proven and tested. We need to be like Job and set our trustworthiness at God's feet when we are at our lowest. We cannot get out of a storm on our own, we need His help. Here we see when Paul was at a low point, he asked the storm to be taken away and he was given the answer that God's grace is sufficient for thee. Such an odd statement to make and one we should briefly investigate. Let's look at the words per Strong's, *grace* G5485 – means graciousness. Not necessarily clear so in *www.merriam-webster.com's* grace is defined as unmerited divine assist-ance given humans for their regeneration or sanctification (purity before God (holiness)). Then per Strong's *sufficient*, G714, is a primary verb to *ward off*. What is being warded off? The storm… God's continual divine assistance in regenerating us into Christ likeness is enough to ward off the storms of life if we focus on Jesus and walk toward Him. When we do that, God's strength (His miraculous power) is made perfect (complete) in our weakness (feebleness). In other words, when we walk through a storm focusing on Jesus, the world takes notices, because what we are doing is not "normal" and it allows God to show His miraculous power to a world that is in dying need of it. The very weakness that satan attempts to use in the storm to take us out, is redeemed by God to show others Who God is… we are beacons of light in the storm, because we are walking toward Jesus. Where is Jesus, He is right where we need to be to reach someone for Him. In summary the reason God allows the storm is for Him to show a dying world how ***GREAT HE IS***.

Hopefully you are gaining some perspective about a storm you may be going through. Let us continue with another perspective topic and that is seeking direction. Storms are redeemed by God because they lead us to seek direction from Him. Remember the wind we discussed earlier? The wind is used to blow us, confuse us, block our way, pick up and hurl doubts at us and to choke us. We are surrounded by a swirling mass of darkness blowing around us. We need direction to navigate in the storm because nothing else we may have done on our own in the past, will work. Let's look at some scriptures that discuss direction.

> [5]"Trust in the LORD with all thine heart; and lean not unto thine own understanding." [6]"In all thy ways acknowledge him, and he shall direct thy paths."
> – Proverbs 3:5 - 6

How do we gain understanding? By reading and studying the Word of God. As we do this and receive God's Word into us and submit to what it says, we are acknowledging Him and are ready to allow Him to direct our paths.

> "I will instruct thee and teach thee in the way which thou shalt go: I will guide thee with mine eye."
> – Psalms 32:8

Remember God's name Jehovah-Jireh... this name speaks that God is watching over the earth, seeing our needs and meeting our needs. This is how God guides us with His eye.

> [104]"Through thy precepts I get understanding: therefore I hate every false way." [105]"Thy word is a lamp unto my feet, and a light unto my path." – Psalms 119:104 - 105

God's Word lights our way in the storm. He illuminates the path we need to take by revealing that path to us so that we can stay focused on Him and not sink.

> *"Thus saith the LORD, thy Redeemer, the Holy One of Israel; I am the LORD thy God which teacheth thee to profit, which leadeth thee by the way that thou shouldest go." – Isaiah 48:17*

God knows what is best for us/what will make us most valuable (our faith's trustworthiness) and leads us in the way we need to go in order for our faith to be developed.

> *⁷"I will bless the LORD, who **hath given me counsel**:^H3289 my **reins**^H3629 also **instruct**^H3256 me in the **night seasons**."^H3915 ⁸"I have set the LORD always before me: because he is at my right hand, I shall not be moved."* – Psalms 16:7 - 8

The Lord gives counsel (advise) and our reins (mind/heart) are also instructed (chastised through physical blows) that we receive in the night seasons (adversity). So we receive advice from God and gain experience from the blows we receive in life's storms. What is neat here is if we set Jesus before us, He stays at our right side as we move through the storm and helps us not to fall or fail.

> *²⁰"And though the Lord give you the bread of **adversity**,^H6862 and the water of **affliction**,^H3906 yet shall not thy teachers be removed into a corner any more, but thine eyes shall see thy teachers:" ²¹"And thine ears shall*

hear a word behind thee, saying, This is the way, walk ye in it, when ye turn to the right hand, and when ye turn to the left." – Isaiah 30:20 - 21

Adversity here means a narrow/tight place and affliction means distress. In order to mature in God and hear His voice, we need to be on the narrow path, which squeezes us tightly and may put us through distress while on it. However, without it we never learn God's voice. We need to know His voice so He can direct us when we are turning right or left off the narrow path. Again just as we discussed in chapter two, God is always communicating with us and one of His important communications is to give us direction to keep us on His path.

The next perspective is rejoicing which is used to show others Jesus shining through us. How will someone else know we are different and reacting different to a storm…by rejoicing (praising and worshipping God) while we go through the storm.

[1]"O God, thou art my God; early will I seek thee: my soul thirsteth for thee, my flesh longeth for thee in a dry and thirsty land, where no water is;" [2]"To see thy power and thy glory, so as I have seen thee in the sanctuary." [3]"Because thy lovingkindness is better than life, my lips shall praise thee." [4]"Thus will I bless thee while I live: I will lift up my hands in thy name." [5]"My soul shall be satisfied as with marrow and fatness; and my mouth shall praise thee with joyful lips:" [6]"When I remember thee upon my bed, and meditate on thee in the night watches." [7]"Because thou hast been my help, therefore in the shadow of thy wings will I rejoice." [8]"My soul followeth hard after thee: thy right hand upholdeth me." – Psalms 63:1 - 8

No one in the Bible did a better job praising and worshipping God than King David. He worshipped and praised when things were going well, he worshipped and praised when things were not going well, he praised and worshipped all the time. The kingdom moved forward and was invigorated with David's worship and praise. He even instituted the praise and worship in the temple courts as God directed. We need to model after King David and worship and praise God, through seeking Him, through reading His Word, through prayer and communicating with God, and through the attitude of our hearts rejoicing in our relationship with God, our very salvation, redemption, and restoration in relationship.

Even Apostle Paul says we are to rejoice, pray and give thanks to God for this is the reason we were created.

> [16] *"Rejoice evermore."* [17] *"Pray without ceasing."* [18] *"In every thing give thanks: for this is the will of God in Christ Jesus concerning you."* – 1 Thessalonians 5:16 - 18

We are to BE this so we can reflect God no matter what situation He allows us to go through. As we are **BEING** this, we show the world we are different because we serve a living God. Rejoicing helps us to focus on Jesus and as we do that the storm gets clearer and starts to dissipate.

And why are we rejoicing? Because we know ultimately *we will have Victory.* The next perception to remember when going through a storm is that no matter what happens, **WE WIN THROUGH GOD**.

> [28] *"Hast thou not known? hast thou not heard, that the everlasting God, the LORD, the Creator of the ends of the earth, fainteth not, neither is weary? there is no searching of his understanding."* [29] *"He giveth power to the faint; and to them that have no might he increaseth strength."*

*30 "Even the youths shall faint and be weary, and the young men shall utterly fall." 31 "But they that **wait upon**H6960 the LORD **shall renew**H2498 their **strength;**H3581 they shall mount up with wings as eagles; they shall run, and not be weary; and **they shall walk,**H1980 and not faint."*
– Isaiah 40:28 - 31

God, our God, the Great I AM, never grows tired or faint in watching over us. He strengthens us when we are exhausted and tired, when we can go no further on our own. When we wait (bind ourselves) on God, He will renew our strength (force). We will ascend as if they were soaring like an eagle. We will run and not be exhausted. We will walk (with purpose) and not grow tired. Why because we are walking toward Jesus!!!

*"These things I have spoken unto you, that in me ye might have peace. In the world ye shall have tribulation: but **be of good cheer;**G2293 I **have overcome**G3528 the **world.**"G2889 – John 16:33*

Even though we face the pressures of this world, we have cheer (comfort / courage) because Jesus has overcome (subdued) the world (satan's domain).

"For God hath not given us the spirit of fear; but of power, and of love, and of a sound mind." – 2 Timothy 1:7

We touched on this already, as we are weak in the storm, God gives us the spirit of power (miraculous power that only He can give) to show the world His love as we walk toward Him ***through*** the storm.

"Now the God of hope fill you with all joy and peace in believing, that ye may abound in hope, through the power of the Holy Ghost." – Romans 15:13

We can have peace in the storm because of our rejoicing in the hope of the victory we will attain.

"I can do all things through Christ which strengtheneth me." – Philippians 4:13

This is such a powerful personal statement. To restate using Strong's, I can exercise force in all things because my empowerment originates in the Messiah. The Messiah, the one anointed to rescue the whole world from the captivity of sin and satan, empowers **ME** to prevail no matter what storm is thrown my way.

And why do we have Victory? **Because God ANSWERS prayer!!!**

[21] "Beloved, if our heart condemn us not, then have we confidence toward God." [22] "And whatsoever we ask, we receive of him, because we keep his commandments, and do those things that are pleasing in his sight." [23] "And this is his commandment, That we should believe on the name of his Son Jesus Christ, and love one another, as he gave us commandment." – 1 John 3:21 - 23

As we have laid the premise in this book as we draw near to God and enter in relationship with Him, submit to Him, grow in confidence in Him, we will hear Him and will desire to ask "Father, what do you want done?", He will answer and we being obedient, ask and act on what He tells us to. As we do these things He will answer and we will receive from Him what we need.

> *14 "And this is the confidence that we have in him, that, if we ask any thing according to his will, he heareth us:" 15 "And if we know that he hear us, whatsoever we ask, we know that we have the petitions that we desired of him." – 1 John 5:14 - 15*

Again the premise of the book, we are asking for the things that God tells us to ask for and this is why we have the confidence He will hear us, and answer our petitions.

> *23 "For verily I say unto you, That whosoever shall say unto this mountain, Be thou removed, and be thou cast into the sea; and shall not doubt in his heart, but shall believe that those things which he saith shall come to pass; he shall have whatsoever he saith." 24 "Therefore I say unto you, What things soever ye desire, when ye pray, believe that ye receive them, and ye shall have them." – Mark 11:23 - 24*

We can believe that He will answer because we are asking for what He wants and we will receive those things when we ask in obedience to the desire of our heart (being and doing what God wants done).

Nothing in the physical realm is impossible for God to do and for us to ask if we are following what has been laid out in this book. **We need to praise God for His goodness toward us. So many things in His Word crescendo into His Greatness and to how much He loves and cares for us!!!!**

We think this is a great place to take a break and look at an example in the Bible with 3 men who put what we have stated above into practice. Let's set the stage: King Nebuchadnezzar conquered Judah and he takes captives back to Babylon. Three of the captives were Hananiah, Mishael, and Azariah who you probably know better by their Chaldean names Shadrach, Meshach, and Abednego. Through partnering with Daniel and resisting the king's earlier edicts regarding food, they came to be administrators of different provinces of the Babylonian empire. These three men knew the king well and the king knew them well as they were the third highest officials in the kingdom. The king, probably through bad advice given to him by his other "wise" men (all who would have been under satan's control), decides to build a statue in his likeness which everyone would bow down and worship. The king makes a great to do and forces everyone in the city to come out and bow down to worship this idol under punishment of being thrown into a furnace if they do not. They all do but these 3 men. You can feel the shock and surprise of the other wise men and they immediately bring this before the king. The king summons them which is where we will pick up:

> ¹³ "*Then Nebuchadnezzar in his rage and fury commanded to bring Shadrach, Meshach, and Abednego. Then they brought these men before the king.*"
> ¹⁴ "*Nebuchadnezzar spake and said unto them, Is it true, O Shadrach, Meshach, and Abednego, do not ye serve my gods, nor worship the golden image which I have set up?*"
> ¹⁵ "*Now if ye be ready that at what time ye hear the sound of the cornet, flute, harp, sackbut, psaltery, and dulcimer, and all kinds of musick, ye fall down and worship the image which I have made; well: but if ye worship not, ye shall be cast the same hour into the midst of a burning fiery furnace; and who is that God that shall deliver you out of my hands?*" – Daniel 3:13 - 15

Let's stop here for a second. Again these three men are known very well by the king, we are sure they meet with him frequently as they were over the affairs of the Babylon provinces. From what we can tell it was the king, then Daniel, then these three men. So it is not like they were strangers to the king and it is not like the king did not know them well. Yet in his rage (loss of self-control) he is going to put three of his most trusted advisors to death. Think about that. Talk about an immediate storm coming out of nowhere that these three men were all of a sudden thrusted into. Let's see how they focus on God and handle this storm they are in. The king "tries" to grant them "grace" by offering them another chance to bow. But receiving grace from anyone other than God, is never really grace if you are being forced to do something you know is wrong. It is a thin veiled attempt by satan to doubt ourselves and who we are trusting in.

> [16]"Shadrach, Meshach, and Abednego, answered and said to the king, O Nebuchadnezzar, we are not careful to answer thee in this matter." [17]"If it be so, our God whom we serve is able to deliver us from the burning fiery furnace, and he will deliver us out of thine hand, O king." [18]"But if not, be it known unto thee, O king, that we will not serve thy gods, nor worship the golden image which thou hast set up." – Daniel 3:16 - 18

Wow, what a response. One cannot have that type of response if one is not daily immersed in an intimate relationship with God, seeking Him in every way possible, becoming more Christ like, and ready to do what God wants done no matter what situation you are put in. Talk about a crescendo response. We can hear the gasps from all those who heard the response. What happens:

"Then was Nebuchadnezzar full of fury, and the form of his visage was changed against Shadrach, Meshach, and Abednego:

> *therefore he spake, and commanded that they should heat the furnace one seven times more than it was wont to be heated."* – Daniel 3:19

His visage (face) changed. Think about that. satan was having a field day with this king falling for the trap of thinking he was a god. This carnival ride slams into 3 men who stand firm resisting this train of thought. We believe when the king's face changed, the demonic presence that was on/in him was forced out and now the physical interplay here becomes a spiritual battle for a winner take all match. satan puffs up and prepares his best battle in the physical realm and the story continues:

> [20] *"And he commanded the most mighty men that were in his army to bind Shadrach, Meshach, and Abednego, and to cast them into the burning fiery furnace."* [21] *"Then these men were bound in their coats, their hosen, and their hats, and their other garments, and were cast into the midst of the burning fiery furnace."* [22] *"Therefore because the king's commandment was urgent, and the furnace exceeding hot, the flame of the fire slew those men that took up Shadrach, Meshach, and Abednego."* [23] *"And these three men, Shadrach, Meshach, and Abednego, fell down bound into the midst of the burning fiery furnace."* [24] *"Then Nebuchadnezzar the king was astonied, and rose up in haste, and spake, and said unto his counsellors, Did not we cast three men bound into the midst of the fire? They*

answered and said unto the king, True, O king." ²⁵"He
answered and said, Lo, I see four men loose, walking in
the midst of the fire, and they have no hurt; and the form
of the fourth is like the Son of God." – Daniel 3:20 - 25

And satan's puny physical battle meets Jesus as He comes and joins the men in the furnace. We would love to think that Jesus is telling them how proud He is for them taking on this battle and instructing them on what to do when the king realizes his folly. We really want to note here, Jesus did not say BE STILL. He joined them in the storm, right by their side, protecting them as they walked into it, through it, and out of it. Jesus always responds to faith. We can extend that to say that God always responds to faith. He desires it and rewards it as we step up and be what He wants us to become and step out and act in obedience to what He wants done. Also notice no one cared about their God until He revealed Himself. Everyone was saying God could not save them. It wasn't until they were in the worst of the storm, being obedient, that God's miraculous power was revealed.

²⁶"Then Nebuchadnezzar came near to the mouth of
the burning fiery furnace, and spake, and said, Shadrach,
Meshach, and Abednego, ye servants of the most high God,
come forth, and come hither. Then Shadrach, Meshach,
and Abednego, came forth of the midst of the fire." ²⁷"And
the princes, governors, and captains, and the king's
counsellors, being gathered together, saw these men, upon
whose bodies the fire had no power, nor was an hair of
their head singed, neither were their coats changed, nor the
smell of fire had passed on them." ²⁸"Then Nebuchadnezzar
spake, and said, Blessed be the God of Shadrach, Meshach,

and Abednego, who hath sent his angel, and delivered his servants that trusted in him, and have changed the king's word, and yielded their bodies, that they might not serve nor worship any god, except their own God." [29] *"Therefore I make a decree, That every people, nation, and language, which speak any thing amiss against the God of Shadrach, Meshach, and Abednego, shall be cut in pieces, and their houses shall be made a dunghill: because there is no other God that can deliver after this sort."* [30] *"Then the king promoted Shadrach, Meshach, and Abednego, in the province of Babylon."* – Daniel 3:26 - 30

What a beautiful conclusion of how to walk through a storm. *God gets all the glory!* Not just with a few people, but with a whole city watching this play out, God gets all the glory, honor and praise. The king makes a decree that no person shall speak anything against God without losing their life. satan loses this battle in a big way, and God's 3 chosen men get promoted even higher to the king's confidence so that they can influence the king and his kingdom to what God wants done. What an awesome short example for us to focus on God: no matter what the odds, trusting that He has our backs, walking through the storm, and allowing Him to show the world who He is through us.

Now that we have an understanding of what a storm is, satan's motivation for the storm, how God redeems the storm, and the perspective we should have in the storm, let's discuss some of the things we can do while we are in a storm.

To protect against the wind, one of the best things are goggles which protect the eyes and a bandana or something similar to protect your nose and mouth so you can breathe. From a spiritual standpoint, the winds are the thoughts thrown our way by satan to make us doubt God. Just as we discussed in Chapter 2, thoughts can bring us closer or further from God if we are not protected. To protect yourself from the spiritual winds, you need to put yourself deeper into God's word through reading and hearing. Immersing yourself in the Bible is like putting on goggles and covering over your nose and mouth. You are feeding yourself God's truth and when you have God's truth flowing into you, the doubts being hurled at you do not seem so big. You can see through them and focus on Jesus. Here are some great scripture nuggets which can be googles and bandanas:

> [7]"Only **be thou strong**[H2388] and very **courageous**,[H553] that thou mayest observe to do according to all the law, which Moses my servant commanded thee: turn not from it to the right hand or to the left, that thou mayest prosper whithersoever thou goest." [8]"This book of the law shall not depart out of thy mouth; but thou shalt meditate therein day and night, that thou mayest observe to do according to all that is written therein: for then thou shalt make thy way prosperous, and then thou shalt have good success." [9]"Have not I commanded thee? Be strong and of a good courage; be not afraid, neither be thou dismayed: for the LORD thy God is with thee whithersoever thou goest."
> – Joshua 1:7 - 9

Strong and courageous here mean, seize and be alert. Joshua is being told to seize God's word (His commandments) and be alert that they are always present and always in the forefront of his mind so he may not turn to the right or the left.

*"There hath no **temptation**^{G3986} taken you but such as is common to man: but God is faithful, who will not suffer you to be tempted above that ye are able; but will with the temptation also make a way to escape, that ye may be able to bear it." – 1 Corinthians 10:13*

There is no temptation (testing) which satan has not already done to someone else. God knows all satan's ways and will provide a way out as God wants to redeem your testing to show the world His glory and honor.

^{33}"Hear instruction, and be wise, and refuse it not." ^{34}"Blessed is the man that heareth me, watching daily at my gates, waiting at the posts of my doors." – Proverbs 8:33 – 34

As we seek God, He sustains us with life, His words (Jesus) the daily bread and wine that we should be eating and drinking to be in fellowship with God. As we do this, we gain the favour (delight) of God as we are in intimate relationship with Him just as He always intended.

"But whoso looketh into the perfect law of liberty, and continueth therein, he being not a forgetful hearer, but a doer of the work, this man shall be blessed in his deed." – James 1:25

God's law, His Word, gives us life the way it was intended to be, in relationship with Him, being and doing what God always had intended (choosing to worship and praise Him and showing others to do the same).

^{26}"But the Comforter, which is the Holy Ghost, whom the Father will send in my name, he shall teach

you all things, and bring all things to your remembrance, whatsoever I have said unto you." [27] "Peace I leave with you, my peace I give unto you: not as the world giveth, give I unto you. Let not your heart be troubled, neither let it be afraid." – John 14:26 - 27

God doesn't leave us, He is always with us through the Holy Spirit who lives in us and shows us the path to take. He is always there reminding us of God and teaching us about God. Because of this closeness with God we can have peace, peace because we know He is with us always and regardless of what we "see" going on in the world, we need not be troubled (agitated) or afraid (timid) because our whole purpose is for God to shine through us to demonstrate peace to the rest of the world.

[1] "Blessed is the man that walketh not in the counsel of the ungodly, nor standeth in the way of sinners, nor sitteth in the seat of the scornful." [2] "But his delight is in the law of the LORD; and in his law doth he meditate day and night." [3] "And he shall be like a tree planted by the rivers of water, that bringeth forth his fruit in his season; his leaf also shall not wither; and whatsoever he doeth shall prosper." – Psalms 1:1 - 3

As we become Christ like, we will be strong trees fed by living water (Jesus) and the fruit of God will be brought forth through us. This bearing of fruit is an interesting thought. Fruit is two things: one, it is food that can be fed to others to strengthen them/nourish them and two, most fruit, if not all, have seeds in them, which if planted in soil, germinate to become another same type seed bearing plant. Our fruit is to do two things then: one, nourish those around us who are faint with hunger (filling the emptiness inside them) and two our fruit should be planting like seeds into those who are ready to receive and also become Christ like.

Finally we can protect our eyes and mouth through trusting in the words of Jesus when He said that we can ask anything and He shall do it for us because we are asking what He wants us to ask of Him. This would be to bring God glory through our abiding in Jesus.

> [13]*"And whatsoever ye shall ask in my name, that will I do, that the Father may be glorified in the Son."* [14]*"If ye shall ask any thing in my name, I will do it."* – John 14:13 - 14*

> *"If ye abide in me, and my words abide in you, ye shall ask what ye will, and it shall be done unto you."* – John 15:7*

As we noted, when we protect our eyes and mouths with God's word, we can see Christ clearly to be an example to the world around us.

Next let's talk about the spiritual rains. We think that the rain is an analogy of feelings that satan throws at us. Remember from chapter two, our thoughts and feelings need to be tested to understand where they are coming from. If we are not careful, the feelings we experience can erode our strong base and trust in God. To protect yourself from the rain put on two things: the helmet of salvation and the shoes of the gospel of peace. Let's look at the helmet of salvation first:

> [17]*"And take the helmet of salvation, and the sword of the Spirit, which is the word of God:"* [18]*"Praying always with all prayer and supplication in the Spirit, and watching thereunto with all perseverance and supplication for all saints;"* – Ephesians 6:17 - 18*

The helmet of salvation is knowing that you have admitted you are a sinner, believe in Jesus and confessed Him Lord of your life. Having done these steps you have invited Jesus to live in your heart and you have all assurances you are His and He is yours. You can then move forward rejoicing in the confidence of your salvation, taking the miraculous power of the Holy Spirt (the Word of God), with praying (supplicate) with all prayer (worship), and supplication (petition) in our spirit. It protects your head from the rain and from the effect rain can have in our thinking processes so we can make clear decisions or wait for clear direction.

Next, the shoes of the gospel of peace are spoken about in, Ephesians 6:15 "And your feet shod with the preparation of the gospel of peace;" We are to be prepared, immersed in, the good message of Christ: what His death and resurrection did for the human race. The peace of this message, and the salvation we have provide us with the solid footing of knowing who God is; His character and His character toward you/us. This is a key point: you have to trust that no matter what is going on and what happens to you, God has your back. If you do not trust that God has your back no matter what, then you will never be able to have faith. This doubt will permeate through you and kill any faith you might have. We do not say this glibly, lightly, jokingly, or harmfully. There are a lot of brothers and sisters in Christ have been subjected to things too horrible to list in this book. Some of our family members are included in this list and we have had to deal with the effects these evil acts have done to them. So please do not think we are glossing over this key point because we are not and we take what is being said here very seriously. ***However, it is absolutely critical that you believe, no matter what has happened or is happening to you, that God has promised He will never leave you nor forsake you. God has your back.*** God intends good toward you, that He will redeem all the evil that has been inflicted on you in your life. Maybe not right away, but down the road. God has your back. God loves you. God created you for a purpose, to become like Him and to allow His glory to shine through you. God will use you to reach people for His Glory. But if you do not believe that He has your back, you cannot have faith in anything He tells you. That is why we listed the example of Shadrach, Meshach, and Abednego as such an awesome one to study. They understood the consequences, they and their families were to be put to death. They were ready to die to allow God to shine through them… showing a king that he was wrong and only God is right. And God proved Himself in a mighty, miraculous way, to a king, "wise men", and a city. God received the glory because of 3 men's sure footing trusting that God had their back no matter what happened. This is our sure footing… the footing rests, stands firm, and resists by placing all one's trust in God, His character, His character towards us, and His Word. Standing on anything else and the spiritual rains (from satan) will muddy up and erode our foundation and we will fall. We will fall because we are not standing firm looking forward at Jesus but rather twisting by turning around looking at our past. One cannot stand firm when they are twisted with their bottom half pointed one way and their top torso pointed another. This causes us to be off balance and we will fall.

Finally, let's talk about hail, lighting, and tornados. Hail, as we mentioned, are harmful / abusive words others have spoken against us, they might not break our bones, but they sure do hurt. They are more general words that make us hurt all over. We would submit that lightning is specific actions or words meant to take out our hearts. Specific words or actions which feel like someone stabbed us and stopped our heart from working. Tornados are high velocity winds that suck us up and smash us back to the ground. It would make us so spiritually dizzy that we are not able to stand. It spiritually twists us up. Now that we have generally defined what these are like, how do we protect ourselves from them? Normally when these things happen in the physical realm, we hide in or under some type of shelter. When these things happen spiritually though, we still hide but rather than in a shelter we withdrawal and hide in ourselves. Instead of hiding in ourselves, we need to seek shelter in our prayer closet and pour out our hearts to God and seek Him in intimate conversation, just between the two of you. Our prayer closet and our connection with God is what shelters us from these things harming us. We have to get gut level with God and realize He is our only source of protection. Here are some scripture nuggets:

> [1]*"God is our refuge and strength, a very present help in trouble."* [2]*"Therefore will not we fear, though the earth be removed, and though the mountains be carried into the midst of the sea;"* [3]*"Though the waters thereof roar and be troubled, though the mountains shake with the swelling thereof. Selah."* – Psalms 46:1 - 3

God is our shelter and force in our time of passing through a narrow place. No matter what we observe as happening in the physical realms, even as our world is shaking apart, our shelter is present with us through the shaking and will be there with us sheltering us.

> [10]*"Fear thou not; for I am with thee: be not dismayed; for I am thy God: I will strengthen thee; yea, I will help thee; yea, I will uphold thee with the right hand of my righteousness."* [11]*"Behold, all they that were incensed against thee shall be ashamed and confounded: they shall be as nothing; and they that strive with thee shall perish."* [12]*"Thou shalt seek them, and shalt not find them, even them that contended with thee: they that war against thee shall be as nothing, and as a thing of nought."* [13]*"For I the LORD thy God will hold thy right hand, saying unto thee, Fear not; I will help thee."* – Isaiah 41:10 - 13

Dismayed here means to gaze about, again not being focused on Christ. God is saying He has this and we will see everything which is against us, diminish to nothing even to the point if we try to find them, they will not be there, because God will help (surround) us with Himself.

> *"And the LORD, he it is that doth go before thee;*
> *he will be with thee, he will not **fail**[H7503] thee, neither*
> ***forsake**[H5800] thee: fear not, neither be **dismayed**.*"[H2865]
> *– Deuteronomy 31:8*

God is always going before us, clearing the way and at the same time He is by our side as we move forward… how awesome is that? He will not fail (slacken) in doing anything for us. He will not forsake (loosen or relinquish) us to the enemy. Therefore, we are free of fear, and free of dismay (breaking down under the weight of what we see and feel).

> *[2] "The LORD is my rock, and my fortress, and my*
> *deliverer; God, my strength, in whom I will trust; my*
> *buckler, and the horn of my salvation, and my high tower."*
> *[3] "I will call upon the LORD, who is worthy to be praised:*
> *so shall I be saved from mine enemies." – Psalms 18:2 - 3*

> *"Yea, though I walk through the valley of the shadow*
> *of death, I will fear no evil: for thou art with me; thy rod*
> *and thy staff they comfort me." – Psalms 23:4*

We need to take our shelter in God not in ourselves. If we take shelter by withdrawing into ourselves, our thoughts, feelings, and isolation will keep us from focusing on God. Ultimately doing this, satan will eventually devour (drown) us because we have cut ourselves of from our life breath… God. We need to allow Him to renew us and rejuvenate us through our brothers and sisters in Christ ministering to us in our deepest time of need.

We know we have talked about this at length, but in short layman's terms we want to state that storms bring uncertainty into our lives. We cannot get the normal information to guide and direct ourselves.

Nothing, as we perceive it, seems to be right. Something is affecting all
of our circumstances of time and place. We are directionless. We are like
a compass which is just spinning round and round. We also want to state
that all storms are unique. They are unique to the individual in the storm
and unique in what God wants done through us as a result of the storm. If
you are going through a storm or want to better be prepared for a storm, we
encourage you to have a scripture reference of different verse that you can
go to for help, comfort, and encouragement. There have been many books
published with different verses. We also came across two good resources
from the internet:

From Rick Warren:

> *http://rockvillecogop.com/blog/2010/10/14/a-list-of-*
> *god%E2%80%99s-promises-of-blessing-by-rick-warren/*

and

From the organization Scripture Promises (Ken and Dorothy Bassett):
http://scripturepromises.com/ This one has 29 categories of scriptures for
different needs we may have.

We would also like you to read Psalms 107. This is a great chapter of
God redeeming the different storms we may go through and shows how
much He cares for us. ***ALWAYS REMEMBER,***

> [38]*"For I am persuaded, that neither death, nor life,*
> *nor angels, nor principalities, nor powers, nor things*
> *present, nor things to come,"* [39]*"Nor height, nor depth,*
> *nor any other creature, shall be able to separate us from*
> *the love of God, which is in Christ Jesus our Lord."*
> *– Romans 8:38 - 39*

During our team meetings, one of the team members showed a cartoon
that has been passed around for many years and is a good pictorial of what

we have been discussing. Before showing the pictorial though we want to share two more verses that are specifically relevant to the pictures:

"Man's goings are of the LORD; how can a man then understand his own way?" – Proverbs 20:24

and

"The steps of a good man are ordered by the LORD: and he delighteth in his way." – Psalms 37:23

We are not artists so forgive us but here is our best attempt. As we go through life we have a plan or God gives us a plan to follow and here what we hear and think of. A non-eventful, smooth, straight, no issues path:

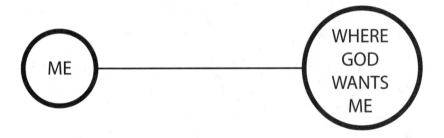

However, God does not work this way and often as we reflect back on our lives our path looks more like the following:

As we look at this path, we chuckle, but when we study it, we really can start to see how being on God's path changed us. As this was being shown, God put it on my (Rich's) heart what this path means. I will do my best to explain what I was revealed.

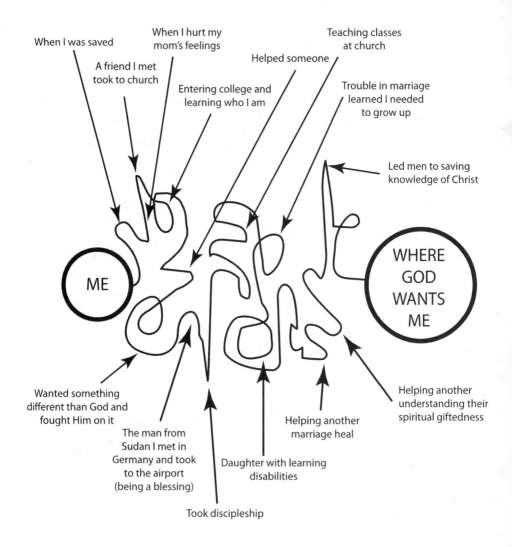

When I was saved

When I hurt my mom's feelings

Teaching classes at church

A friend I met took to church

Helped someone

Entering college and learning who I am

Trouble in marriage learned I needed to grow up

Led men to saving knowledge of Christ

ME

WHERE GOD WANTS ME

Wanted something different than God and fought Him on it

The man from Sudan I met in Germany and took to the airport (being a blessing)

Daughter with learning disabilities

Helping another marriage heal

Helping another understanding their spiritual giftedness

Took discipleship

Each curve, each point, each change in direction, is God leading, changing, molding, maturing you so that you can reach a lost and dying world for Him... to **show** the world *Who He Is* so that they can choose to follow Him. Each event is meant to bring Him glory and honor. Oh we may have circles where we spin for a while till we learn and understand a lesson, but we keep pressing on with God and as we reach those for Him or help our brothers and sisters in Christ to grow, He gets all the glory and honor. That is why God's plan, His path for us, is never straight. If it were straight, we would not be able to reach those He needs reach. He wants us to meet others where they are at and bring them to Him. The items above are points from my life to date. Think back through your life and put your events into a path. You'll see how God has used you in small and mighty ways. Remember in Chapter 7 we discussed return on investment (ROI)? Your path represents God's ROI in your life. Who did you touch in His name? How did you touch them? What example were you to another of God's mercy, grace, love, shelter, strength, compassion? Then stop and think deep of how the joy in your life was restored while you did that ministry for the other person. You may have felt their pain and empathized with them, but you also experienced a joy while walking with the Holy Spirit doing what you know God wanted you to do. Your joy grew, expanded, and overflowed. Your compass, which may have been spinning out of control in your own situation, was reset and pointed back to God and your focus was restored. What an awesome picture of what God does through us to reach this lost and dying world!!!

Well our new friend, we are coming to the end of this chapter and the end of this book. We have discussed faith in depth and given you a strong foundation to build upon as God leads you to become Christ like. We hope this chapter has given you perspective, hope, a renewed trust in

God, and an intense focus on Jesus. We hope and pray that this book has touched you in a mighty way by allowing the Holy Spirit to speak to you, encouraging you, uplifting you, and instructing you. May your faith be forever changed as you submit yourself to God and allow Him to mature you and do great things through you while you become Christ like!! We would like to discuss one more storm from the Bible to bring the point of this chapter and book to a close.

> [35] "And the same day, when the even was come, he [Jesus] saith unto them, Let us pass over unto the other side." [36] "And when they had sent away the multitude, they took him even as he was in the ship. And there were also with him other little ships." [37] "And there arose a great storm[G2978] of wind,[G417] and the waves beat into the ship, so that it was now full." [38] "And he was in the hinder part of the ship, asleep on a pillow: and they awake him, and say unto him, Master, carest thou not that we perish?" [39] "And he arose, and rebuked[G2008] the wind, and said unto the sea, Peace,[G4623] be still.[G5392] And the wind ceased, and there was a great calm." [40] "And he said unto them, Why are ye so fearful?[G1169] how is it that ye have no faith?" [41] "And they feared exceedingly, and said one to another, What manner of man is this, that even the wind and the sea obey him?" – Mark 4:35 - 41

We want to discuss this story a little deeper than what we may have thought about it before. First, let's reiterate the scene: after a day of preaching and instruction, Jesus asks to go to the other side of the Sea of Galilee. He does not explain why He wanted to go. The disciples, *in obedience*, load the boat and set off. At some point in the crossing, a great storm (whirlwind /

squall) of wind came up. The NIV translates *storm* Strong's G2978 this as a squall. Remember one of the storms that can take place is a squall line and it is a line of very strong winds meant to knock things over. The sea is roused into swells of waves which swamp the boat to the point of it being full. At this point, the disciples were afraid and decided to wake Jesus and let Him know what was going on. Jesus rebukes (forbids) the wind by saying Peace (hush) be still (muzzle) meaning stop blowing and howling. Then He asks the disciples why they are so fearful (timid) and why do they not have faith.

Now let's pick the story apart: Jesus tells the disciples He wishes to go to the other side of the lake. This is not a normal request. From our study Bible, Jesus only went to the east/south east side of the lake twice. We know if we continue reading Mark Chapter 5, Jesus is going to the other side of the lake to free the man (of the tombs) from legion. Since we know that Jesus was in close communication with God, we may assume God gave Jesus instructions to go there to set the man free. satan, we can assume then, also heard this. Now the question becomes, why the storm? As we have laid out in this chapter, spiritual storms are meant to take us out so we cannot either become Christ like or so we are not able to do what God wants done. satan has no power in the spiritual realms as he has been cut off from there by God. However, his domain is the earth and we believe that satan caused this fast moving un-natural storm to take Jesus and the disciples out from getting to the other side. Another thing that is interesting, either the storm came so fast that the disciples were not able to react quickly or they waited till the last possible second to get Jesus involved. The boat was full of water. It was about ready to sink. We wonder how long the disciples tried to "handle" this storm on their own before waking Jesus... something to think about as we face our own storms. Notice that Jesus is with them in the storm. He entered the storm with them, He stayed with them, He ended the storm with them, and they reached the other side with Him. ***HE NEVER LEFT THEM***. However, Jesus was asleep in the boat. He was not engaged in the storm like the disciples. Think about that, the wind is howling, the boat is tossing, the boat is filling with water, Jesus had to be getting wet, He had to be feeling this storm from some physical standpoint, but He was fast asleep in the boat. He is so asleep, that the disciples had to wake Him to let Him know what was going on. He sees the storm and hushes it, like putting a muzzle on something to prevent it from doing damage. Immediately the storm stops and there is total tranquility in the sea. Then Jesus asks two most amazing questions: why are you timid and where is your faith? The disciples, just as we today, totally miss the questions because they / we are focused on what Jesus did with the storm. We miss the question of faith. Since this is a book explaining faith through life's storms, we are going to stop here and work our way backward.

We, just like the disciples, are always so focused on what is going on around us that we do not pay attention to what God is telling us. What He speaks so clearly to us and we, not paying attention, miss what He says. We are so awed with what Jesus does with the storm, we miss the beginning. We do not stop and go back and read between the lines to understand what is going on… shame on us for not taking the time to meditate on the scriptures. We see that Jesus can calm the storm and that is all we seek from Him for our own storms we go through. However, we need to understand, *HE NEVER PROMISED* to calm the storms in our lives. In John 17:15 "I [Jesus] pray not that thou shouldest take them out of the world, but that thou shouldest keep them from the evil." … *HE ASKED* that we be protected.

Again, why did Jesus question the disciple's faith? What was this so important faith point they missed? What was this deep faith they needed to have, to make it through this storm? What were they to attain that they so blatantly missed according to Jesus? After all, were they not being obedient doing what He asked them to do? Weren't they following His directions? Why wasn't Jesus protecting them? Why was He asleep in the boat not engaged like they were trying to survive the storm? Why wasn't the way smooth across the lake with a bright moon and stars shining to light the way and a calm breeze blowing at their backs to help push them along? After all, they were ferrying the SON of GOD. Why the hardship? Why the battle? What did they miss to be so punished to have this storm from satan try to kill them? How could they be punished for doing good helping Jesus? For that matter, since we are on the topic, how dare God let them go through this storm! It wasn't fair! After all, it is not like they could make it to the other side without their boat… or could they?

They missed or forgot a crucial statement that Jesus made. A very simple one liner… nothing that was transcendent, nothing that seemed out of the ordinary, nothing that had heaven part and a dove rest on His head, no voice from heaven, just a simple statement: Mark 4:35 "… he [Jesus] saith unto them, Let us pass over unto the other side."

Did you catch it? Do you see it? Do you understand the statement? I (Rich) have read this story many times during my life and until co-authoring this book, I missed this phrase. This simple but critical statement that Jesus made to the disciples that seems like nothing, but it is everything and here is where faith comes into play. Let us reiterate it for you in simple layman terms: *JESUS SAID LET'S GO OVER TO THE OTHER SIDE.* Do you understand? Do you see? Put yourself into the disciple's' shoes, as if you were one of them that day who Jesus was speaking to. Did this statement move from your ears, into your mind, sinking deep into your heart and get absorbed into your soul? Just like the disciples, we miss the simple things God tells us because they seem so mundane and un-important… but we want you to understand that *NOTHING* God says to us is mundane and *IT IS ALL IMPORTANT*. Jesus said LET'S GO TO THE OTHER SIDE, and as soon as He spoke this, nothing else mattered. *Nothing else mattered*… Jesus spoke something and now all the disciples needed to do was put their belief in Jesus into action. They started well, but when the physical turned on them, they forgot the simple statement Jesus said… LET'S GO TO THE OTHER SIDE. We cannot make this clear enough for you… in this instance it did not matter if there was a storm; if the storm raged worse; if the storm stopped; if the wind destroyed the boat; if the boat sank; if the boat was overturned; if the boat disappeared; if the boat struck something; if something struck the boat; or anything else that may have stopped them… *nothing else mattered*, **nothing else mattered**, because JESUS SAID LET'S GO TO THE OTHER SIDE. He meant they were going to the other side, nothing was going to stop them from reaching the other side, like a covert ops team sent in to destroy an enemy, they were going to the other side, nothing satan had in his arsenal was going to stop them from going to the other side. satan himself could have showed up with all his armies and they could not have stopped them from reaching the other side. You see JESUS SAID LET'S GO TO THE OTHER SIDE. JESUS holds the keys to all of creation: all heaven is subjected to Him; all earth is subjected to Him; the universe is subjected to Him; satan and all the spiritual world are subjected to Him; and JESUS SAID LET'S GO TO THE OTHER SIDE. The sheer hilarity of satan trying to prevent them from reaching the other side should make us fall over in laughter… satan, the created and defeated being, was going to stop Jesus from getting to the other side by a storm. Really… Seriously… You're kidding right? A physical realm storm? This is the best he can do to the SON of GOD, trying to sink the boat He was in?

Because, JESUS SAID LET'S GO TO THE OTHER SIDE… the boat was irrelevant, the sea was irrelevant, the water was irrelevant, the storm was irrelevant, the waves were irrelevant, the dark clouds were irrelevant, the distance was irrelevant, time was irrelevant, the spiritual darkness was irrelevant, legion who would meet them on the other side was irrelevant, the only thing that was *relevant* was JESUS SAID LET'S GO TO THE OTHER SIDE. They could have walked on the water to get to the other side, they could have walked under the water to get to the other side, Jesus could have parted the water so they could get to the other side, He could have teleported them to the other side (seriously that is in the Bible John 6:21 and Acts 8:39), they could have flown to the other side, think of any number of ways that *Jesus, THE CREATOR OF ALL*, could have gotten to the other side. Nothing is impossible for Jesus, all physical rules we know get thrown out the window with Jesus. When He says He wants something done, we need to have faith that HE is going to do it and be obedient in the process totally focused on Him and Him alone. That is the lesson here, yes His command over the storm is aweing, but even more so is that we believe in Him and trust what He says. May we forever keep our minds and hearts alert to truly hear, listen, believe, and do what He wants done.

We would like to close this chapter with the song *"Thy Will"*. We recommend that you go to *www.youtube.com* and in the YouTube search bar, search for *"Thy Will by Hillary Scott & The Scott Family"* minus the quotation marks.

IN SUMMARY _____

- God Loves YOU

- God wants the best FOR YOU

- GOD HAS YOUR BACK!

- The storms of life are satan trying to distract us from Jesus our rock, fortress, and our ever present help in the time of need

- Our reaction to the storm either feeds it or calms it

- God redeems the storms in our lives to show others His Greatness

- How we live through the storm is God Return on Investment in us

- We need to dig deep in the perspectives of the storm

  ▶ Our trustworthiness is perfected

  ▶ We need to seek God

  ▶ We need to be shaken of things which are temporal so we understand and hold to the eternal

  ▶ We learn to focus/refocus on Jesus and walk through the storm to Him

  ▶ We learn how God's grace is sufficient for us

  ▶ We learn to rejoice through the storms of life

- We need to be seeking God so we are protected from how the storms can hurt us

- God's path is a path to lead us to others so we can reach them to a saving knowledge of Jesus Christ

And lastly the most important point to this whole book, faith allows us to know what is irrelevant (everything other than what God says), and what is relevant (only what God says/tells us).

CLOSING

I (Walter) and the rest of the team, want to congratulate you and thank you for acting on the thought that God gave you…that you needed to read this book. You have already exhibited faith.

We hope that this book has helped you understand faith and that you can now see you can act in faith to become Christ like so God can put you into any situation He needs to put you into, lighting the way of others to Him.

It is my sincere hope that you pass this information along to others in your sphere of influence so we, as the Christian body at this time, can move forward and bring others to the saving knowledge of Jesus Christ.

May God bless you as He formulates this in your mind and starts to move you into practicing what He has revealed to you.

Again can you even imagine, can you see, how many we can reach, help, and bring to Jesus if we all understood faith and properly applied it, not for our own gain, but to further the kingdom of God. I want heaven to be full when I get there. I hope you do too.

We want to leave you with the following verses to capstone this book,

"In God is my salvation and my glory: the rock of my strength, and my refuge, is in God." – Psalms 62:7

For whatsoever things were written aforetime were written for our learning, that we through patience and comfort of the scriptures might have hope." – Romans 15:4

" These things I [Jesus] have spoken unto you, that in me ye might have peace. In the world ye shall have tribulation: but be of good cheer; I have overcome the world." – John 16:33

"For whatsoever is born of God overcometh the world: and[G2532] this is the victory that overcometh the world, even our faith." – 1 John 5:4

We would also like to end this book with an awesome song, **"Victor's Crown"**. We recommend that you go to *www.youtube .com* and in the YouTube search bar, search for *"Victor's Crown by Darlene Zschech"* minus the quotation marks. We recommend the one with this title if it is listed *"Victor's Crown (OFFICIAL VIDEO) by Darlene Zschech from REVEALING JESUS".*

Always remember God has already overcome, He has won, the rest of the story just plays out till Jesus comes back, and the final battle is fought and through ***JESUS YOU HAVE OVERCOME!!***

Sincerely,
Walter Davitz

APPENDIX A

Strong's Word Definitions

In http://en.wikipedia.org/wiki/Strong%27s_Concordance, "Strong's Exhaustive Concordance of the Bible, generally known as Strong's Concordance, is a concordance of the King James Bible (KJV) that was constructed under the direction of Dr. James Strong (1822–1894) and first published in 1890. Dr. Strong was Professor of exegetical theology at Drew Theological Seminary at the time. It is an exhaustive cross-reference of every word in the KJV back to the word in the original text. Unlike other Biblical reference books, the purpose of Strong's Concordance is not to provide content or commentary about the Bible, but to provide an index to the Bible. This allows the reader to find words where they appear in the Bible. This index allows a student of the Bible to re-find a phrase or passage previously studied. It also lets the reader directly compare how the same word may be used elsewhere in the Bible. In this way Strong's Notes provides an independent check against translations, and offers an opportunity for greater, and more technically accurate understanding of text."

WORDS FROM CHAPTER ONE

G4102 - Faith

From *G3982*; *persuasion*, that is, *credence*; moral *conviction* (of *religious* truth, or the truthfulness of God or a religious teacher), especially *reliance* upon Christ for salvation; abstractly *constancy* in such profession; by extension the system of religious (Gospel) *truth* itself: - assurance, belief, believe, faith, fidelity.

G3982

A primary verb; to *convince* (by argument, true or false); by analogy to *pacify* or *conciliate* (by other fair means); reflexively or passively to *assent* (to evidence or authority), to *rely* (by inward certainty): - agree, assure, believe, have confidence, be (wax) content, make friend, obey, persuade, trust, yield.

G5287 - Substance

This word occurs in the New Testament only in the following places. In 2Co 9:4; 2Co 11:17; Heb 3:14, where it is rendered "confident" and "confidence;" and in Heb 1:3, Now faith is the "substance" of these things; it is the ground and foundation of them, in which there is some standing hope. The word of promise is principal ground and foundation of hope; and faith, as leaning on the word, is a less principal ground; it is a confident persuasion, expectation, and assurance.

G1679 – Hoped for

From *G1680*; to *expect* or *confide:* - (have, thing) hope (-d) (for), trust.

G1680

A primary word (to *anticipate*, usually with pleasure); *expectation* (abstract or concrete) or *confidence:* - faith, hope.

G1650 – Evidence

From G1651; proof, conviction: - evidence, reproof.

G1651

Of uncertain affinity; to *confute, admonish:* - convict, convince, tell a fault, rebuke, reprove.

WORDS FROM CHAPTER TWO

H4284 - thoughts

From *H2803*; a contrivance, that is, (concretely) a texture, machine, or (abstractly) intention, plan (whether bad, a plot; or good, advice): - cunning (work), curious work, device (-sed), imagination, invented, means, purpose, thought.

H2803

A primitive root; properly to *plait* or interpenetrate, that is, (literally) to *weave* or (generally) to *fabricate*; figuratively to *plot* or contrive (usually in a malicious sense); hence (from the mental effort) to *think, regard, value, compute :* - (make) account (of), conceive, consider, count, cunning (man, work, workman), devise, esteem, find out, forecast, hold, imagine, impute, invent, be like, mean, purpose, reckon (-ing be made), regard, think.

H4209 - thoughts

From *H2161*; a plan, usually evil (*machination*), sometimes good (*sagacity*): - (wicked) device, discretion, intent, witty invention, lewdness, mischievous (device), thought, wickedly.

H2161

A primitive root; to *plan*, usually in a bad sense: - consider, devise, imagine, plot, purpose, think (evil).

H7454 - thoughts

From *H7462*; a *thought* (as *association* of ideas): - thought.

H7462

A primitive root; to *tend* a flock, that is, *pasture* it; intransitively to *graze* (literally or figuratively); generally to *rule*; by extension to *associate* with (as a friend): - X break, companion, keep company with, devour, eat up, evil entreat, feed, use as a friend, make friendship with, herdman, keep [sheep] (-er), pastor, + shearing house, shepherd, wander, waste.

H7808 - thought

From *H7879*; *communion*, that is, (reflexively) *meditation:* - thought

H7879

From *H7878*; a *contemplation*; by implication an *utterance:* - babbling, communication, complaint, meditation, prayer, talk.

H7878

A primitive root; to *ponder*, that is, (by implication) *converse* (with oneself, and hence aloud) or (transitively) *utter:* - commune, complain, declare, meditate, muse, pray, speak, talk (with).

G3540 - thought

From *G3539*; a *perception*, that is, *purpose*, or (by implication) the *intellect, disposition*, itself: - device, mind, thought.

G3539

From *G3563*; to *exercise* the *mind* (*observe*), that is, (figuratively) to *comprehend, heed:* - consider, perceive, think, understand.

G3563

Probably from the base of *G1097*; the *intellect*, that is, *mind* (divine or human; in thought, feeling, or will); by implication *meaning:* - mind, understanding. Compare *G5590*.

G1271 - mind

From *G1223* and *G3563*; *deep thought*, properly the faculty (*mind* or its *disposition*), by implication its exercise: - imagination, mind, understanding.

G601 - revealed

From *G575* and *G2572*; to take *off the cover*, that is, *disclose:* - reveal.

WORDS FROM CHAPTER FOUR

H3068 - Yahweh

From *H1961*; (the) *self Existent* or eternal; *Jehovah*, Jewish national name of God: - Jehovah, the Lord. Compare *H3050, H3069*.

H1961

A primitive root (compare *H1933*); to *exist*, that is, *be* or *become, come to pass* (always emphatic, and not a mere copula or auxiliary): - beacon, X altogether, be (-come, accomplished, committed, like), break, cause, come (to pass), continue, do, faint, fall, + follow, happen, X have, last, pertain, quit (one-) self, require, X use.

H430 - Elohim

Plural of *H433*; *gods* in the ordinary sense; but specifically used (in the plural thus, especially with the article) of the supreme *God*; occasionally applied by way of deference to *magistrates*; and sometimes as a superlative: - angels, X exceeding, God (gods) (-dess, -ly), X (very) great, judges, X mighty.

H433

(The second form is rare); probably prolonged (emphatically) from H410; a *deity* or the *deity*: - God, god. See *H430*.

H410

Shortened from *H352*; *strength*; as adjective *mighty*; especially the *Almighty* (but used also of any *deity*): - God (god), X goodly, X great, idol, might (-y one), power, strong. Compare names in "-el."

H5945 - Elyon

From *H5927*; an *elevation*, that is, (adjectively) *lofty* (comparatively); as title, the *Supreme:* - (Most, on) high (-er, -est), upper (-most).

H5943 – the most high

(Chaldee); corresponding to *H5942*; *supreme* (that is, *God*): - (most) high.

H8033 - Shamah

A primitive particle (rather from the relative *H834*); *there* (transfered to time) *then*; often *thither*, or *thence:* - in it, + thence, there (-in, + of, + out), + thither, + whither.

H7138 – Qârôb

From *H7126*; *near* (in place, kindred or time): - allied, approach, at hand, + any of kin, kinsfolk (-sman), (that is) near (of kin), neighbour, (that is) next, (them that come) nigh (at hand), more ready, short (-ly).

H7126

A primitive root; to *approach* (causatively *bring near*) for whatever purpose: - (cause to) approach, (cause to) bring (forth, near), (cause to) come (near, nigh), (cause to) draw near (nigh), go (near), be at hand, join, be near, offer, present, produce, make ready, stand, take.

H7706 - Shaddai

From *H7703*; the *Almighty:* - Almighty.

H7703

A primitive root; properly to *be burly*, that is, (figuratively) *powerful* (passively *impregnable*); by implication to *ravage:* - dead, destroy (-er), oppress, robber, spoil (-er), X utterly, (lay) waste.

H3070 - Jireh

From *H3068* and *H7200*; *Jehovah will see* (to it); *Jehovah-Jireh*, a symbolical name for Mt. Moriah: - Jehovah-jireh.

H7200

A primitive root; to *see*, literally or figuratively (in numerous applications, direct and implied, transitively, intransitively and causatively): - advise self, appear, approve, behold, X certainly, consider, discern, (make to) enjoy, have experience, gaze, take heed, X indeed, X joyfully, lo, look (on, one another, one on another, one upon another, out, up, upon), mark, meet, X be near, perceive, present, provide, regard, (have) respect, (fore-, cause to, let) see (-r, -m, one another), shew (self), X sight of others, (e-) spy, stare, X surely, X think, view, visions.

H7495 - Repheka

A primitive root; properly to *mend* (by stitching), that is, (figuratively) to *cure*: - cure, (cause to) heal, physician, repair, X thoroughly, make whole. See *H7503*.

H2483 - griefs

From *H2470*; *malady, anxiety, calamity:* - disease, grief, (is) sick (-ness).

H2470

A primitive root (compare *H2342, H2490*); properly to *be rubbed* or *worn*; hence (figuratively) to *be weak, sick, afflicted*; or (causatively) to *grieve, make sick*; also to *stroke* (in flattering), *entreat*: - beseech, (be) diseased, (put to) grief, be grieved, (be) grievous, infirmity, intreat, lay to, put to pain, X pray, make prayer, be (fall, make) sick, sore, be sorry, make suit (X supplication), woman in travail, be (become) weak, be wounded.

H4341 - sorrows

From *H3510*; *anguish* or (figuratively) *affliction:* - grief, pain, sorrow.

H3510

A primitive root; properly to feel *pain*; by implication to *grieve*; figuratively to *spoil:* - grieving, mar, have pain, make sad (sore), (be) sorrowful.

H5060 - stricken

A primitive root; properly to *touch*, that is, *lay the hand upon* (for any purpose; euphemistically, to *lie with* a woman); by implication to *reach* (figuratively to *arrive, acquire*); violently, to *strike* (punish, defeat, destroy, etc.): - beat, (X be able to) bring (down), cast, come (nigh), draw near (nigh), get up, happen, join, near, plague, reach (up), smite, strike, touch.

H5221 - smitten

A primitive root; to *strike* (lightly or severely, literally or figuratively): - beat, cast forth, clap, give [wounds], X go forward, X indeed, kill, make [slaughter], murderer, punish, slaughter, slay (-er, -ing), smite (-r, -ing), strike, be stricken, (give) stripes, X surely, wound.

H6588 - transgressions

From *H6586*; a *revolt* (national, moral or religious): - rebellion, sin, transgression, trespassive

H6586

A primitive root (rather identical with H6585 through the idea of *expansion*); to *break* away (from just authority), that is, *trespass, apostatize, quarrel:* - offend, rebel, revolt, transgress (-ion, -or).

H5771 - iniquity

From *H5753; perversity,* that is, (moral) *evil:* - fault, iniquity, mischief, punishment (of iniquity), sin.

H5753

A primitive root; to *crook,* literally or figuratively: - do amiss, bow down, make crooked, commit iniquity, pervert, (do) perverse (-ly), trouble, X turn, do wickedly, do wrong.

H6664 - Tsidqenu

From *H6663;* the *right* (natural, moral or legal); also (abstractly) *equity* or (figuratively) *prosperity:* - X even, (X that which is altogether) just (-ice), ([un-]) right (-eous) (cause, -ly, -ness).

H6663

A primitive root; to *be* (causatively *make*) *right* (in a moral or forensic sense): - cleanse, clear self, (be, do) just (-ice, -ify, -ify self), (be, turn to) righteous (-ness).

H6918 - Qâdôsh

From *H6942; sacred* (ceremonially or morally); (as noun) *God* (by eminence), an *angel,* a *saint,* a *sanctuary:* - holy (One), saint.

H6942

A primitive root; to *be* (causatively *make, pronounce* or *observe* as) *clean* (ceremonially or morally): - appoint, bid, consecrate, dedicate, defile, hallow, (be, keep) holy (-er, place), keep, prepare, proclaim, purify, sanctify (-ied one, self), X wholly.

H6635 - Tsebaoth

From *H6633*; a *mass* of persons (or figurative things), especially regularly organized for war (an *army*); by implication a *campaign*, literally or figuratively (specifically *hardship*, *worship*): - appointed time, (+) army, (+) battle, company, host, service, soldiers, waiting upon, war (-fare).

H6633

A primitive root; to *mass* (an army or servants): - assemble, fight, perform, muster, wait upon, war.

H3478 - Israel

From *H8280* and *H410*; *he will rule* as *God*; *Jisrael*, a symbolical name of Jacob; also (typically) of his posterity: - Israel.

H8280

A primitive root; to *prevail:* - have power (as a prince).

H410

Shortened from *H352*; *strength*; as adjective *mighty*; especially the *Almighty* (but used also of any *deity*): - God (god), X goodly, X great, idol, might (-y one), power, strong. Compare names in "-el."

H4634 - armies

Feminine of *H4633*; an *arrangement*; concretely a *pile*; specifically a military *array:* - army, fight, be set in order, ordered place, rank, row.

H4633

From *H6168*; an *arrangement*, that is, (figuratively) mental *disposition:* - preparation.

H5462 – deliver

A primitive root; to *shut* up; figuratively to *surrender:* - close up, deliver (up), give over (up), inclose, X pure, repair, shut (in, self, out, up, up together), stop, X straitly.

H3071 - Nissi

From *H3068* and *H5251* with pronominal suffix.; *Jehovah* (is) *my banner*; *Jehovah-Nissi*, a symbolical name of an altar in the Desert: - Jehovah-nissi.

H5251

From *H5264*; a *flag*; also a *sail*; by implication a *flagstaff*; generally a *signal*; figuratively a *token:* - banner, pole, sail, (en-) sign, standard.

H3073 - Shalom

From *H3068* and *H7965*; *Jehovah* (is) *peace*; *Jehovah-Shalom*, a symbolical name of an altar in Palestine: - Jehovah-shalom.

H7965

From *H7999*; *safe*, that is, (figuratively) *well, happy, friendly*; also (abstractly) *welfare*, that is, health, prosperity, peace: - X do, familiar, X fare, favour, + friend, X greet, (good) health, (X perfect, such as be at) peace (-able, -ably), prosper (-ity, -ous), rest, safe (-ly), salute, welfare, (X all is, be) well, X wholly.

H7999

A primitive root; to *be safe* (in mind, body or estate); figuratively to *be* (causatively *make*) *completed*; by implication to *be friendly*; by extension to *reciprocate* (in various applications): - make amends, (make an) end, finish, full, give again, make good, (re-) pay (again), (make) (to) (be at) peace (-able), that is perfect, perform, (make) prosper (-ous), recompense, render, requite, make restitution, restore, reward, X surely.

H7349 – Rachûm

From *H7355*; *compassionate:* - full of compassion, merciful.

H7355

A primitive root; to *fondle*; by implication to *love*, especially to *compassionate:* - have compassion (on, upon), love, (find, have, obtain, shew) mercy (-iful, on, upon), (have) pity, Ruhamah, X surely.

H2587 - Channûn

From *H2603*; *gracious:* - gracious.

H2603

A primitive root (compare *H2583*); properly to *bend* or stoop in kindness to an inferior; to *favor*, *bestow*; causatively to *implore* (that is, move to favor by petition): - beseech, X fair, (be, find, shew) favour (-able), be (deal, give, grant (gracious (-ly), intreat, (be) merciful, have (shew) mercy (on, upon), have pity upon, pray, make supplication, X very.

H2617 - mercy

From *H2616*; *kindness*; by implication (towards God) *piety*; rarely (by opprobrium) *reproof*, or (subjectively) *beauty:* - favour, good deed (-liness, -ness), kindly, (loving-) kindness, merciful (kindness), mercy, pity, reproach, wicked thing.

H2616

A primitive root; properly perhaps to *bow* (the neck only (compare *H2603*) in courtesy to an equal), that is, to *be kind*; also (by euphemism (compare *H1288*), but rarely) to *reprove:* - shew self merciful, put to shame.

G26 - Agapē

From *G25*; *love*, that is, *affection* or *benevolence*; specifically (plural) a *love feast:* - (feast of) charity ([-ably]), dear, love.

G25

Perhaps from ἄγαν agan (*much*; or compare [*H5689*]); to *love* (in a social or moral sense): - (be-) love (-ed). Compare *G5368*.

G5368

From *G5384*; to *be a friend to* (*fond of* [an individual or an object]), that is, *have affection* for (denoting *personal* attachment, as a matter of sentiment or feeling; while *G25* is wider, embracing especially the judgment and the *deliberate* assent of the will as a matter of principle, duty and propriety: the two thus stand related very much as *G2309* and *G1014,* or as *G2372* and *G3563* respectively; the former being chiefly of the *heart* and the latter of the *head*); specifically to *kiss* (as a mark of tenderness): - kiss, love.

WORDS FROM CHAPTER FIVE

H2896 - good

From *H2895*; *good* (as an adjective) in the widest sense; used likewise as a noun, both in the masculine and the feminine, the singular and the plural (*good*, a *good* or *good* thing, a *good* man or woman; the *good*, *goods* or *good* things, *good* men or women), also as an adverb (*well*): - beautiful, best, better, bountiful, cheerful, at ease, X fair (word), (be in) favour, fine, glad, good (deed, -lier, liest, -ly, -ness, -s), graciously, joyful, kindly, kindness, liketh (best), loving, merry, X most, pleasant, + pleaseth, pleasure, precious, prosperity, ready, sweet, wealth, welfare, (be) well ([-favoured]).

H2895

A primitive root, to *be* (transitively *do* or *make*) *good* (or *well*) in the widest sense: - be (do) better, cheer, be (do, seem) good, (make), goodly, X please, (be, do, go, play) well.

WORDS FROM CHAPTER SIX

G1860 – Hope

From *G1861*; an *announcement* (for information, assent or pledge; especially a divine *assurance* of good): - message, promise.

G1861 - Promise

To *announce upon* (reflexively), that is, (by implication) to *engage* to do something, to *assert* something respecting oneself: - profess, (make) promise.

G3727 - oath

From ἕρκος herkos (a *fence*; perhaps akin to *G3725*); a *limit*, that is, (sacred) *restraint* (specifically *oath*): - oath.

G276 – Immutable

From *G1* (as a negative particle) and a derivative of *G3346*; *unchangeable*, or (neuter as abstract) *unchangeability:* - immutable

G1679 - things hoped for

From *G1680*; to *expect* or *confide:* - (have, thing) hope (-d) (for), trust.

G2192 - hope we have

A primary verb to *hold* (used in very various applications, literally or figuratively, direct or remote; such as *possession*, *ability*, *contiguity*, *relation* or *condition*)

G4198 - Went

Middle voice from a derivative of the same as *G3984*; to *traverse*, that is, *travel* (literally or figuratively; especially to *remove* [figuratively *die*], *live*, etc.)

G3984

From the base of *G4008* (through the idea of *piercing*); a *test*, that is, *attempt*, *experience:* - assaying, trial.

G4008

Apparently the accusative case of an obsolete derivation of πείρω peirō (to "peirce")

G565 - went

From *G575* and *G2064*; to *go off* (that is, *depart*), *aside* (that is, *apart*) or *behind* (that is, *follow*), literally or figuratively: - come

G575

A primary particle; *"off"*, that is, *away* (from something near), in various senses (of place, time, or relation; literally or figuratively): - (X here-) after, ago, at, because of, before, by (the space of), for (-th), from, in, (out) of, off, (up-) on (-ce), since, with. In composition (as a prefix) it usually denotes *separation, departure, cessation, completion, reversal,* etc.

G2064

to *come* or *go* (in a great variety of applications, literally and figuratively)

G4100 - believe

From *G4102*; to *have faith* (in, upon, or with respect to, a person or thing), that is, *credit*; by implication to *entrust* (especially one's spiritual well being to Christ): - believe (-r), commit (to trust), put in trust with.

G4102

From *G3982*; *persuasion*, that is, *credence*; moral *conviction* (of *religious* truth, or the truthfulness of God or a religious teacher), especially *reliance* upon Christ for salvation; abstractly *constancy* in such profession; by extension the system of religious (Gospel) *truth* itself: - assurance, belief, believe, faith, fidelity.

G3982

A primary verb; to *convince* (by argument, true or false); by analogy to *pacify* or *conciliate* (by other fair means); reflexively or passively to *assent* (to evidence or authority), to *rely* (by inward certainty): - agree, assure, believe, have confidence, be (wax) content, make friend, obey, persuade, trust, yield.

WORDS FROM CHAPTER SEVEN

G2041 - works

From ἔργω ergō (a primary but obsolete word; to *work*); *toil* (as an effort or occupation); by implication an *act:* - deed, doing, labour, work.

G3786 - profit

From ὀφέλλω ophellō (to *heap* up, that is, *accumulate* or *benefit*); *gain:* - advantageth, profit.

G3498 - dead

From an apparently primary word νέκυς nekus (a *corpse*); *dead* (literally or figuratively; also as noun): - dead.

H8085 – obedience

A primitive root; to *hear* intelligently (often with implication of attention, obedience, etc.; causatively to *tell*, etc.): - X attentively, call (gather) together, X carefully, X certainly, consent, consider, be content, declare, X diligently, discern, give ear, (cause to, let, make to) hear (-ken, tell), X indeed, listen, make (a) noise, (be) obedient, obey, perceive, (make a) proclaim (-ation), publish, regard, report, shew (forth), (make a) sound, X surely, tell, understand, whosoever [heareth], witness.

H4805 - rebellion

From *H4784*; *bitterness*, that is, (figuratively) *rebellion*; concretely *bitter*, or *rebellious:* - bitter, (most) rebel (-ion, -lious).

H6484 - stubborness

A primitive root; to *peck* at, that is, (figuratively) *stun* or *dull:* - press, urge, stubbornness.

H8655 - idolatry

Plural perhaps from *H7495*; a *healer*; *Teraphim* (singular or plural) a family idol: - idols (-atry), images, teraphim.

G2983 - receives

A prolonged form of a primary verb, which is used only as an alternate in certain tenses; to *take* (in very many applications, literally and figuratively [probably objective or active, to *get hold* of; whereas G1209 is rather subjective or passive, to *have offered* to one; while G138 is more violent, to *seize* or *remove*]): - accept, + be amazed, assay, attain, bring, X when I call, catch, come on (X unto), + forget, have, hold, obtain, receive (X after), take (away, up).

WORDS FROM CHAPTER EIGHT

G4100 – believe

From *G4102* [faith]; to *have faith* (in, upon, or with respect to, a person or thing), that is, *credit*; by implication to *entrust* (especially one's spiritual well being to Christ): - believe (-r), commit (to trust), put in trust with.

WORDS FROM CHAPTER NINE

G1252 – wavering / doubt

From *G1223* and *G2919*; to *separate thoroughly*, that is, (literally and reflexively) to *withdraw* from, or (by implication) *oppose*; figuratively to *discriminate* (by implication *decide*), or (reflexively) *hesitate:* - contend, make (to) differ (-ence), discern, doubt, judge, be partial, stagger, waver.

G2919

Properly to *distinguish*, that is, *decide* (mentally or judicially); by implication to *try, condemn, punish:* - avenge, conclude, condemn, damn, decree, determine, esteem, judge, go to (sue at the) law, ordain, call in question, sentence to, think.

G1374 – double minded

From *G1364* and *G5590*; *two spirited*, that is, *vacillating* (in opinion or purpose): - double minded.

G182 – unstable

From *G1* (as a negative particle) and a derivative of *G2525*; *inconstant:* - unstable

G570 – Unbelief

From *G571*; *faithlessness*, that is, (negatively) *disbelief* (*want of* Christian *faith*), or (positively) *unfaithfulness* (*disobedience*): - unbelief.

G571

From *G1* (as a negative particle) and *G4103*; (actively) *disbelieving*, that is, *without* Christian *faith* (specifically a *heathen*); (passively) *untrustworthy* (person), or *incredible* (thing): - that believeth not, faithless, incredible thing, infidel, unbeliever (-ing).

G4100 – Believe

From *G4102*; to *have faith* (in, upon, or with respect to, a person or thing), that is, *credit*; by implication to *entrust* (especially one's spiritual well being to Christ): - believe (-r), commit (to trust), put in trust with.

WORDS FROM CHAPTER TEN

G863 - forgive

From *G575* and ἵημι hiēmi (to *send*; an intensive form of εἶμι eimi (to *go*)); to *send forth*, in various applications: - cry, forgive, forsake, lay aside, leave, let (alone, be, go, have), omit, put (send) away, remit, suffer, yield up.

G3783 - debts

From (the alternate of) *G3784*; *something owed*, that is, (figuratively) a *due*.; morally a *fault:* - debt.

G3784

Including its prolonged form (second form) used in certain tenses. Probably from the base of G3786 (through the idea of *accruing*); to *owe* (pecuniarily); figuratively to *be under obligation* (*ought, must, should*); morally to *fail* in duty: - behove, be bound, (be) debt (-or), (be) due (-ty), be guilty (indebted), (must) need (-s), ought, owe, should. See also *G3785*.

G3781 - debtor

From *G3784*; an *ower*, that is, a person *indebted*; figuratively a *delinquent*; morally a *transgressor* (against God): - debtor, which owed, sinner.

G3900 - trespasses

From *G3895*; a *side slip* (*lapse* or *deviation*), that is, (unintentional) *error* or (wilful) *transgression:* - fall, fault, offence, sin, trespass.

G3895

From *G3844* and *G4098*; to *fall aside*, that is, (figuratively) to *apostatize:* - fall away.

WORDS FROM CHAPTER ELEVEN

G1210 - bind

A primary verb; to *bind* (in various applications, literally or figuratively): - bind, be in bonds, knit, tie, wind. See also *G1163, G1189.*

G1189

Middle voice of *G1210*; to *beg* (as *binding oneself*), that is, *petition:* - beseech, pray (to), make request. Compare *G4441.*

G3089 - loosed

A primary verb; to "loosen" (literally or figuratively): - break (up), destroy, dissolve, (un-) loose, melt, put off. Compare *G4486.*

Good - H2896

From *H2895*; *good* (as an adjective) in the widest sense; used likewise as a noun, both in the masculine and the feminine, the singular and the plural (*good*, a *good* or *good* thing, a *good* man or woman; the *good*, *goods* or *good* things, *good* men or women), also as an adverb (*well*): - beautiful, best, better, bountiful, cheerful, at ease, X fair (word), (be in) favour, fine, glad, good (deed, -lier, liest, -ly, -ness, -s), graciously, joyful, kindly, kindness, liketh (best), loving, merry, X most, pleasant, + pleaseth, pleasure, precious, prosperity, ready, sweet, wealth, welfare, (be) well ([-favoured]).

H2895

A primitive root, to *be* (transitively *do* or *make*) *good* (or *well*) in the widest sense: - be (do) better, cheer, be (do, seem) good, (make), goodly, X please, (be, do, go, play) well.

H7451 - Evil

From *H7489*; *bad* or (as noun) *evil* (naturally or morally). This includes the second (feminine) form; as adjective or noun: - adversity, affliction, bad, calamity, + displease (-ure), distress, evil ([-favouredness], man, thing), + exceedingly, X great, grief (-vous), harm, heavy, hurt (-ful), ill (favoured), + mark, mischief, (-vous), misery, naught (-ty), noisome, + not please, sad (-ly), sore, sorrow, trouble, vex, wicked (-ly, -ness, one), worse (-st) wretchedness, wrong. [Including feminine ra'ah; as adjective or noun.]

H7489

A primitive root; properly to *spoil* (literally by *breaking* to pieces); figuratively to *make* (or *be*) *good for nothing*, that is, *bad* (physically, socially or morally). (*associate selves* and *show self friendly* are by mistake for *H7462*.): - afflict, associate selves [by mistake for *H7462*], break (down, in pieces), + displease, (be, bring, do) evil (doer, entreat, man), show self friendly [by mistake for *H7462*], do harm, (do) hurt, (behave self, deal) ill, X indeed, do mischief, punish, still vex, (do) wicked (doer, -ly), be (deal, do) worse.

H7307 - Spirit

From *H7306*; *wind*; by resemblance *breath*, that is, a sensible (or even violent) exhalation; figuratively *life, anger, unsubstantiality*; by extension a *region* of the sky; by resemblance *spirit*, but only of a rational being (including its expression and functions): - air, anger, blast, breath, X cool, courage, mind, X quarter, X side, spirit ([-ual]), tempest, X vain, ([whirl-]) wind (-y).

H7306

A primitive root; properly to *blow*, that is, *breathe*; only (literally) to *smell* or (by implication *perceive* (figuratively to *anticipate*, *enjoy*): - accept, smell, X touch, make of quick understanding.

H430 - of God

Plural of *H433*; *gods* in the ordinary sense; but specifically used (in the plural thus, especially with the article) of the supreme *God*; occasionally applied by way of deference to *magistrates*; and sometimes as a superlative: - angels, X exceeding, God (gods) (-dess, -ly), X (very) great, judges, X mighty.

G4151 - Spirit (New Testament)

From *G4154*; a *current* of air, that is, *breath* (*blast*) or a *breeze*; by analogy or figuratively a *spirit*, that is, (human) the rational *soul*, (by implication) *vital principle*, mental *disposition*, etc., or (superhuman) an *angel*, *daemon*, or (divine) God, Christ's *spirit*, the Holy *spirit*: - ghost, life, spirit (-ual, -ually), mind. Compare *G5590*.

G4154

A primary word; to *breathe* hard, that is, *breeze*: - blow. Compare *G5594*.

H5771 - sin

From *H5753*; *perversity*, that is, (moral) *evil*: - fault, iniquity, mischief, punishment (of iniquity), sin.

H5753

A primitive root; to *crook*, literally or figuratively: - do amiss, bow down, make crooked, commit iniquity, pervert, (do) perverse (-ly), trouble, X turn, do wickedly, do wrong.

G3614 - house

From *G3624*; properly *residence* (abstractly), but usually (concretely) an *abode* (literally or figuratively); by implication a *family* (especially *domestics*): - home, house (-hold).

G3624

Of uncertain affinity; a *dwelling* (more or less extensive, literally or figuratively); by implication a *family* (more or less related, literally or figuratively): - home, house (-hold), temple.

G833 - palace

From the same as *G109*; a *yard* (as open to the *wind*); by implication a *mansion:* - court, ([sheep-]) fold, hall, palace.

G2478 - Strongman

From *G2479*; *forcible* (literally or figuratively): - boisterous, mighty (-ier), powerful, strong (-er, man), valiant.

G2479

From a derivative of ἴς his (*force*; compare ἔσχον eschon; a form of *G2192*); *forcefulness* (literally or figuratively): - ability, might ([-ily]), power, strength.

G2192

A primary verb (including an alternate form σχέω scheō *skheh'-o* used in certain tenses only); to *hold* (used in very various applications, literally or figuratively, direct or remote; such as *possession, ability, contiguity, relation* or *condition*): - be (able, X hold, possessed with), accompany, + begin to amend, can (+ -not), X conceive, count, diseased, do, + eat, + enjoy, + fear, following, have, hold, keep, + lack, + go to law, lie, + must needs, + of necessity, + need, next, + recover, + reign, + rest, return, X sick, take for, + tremble, + uncircumcised, use.

G758 - Prince

Present participle of *G757*; a *first* (in rank or power): - chief (ruler), magistrate, prince, ruler.

G2666 - devour

From *G2596* and *G4095*; to *drink down*, that is, *gulp entire* (literally or figuratively): - devour, drown, swallow (up).

H4668 - key

From *H6605*; an *opener*, that is, a *key:* - key.

G2807 - key

From *G2808*; a *key* (as *shutting* a lock), literally or figuratively: - key.

G1793 – make intercession

From *G1722* and *G5177*; to *chance upon*, that is, (by implication) *confer with*; by extension to *entreat* (in favor or against): - deal with, make intercession.

G1283 - spoil

From *G1223* and *G726;* to *seize asunder*, that is, *plunder:* - spoil.

G726

From a derivative of *G138*; to *seize* (in various applications): - catch (away, up), pluck, pull, take (by force).

G1659 - free

From *G1658*; to *liberate*, that is, (figuratively) to *exempt* (from moral, ceremonial or mortal liability): - deliver, make free.

G1658 - free

Probably from the alternate of *G2064*; *unrestrained* (to *go* at pleasure), that is, (as a citizen) *not a slave* (whether *freeborn* or *manumitted*), or (generally) *exempt* (from obligation or liability): - free (man, woman), at liberty.

G763 - wickedness

From *G765*; *impiety*, that is, (by implication) *wickedness:* - ungodly (-liness).

G765

From *G1* (as a negative particle) and a presumed derivative of *G4576*; *irreverent*, that is, (by extension) *impious* or *wicked:* - ungodly (man).

G2886 - worldly

From *G2889* (in its secondary sense); *terrene* ("cosmic"), literally (*mundane*) or figuratively (*corrupt*): - worldly.

G1939 - lusts

From *G1937*; a *longing* (especially for what is forbidden): - concupiscence, desire, lust (after).

G1937

From *G1909* and *G2372*; to set the *heart upon*, that is, *long* for (rightfully or otherwise): - covet, desire, would fain, lust (after).

G2168 – giving thanks

From *G2170*; to *be grateful*, that is, (actually) to *express gratitude* (towards); specifically to *say grace* at a meal: - (give) thank (-ful, -s).

G2170

From *G2095* and a derivative of *G5483*; *well favored*, that is, (by implication) *grateful:* - thankful.

G1654 - alms

From *G1656*; *compassionateness*, that is, (as exercised towards the poor) *beneficence*, or (concretely) a *benefaction:* - alms (-deeds).

G1656

Of uncertain affinity; *compassion* (human or divine, especially active): - (+ tender) mercy.

G1342 – righteous man

From *G1349*; *equitable* (in character or act); by implication *innocent, holy* (absolutely or relatively): - just, meet, right (-eous).

G1349

Probably from *G1166*; *right* (as self *evident*), that is, *justice* (the principle, a decision, or its execution): - judgment, punish, vengeance.

G1754 – effectual fervent

From *G1756*; to *be active, efficient:* - do, (be) effectual (fervent), be mighty in, shew forth self, work (effectually in).

G1756

From *G1722* and *G2041*; *active, operative:* - effectual, powerful.

G436 - resist

From *G473* and *G2476*; to *stand against,* that is, *oppose:* - resist, withstand.

G2476

A prolonged form of a primary word στάω staō (of the same meaning, and used for it in certain tenses); to *stand* (transitively or intransitively), used in various applications (literally or figuratively): - abide, appoint, bring, continue, covenant, establish, hold up, lay, present, set (up), stanch, stand (by, forth, still, up). Compare *G5087*.

H1605 - rebuke

A primitive root; to *chide:* - corrupt, rebuke, reprove.

G2008 - rebuke

From *G1909* and *G5091*; to *tax upon,* that is, *censure* or *admonish*; by implication *forbid:* - (straitly) charge, rebuke.

G5091

From *G5093*; to *prize*, that is, *fix* a *valuation* upon; by implication to *revere:* - honour, value.

G1849 – power / authority

From *G1832* (in the sense of *ability*); *privilege*, that is, (subjectively) *force, capacity, competency, freedom*, or (objectively) *mastery* (concretely *magistrate, superhuman, potentate, token of control*), delegated *influence:* - authority, jurisdiction, liberty, power, right, strength.

G1411 – power / miracles

From *G1410*; *force* (literally or figuratively); specifically miraculous *power* (usually by implication a *miracle* itself): - ability, abundance, meaning, might (-ily, -y, -y deed), (worker of) miracle (-s), power, strength, violence, mighty (wonderful) work.

G1410

Of uncertain affinity; to *be able* or *possible:* - be able, can (do, + -not), could, may, might, be possible, be of power.

G1845 - exorcists

From *G1844*; *one that binds by an oath* (or *spell*), that is, (by implication) an "exorcist" (*conjurer*): - exorcist.

G1844

From *G1537* and *G3726*; to *exact an oath*, that is, *conjure:* - adjure.

G3726

From *G3727*; to *put on oath*, that is, *make swear*; by analogy to solemnly *enjoin:* - adjure, charge.

WORDS FROM CHAPTER THIRTEEN

G4856 - agree

From *G4859*; to be *harmonious*, that is, (figuratively) to *accord* (*be suitable, concur*) or *stipulate* (by compact): - agree (together, with).

G4859

From *G4862* and *G5456*; *sounding together* (*alike*), that is, (figuratively) *accordant* (neuter as noun, *agreement*): - consent.

G4863 – gathered together

From *G4862* and *G71*; to *lead together*, that is, *collect* or *convene*; specifically to *entertain* (hospitably): - + accompany, assemble (selves, together), bestow, come together, gather (selves together, up, together), lead into, resort, take in.

G4862

A primary preposition denoting *union*; *with* or *together* (but much closer than *G3326* or *G3844*), that is, by association, companionship, process, resemblance, possession, instrumentality, addition, etc.: - beside, with. In compounds it has similar applications, including *completeness*.

WORDS FROM CHAPTER FOURTEEN

G3100 - Teach

From *G3101*; intransitively to *become a pupil*; transitively to *disciple*, that is, enrol as scholar: - be disciple, instruct, teach.

G3101

From *G3129*; a *learner*, that is, *pupil:* - disciple.

G3129

Prolonged from a primary verb, another form of which, μαθέω matheō, is used as an alternate in certain tenses; to *learn* (in any way): - learn, understand.

H6556 - Gap

From *H6555*; a *break* (literally or figuratively): - breach, breaking forth (in), X forth, gap.

H6555

A primitive root; to *break* out (in many applications, direct and indirect, literally and figuratively): - X abroad, (make a) breach, break (away, down, -er, forth, in, up), burst out come (spread) abroad, compel, disperse, grow, increase, open, press, scatter, urge.

G2368 - Odours

From *G2370*; an *aroma*, that is, fragrant *powder* burnt in religious service; by implication the *burning* itself: - incense, odour.

G2370

From a derivative of *G2380* (in the sense of *smoking*); to *fumigate*, that is, *offer* aromatic *fumes:* - burn incense.

G2380

A primary verb; properly to *rush* (*breathe* hard, *blow*, *smoke*), that is, (by implication) to *sacrifice* (properly by fire, but generally); by extension to *immolate* (*slaughter* for any purpose): - kill, (do) sacrifice, slay

G1754 – effectual fervent

From *G1756*; to *be active, efficient:* - do, (be) effectual (fervent), be mighty in, shew forth self, work (effectually in).

G1756

From *G1722* and *G2041*; *active, operative:* - effectual, powerful.

G1162 - prayer

From *G1189*; a *petition:* - prayer, request, supplication.

G1189

Middle voice of *G1210*; to *beg* (as *binding oneself*), that is, *petition:* - beseech, pray (to), make request. Compare *G4441*.

G1210

A primary verb; to *bind* (in various applications, literally or figuratively): - bind, be in bonds, knit, tie, wind

G1342 – righteous man

From *G1349*; *equitable* (in character or act); by implication *innocent, holy* (absolutely or relatively): - just, meet, right (-eous).

G1349

Probably from *G1166*; *right* (as self *evident*), that is, *justice* (the principle, a decision, or its execution): - judgment, punish, vengeance.

G2480 - availeth

From *G2479*; to *have* (or *exercise*) *force* (literally or figuratively): - beable, avail, can do ([-not]), could, be good, might, prevail, be of strength, be whole, + much work.

G2479

From a derivative of ἰς his (*force*; compare ἔσχον eschon; a form of *G2192*); *forcefulness* (literally or figuratively): - ability, might ([-ily]), power, strength.

G4183 - much

Including the forms from the alternate "pollos"; (singular) *much* (in any respect) or (plural) *many*; neuter (singular) as adverb *largely*; neuter (plural) as adverb or noun *often, mostly, largely*: - abundant, + altogether, common, + far (passed, spent), (+ be of a) great (age, deal, -ly, while), long, many, much, oft (-en [-times]), plenteous, sore, straitly.

H1961 – minister (first part)

A primitive root (compare *H1933*); to *exist*, that is, *be* or *become, come to pass* (always emphatic, and not a mere copula or auxiliary): - beacon, X altogether, be (-come, accomplished, committed, like), break, cause, come (to pass), continue, do, faint, fall, + follow, happen, X have, last, pertain, quit (one-) self, require, X use.

H8334 – minister (second part)

A primitive root; to *attend* as a menial or worshipper; figuratively to *contribute* to: - minister (unto), (do) serve (-ant, -ice, -itor), wait on.

WORDS FROM CHAPTER FIFTEEN

G591 - Reward

From *G575* and *G1325*; to *give away*, that is, *up, over, back*, etc. (in various applications): - deliver (again), give (again), (re-) pay (-ment be made), perform, recompense, render, requite, restore, reward, sell, yield,

G1325

A prolonged form of a primary verb (which is used as an alternate in most of the tenses); to *give* (used in a very wide application, properly or by implication, literally or figuratively; greatly modified by the connection): - adventure, bestow, bring forth, commit, deliver (up), give, grant, hinder, make, minister, number, offer, have power, put, receive, set, shew, smite (+ with the hand), strike (+ with the palm of the hand), suffer, take, utter, yield.

G3900 - Trespasses

From *G3895*; a *side slip* (*lapse* or *deviation*), that is, (unintentional) *error* or (wilful) *transgression:* - fall, fault, offence, sin, trespass.

G3895

From *G3844* and *G4098*; to *fall aside*, that is, (figuratively) to *apostatize:* - fall away.

G740 - Bread

From *G142*; *bread* (as *raised*) or a *loaf:* - (shew-) bread, loaf.

G2315 – given by inspiration of God

From *G2316* and a presumed derivative of *G4154*; *divinely breathed in:* - given by inspiration of God.

G3056 – Word or The Word

From *G3004*; something *said* (including the *thought*); by implication a *topic* (subject of discourse), also *reasoning* (the mental faculty) or *motive*; by extension a *computation*; specifically (with the article in John) the Divine *Expression* (that is, *Christ*): - account, cause, communication, X concerning, doctrine, fame, X have to do, intent, matter, mouth, preaching, question, reason, + reckon, remove, say (-ing), shew, X speaker, speech, talk, thing, + none of these things move me, tidings, treatise, utterance, word, work.

G335 - importunity

From a compound of *G1* (as a negative particle (compare *G427*)) and *G127*; *impudence*, that is, (by implication) *importunity:* - importunity.

WORDS FROM CHAPTER SIXTEEN

G2098 - Gospel

From the same as *G2097*; a *good message*, that is, the *gospel:* - gospel.

G2097

From *G2095* and *G32*; to *announce good* news ("evangelize") especially the gospel: - declare, bring (declare, show) glad (good) tidings, preach (the gospel).

G1515 - Peace

Probably from a primary verb εἴρω eirō (to *join*); *peace* (literally or figuratively); by implication *prosperity:* - one, peace, quietness, rest, + set at one again.

G3306 - Abide

A primary verb; to *stay* (in a given place, state, relation or expectancy): - abide, continue, dwell, endure, be present, remain, stand, tarry (for), X thine own

WORDS FROM CHAPTER SEVENTEEN

G2008 - Rebuke

From *G1909* and *G5091*; to *tax upon*, that is, *censure* or *admonish*; by implication *forbid:* - (straitly) charge, rebuke.

G1909

A primary preposition properly meaning *superimposition* (of time, place, order, etc.), as a relation of *distribution* [with the genitive case], that is, *over, upon*, etc.; of *rest* (with the dative case) *at, on*, etc.; of *direction* (with the accusative case) *towards, upon*, etc.: - about (the times), above, after, against, among, as long as (touching), at, beside,

X have charge of, (be-, [where-]) fore, in (a place, as much as, the time of, -to), (because) of, (up-) on (behalf of) over, (by, for) the space of, through (-out), (un-) to (-ward), with. In compounds it retains essentially the same import, *at*, *upon*, etc. (literally or figuratively).

G5091

From *G5093*; to *prize*, that is, *fix* a *valuation* upon; by implication to *revere:* - honour, value.

G5093

Including the comparative τιμιώτερος timiōteros and the superlative τιμιώτατος timiōtatos; from *G5092*; *valuable*, that is, (objectively) *costly*, or (subjectively) *honored, esteemed*, or (figuratively) *beloved:* - dear, honourable, (more, most) precious, had in reputation.

G5092

From *G5099*; a *value*, that is, *money* paid, or (concretely and collectively) *valuables*; by analogy *esteem* (especially of the highest degree), or the *dignity* itself: - honour, precious, price, some.

G5099

Strengthened for a primary word τίω tiō (which is only used as an alternate in certain tenses); to *pay* a price, that is, as a *penalty:* - be punished with.

G142 – Be thou removed

A primary verb; to *lift*; by implication to *take up* or *away*; figuratively to *raise* (the voice), *keep in suspense* (the mind); specifically to *sail* away (that is, *weigh anchor*); by Hebraism (compare [*H5375*]) to *expiate* sin: - away with, bear (up), carry, lift up, loose, make to doubt, put away, remove, take (away, up).

H5375

A primitive root; to *lift*, in a great variety of applications, literally and figuratively, absolutely and relatively: - accept, advance, arise, (able to, [armour], suffer to) bear (-er, up), bring (forth), burn, carry (away), cast, contain, desire, ease, exact, exalt (self), extol, fetch, forgive, furnish, further, give, go on, help, high, hold up, honourable (+ man), lade, lay, lift (self) up, lofty, marry, magnify, X needs, obtain, pardon, raise (up), receive, regard, respect, set (up), spare, stir up, + swear, take (away, up), X utterly, wear, yield.

WORDS FROM CHAPTER EIGHTEEN

G5083 - Keep

From τηρός teros (a *watch*; perhaps akin to *G2334*); to *guard* (from *loss* or *injury*, properly by keeping *the eye* upon)

G4190 - Evil

From a derivative of *G4192*; *hurtful*, that is, *evil* (properly in effect or influence)

G4192

toil, that is, (by implication) *anguish:* - pain.

G436 - Resist

From *G473* and *G2476*; to *stand against*, that is, *oppose:* - resist, withstand.

G473

A primary particle; *opposite*, that is, *instead* or *because* of (rarely *in addition* to)

G2476

to *stand* (transitively or intransitively), used in various applications (literally or figuratively): - abide, appoint, bring, continue, covenant, establish, hold up, lay, present, set (up), stanch, stand (by, forth, still, up).

G2666 - Devour

From *G2596* and *G4095*; to *drink down*, that is, *gulp entire* (literally or figuratively): - devour, drown, swallow (up).

G2596

A primary particle; (preposition) *down* (in place or time), in varied relations

G4095

to *imbibe* (literally or figuratively): - drink.

G2212 - Seeking

Of uncertain affinity; to *seek* (literally or figuratively); specifically (by Hebraism) to *worship* (God), or (in a bad sense) to *plot* (against life)

G4617 - Sift

From σινιον sinion (a *sieve*); to *riddle* (figuratively): - sift.

H7753 - Hedge

A primitive root; to *entwine*, that is, *shut* in (for formation, protection or restraint): - fence. (make an) hedge (up).

G1383 - Trial

Neuter of a presumed derivative of *G1382*; a *testing*; by implication *trustworthiness:* - trial, trying.

G1382

From the same as *G1384*; *test* (abstractly or concretely); by implication *trustiness:* - experience (-riment), proof, trial.

G1384

From *G1380*; properly *acceptable* (*current* after assayal), that is, *approved:* - approved, tried.

G1380

to *think*; by implication to *seem* (truthfully or uncertainly): - be accounted, (of own) please (-ure), be of reputation, seem (good), suppose, think, trow.

G5093 - Precious

from *G5092*; *valuable*, that is, (objectively) *costly*, or (subjectively) *honored, esteemed*, or (figuratively) *beloved:* - dear, honourable, (more, most) precious, had in reputation.

G5092

From *G5099*; a *value*, that is, *money* paid, or (concretely and collectively) *valuables*; by analogy *esteem* (especially of the highest degree), or the *dignity* itself: - honour, precious, price, some.

G5099

to *pay* a price, that is, as a *penalty:* - be punished with.

G3641 - Season

puny (in extent, degree, number, duration or value); especially neuter (adverbially) *somewhat:* - + almost, brief [-ly], few, (a) little, + long, a season, short, small, a while.

G3076 - Heaviness

From *G3077*; to *distress*; reflexively or passively to *be sad:* - cause grief, grieve, be in heaviness, (be) sorrow (-ful), be (make) sorry.

G3077

Apparently a primary word; *sadness:* - grief, grievous, + grudgingly, heaviness, sorrow.

G4164 - Manifold

motley, that is, *various* in character: - divers, manifold.

G3986 - Temptations

From *G3985*; a putting to *proof* (by experiment [of good], *experience* [of evil], solicitation, discipline or provocation); by implication *adversity:* - temptation, X try.

G3985

From *G3984*; to *test* (objectively), that is, *endeavor, scrutinize, entice, discipline:* - assay, examine, go about, prove, tempt (-er), try.

G3984

From the base of *G4008* (through the idea of *piercing*); a *test*, that is, *attempt, experience:* - assaying, trial.

G4008

to "peirce"; *through* (as adverb or preposition), that is, *across:* - beyond, farther (other) side, over.

G1391 - Glory

glory (as very *apparent*), in a wide application (literally or figuratively, objectively or subjectively): - dignity, glory (-ious), honour, praise, worship.

G5092 - Honour

From *G5099*; a *value*, that is, *money* paid, or (concretely and collectively) *valuables*; by analogy *esteem* (especially of the highest degree), or the *dignity* itself: - honour, precious, price, some.

G5099

to *pay* a price, that is, as a *penalty:* - be punished with.

H6031 - Afflicted

A primitive root (possibly rather identical with *H6030* through the idea of *looking* down or *browbeating*); to *depress* literally or figuratively, transitively or intransitively (in various applications).: - abase self, afflict (-ion, self), answer [by mistake for *H6030*], chasten self, deal hardly with, defile, exercise, force, gentleness, humble (self), hurt, ravish

H6030

A primitive root; properly to *eye* or (generally) to *heed*, that is, *pay attention*; by implication to *respond*; by extension to *begin* to speak; specifically to *sing, shout, testify, announce*

H2706 - Statues

From *H2710*; an *enactment*; hence an *appointment* (of time, space, quantity, labor or usage): - appointed, bound, commandment, convenient, custom, decree (-d), due, law, measure, X necessary, ordinance (-nary), portion, set time, statute, task.

H2710

A primitive root; properly to *hack*, that is, *engrave* (Jdg_5:14, to *be a scribe* simply); by implication to *enact* (laws being *cut* in stone or metal tablets in primitive times) or (generally) *prescribe*

G4531 – Shake (Shook)

From *G4535*; to *waver*, that is, *agitate, rock, topple* or (by implication) *destroy*; figuratively to *disturb, incite: -* move, shake (together), which can [-not] be shaken, stir up.

G4535

Probably from the base of *G4525*; a *vibration*, that is, (specifically) *billow: -* wave.

G4525

A to *shake* (figuratively *disturb*): - move.

G2347 - Tribulations

From *G2346*; *pressure* (literally or figuratively): - afflicted, (-tion), anguish, burdened, persecution, tribulation, trouble.

G2346

to *crowd* (literally or figuratively): - afflict, narrow, throng, suffer tribulation, trouble.

G2716 - Worketh

From *G2596* and *G2038*; to *work fully*, that is, *accomplish*; by implication to *finish, fashion:* - cause, do (deed), perform, work (out).

G2596

down (in place or time), in varied relations

G2038

Middle voice from *G2041*; to *toil* (as a task, occupation, etc.), (by implication) *effect, be engaged in* or *with*, etc.: - commit, do, labor for, minister about, trade (by), work.

G2041

to *work*; *toil* (as an effort or occupation); by implication an *act:* - deed, doing, labour, work.

G5281 - Patience

From *G5278*; cheerful (or hopeful) *endurance, constancy:* - enduring, patience, patient continuance (waiting).

G5278

From *G5259* and *G3306*; to *stay under* (*behind*), that is, *remain*; figuratively to *undergo*, that is, *bear* (trials), *have fortitude, persevere:* - abide, endure, (take) patient (-ly), suffer, tarry behind.

G5259

A primary preposition; *under*, that is, (with the genitive) of place (*beneath*), or with verbs (the agency or means, *through*)

G3306

A primary verb; to *stay* (in a given place, state, relation or expectancy): - abide, continue, dwell, endure, be present, remain, stand, tarry (for), X thine own

G1382 - Experience

From the same as *G1384*; *test* (abstractly or concretely); by implication *trustiness:* - experience (-riment), proof, trial.

G1384

properly *acceptable* (*current* after assayal), that is, *approved:* - approved, tried.

G1680 - Hope

From ἔλπω elpō which is a primary word (to *anticipate*, usually with pleasure); *expectation* (abstract or concrete) or *confidence:* - faith, hope.

G4728 - Strait

Probably from the base of *G2476*; *narrow* (from obstacles *standing* close about): - strait.

G2476

to stand

G4439 - Gate

Apparently a primary word; a *gate*, that is, the leaf or wing of a folding *entrance* (literally or figuratively): - gate.

G1311 - Perish

From *G1223* and *G5351*; to *rot thoroughly*, that is, (by implication) to *ruin* (passively *decay* utterly, figuratively *pervert*): - corrupt, destroy, perish.

G5351

to *pine* or *waste*: properly to *shrivel* or *wither*, that is, to *spoil* (by any process) or (genitive) to *ruin* (especially figuratively by moral influences, to *deprave*): - corrupt (self), defile, destroy.

G341 – Renew (ed)

From *G303* and a derivative of *G2537*; to *renovate:* - renew.

G303

properly *up*; but (by extension) used (distributively) *severally*, or (locally) *at* (etc.): - and, apiece, by, each, every (man), in, through. In compounds (as a prefix) it often means (by implication) *repetition*, *intensity*, *reversal*, etc.

G2537

new (especially in *freshness*)

G5485 - Graciousness

From *G5463*; *graciousness* (as *gratifying*), of manner or act (abstract or concrete; literal, figurative or spiritual; especially the divine influence upon the heart, and its reflection in the life; including *gratitude*): - acceptable, benefit, favour, gift, grace (-ious), joy liberality, pleasure, thank (-s, -worthy).

G5463

A primary verb; to be full of *"cheer"*, that is, calmly *happy* or well off; impersonal especially as a salutation (on meeting or parting), *be well:* - farewell, be glad, God speed, greeting, hail, joy (-fully), rejoice.

G714 - Sufficient

Apparently a primary verb (through the idea of *raising* a barrier); properly to *ward off*, that is, (by implication) to *avail* (figuratively *be satisfactory*): - be content, be enough, suffice, be sufficient.

G1411 - Strength

From *G1410*; *force* (literally or figuratively); specifically miraculous *power* (usually by implication a *miracle* itself): - ability, abundance, meaning, might (-ily, -y, -y deed), (worker of) miracle (-s), power, strength, violence, mighty (wonderful) work.

G1410

Of uncertain affinity; to *be able* or *possible:* - be able, can (do, + -not), could, may, might, be possible, be of power.

G5048 - Prefect

From *G5046*; to *complete*, that is, (literally) *accomplish*, or (figuratively) *consummate* (in character): - consecrate, finish, fulfil, (make) perfect.

G5046

complete (in various applications of labor, growth, mental and moral character, etc.); *completeness:*

G769 - Weakness

From *G772*; *feebleness* (of body or mind); by implication *malady*; moral *frailty:* - disease, infirmity, sickness, weakness.

G772

strengthless

H3045 - Acknowledge

A primitive root; to *know* (properly to ascertain by *seeing*); used in a great variety of senses, figuratively, literally, euphemistically and inferentially (including *observation, care, recognition*; and causatively *instruction, designation, punishment,* etc.): - acknowledge, acquaintance (-ted with), advise, answer, appoint, assuredly, be aware.

H3289 - Counsel

A primitive root; to *advise*; reflexively to *deliberate* or *resolve:* - advertise, take advice, advise (well), consult, (give take) counsel (-lor), determine, devise, guide, purpose.

H3629 - Reins

Feminine of *H3627* (only in the plural); a *kidney* (as an essential *organ*); figuratively the *mind* (as the interior self): - kidneys, reins.

H3267

A primitive root; to be *bold* or *obstinate:* - fierce.

H3256 - Instruct

A primitive root; to *chastise*, literally (with blows) or figuratively (with words); hence to *instruct:* - bind, chasten, chastise, correct, instruct, punish, reform, reprove, sore, teach.

H3915 – Night seasons

From the same as *H3883*; properly a *twist* (away of the light), that is, *night*; figuratively *adversity:* - ([mid-]) night (season).

H3883

From an unused root meaning to *fold* back; a *spiral* step: - winding stair.

H6862 - Adversity

From *H6887*; *narrow*; (as a noun) a *tight* place (usually figuratively, that is, *trouble*); (transitively) an *opponent* (as *crowding*): - adversary, afflicted (-tion), anguish, close, distress, enemy, flint, foe, narrow, small, sorrow, strait, tribulation, trouble.

H6887

A primitive root; to *cramp*, literally or figuratively, transitively or intransitively: - adversary, (be in) afflict (-ion), besiege, bind (up), (be in, bring) distress, enemy, narrower, oppress, pangs, shut up, be in a strait (trouble), vex.

H3906 - Affliction

From *H3905*; *distress:* - affliction, oppression.

H3905

A primitive root; properly to *press*, that is, (figuratively) to *distress:* - afflict, crush, force, hold fast, oppress (-or), thrust self.

H6960 – Wait Upon

A primitive root; to *bind* together (perhaps by *twisting*), that is, *collect*; (figuratively) to *expect:* - gather (together), look, patiently, tarry, wait (for, on, upon).

H3581 - Strength

From an unused root meaning to *be firm*; *vigor*, literally (*force*, in a good or a bad sense) or figuratively (*capacity, means, produce*); also (from its hardiness) a large *lizard:* - ability, able, chameleon, force, fruits, might, power (-ful), strength, substance, wealth.

H1980 - Walk

a primitive root; to *walk* (in a great variety of applications, literally and figuratively

G2293 - Cheer

From *G2294*; to *have courage:* - be of good cheer (comfort).

G2294

daring; boldness (subjectively): - courage.

G3528 - Overcome

From *G3529*; to *subdue* (literally or figuratively): - conquer, overcome, prevail, get the victory.

G3529

conquest (abstractly), that is, (figuratively) the *means of success:* - victory.

G1411 - Power

From *G1410*; *force* (literally or figuratively); specifically miraculous *power* (usually by implication a *miracle* itself): - ability, abundance, meaning, might (-ily, -y, -y deed), (worker of) miracle (-s), power, strength, violence, mighty (wonderful) work.

G1410

Of uncertain affinity; to *be able* or *possible:* - be able, can (do, + -not), could, may, might, be possible, be of power

G2480 – Can Do

From *G2479*; to *have* (or *exercise*) *force* (literally or figuratively): - beable, avail, can do ([-not]), could, be good, might, prevail, be of strength, be whole, + much work.

G2479

forcefulness (literally or figuratively): - ability, might ([-ily]), power, strength.

G1743 - Strengthen

From *G1722* and *G1412*; to *empower:* - enable, (increase in) strength (-en), be (make) strong.

G1412

to *enable:* - strengthen.

G154 - Desire

Of uncertain derivation; to *ask* (in generally): - ask, beg, call for, crave, desire, require.

H7266 - Rage

(Chaldee); from *H7265*; violent *anger:* - rage.

H7265

(Chaldee); corresponding to *H7264*: - provoke unto wrath.

H7264

A primitive root; to *quiver* (with any violent emotion, especially anger or fear)

H600 - Visage

(Chaldee); the *face:* - face, visage.

H2388 - Strong

A primitive root; to *fasten* upon; hence to *seize, be strong* (figuratively *courageous*, causatively *strengthen, cure, help, repair, fortify*), *obstinate*; to *bind, restrain, conquer,* withstand.

H553 - Courageous

A primitive root; to *be alert,* physically (on foot) or mentally (in courage): - confirm, be courageous (of good courage, stedfastly minded, strong, stronger), establish, fortify, harden, increase, prevail, strengthen (self), make strong (obstinate, speed).

G3986 - Temptation

From *G3985*; a putting to *proof* (by experiment [of good], *experience* [of evil], solicitation, discipline or provocation); by implication *adversity:* - temptation,.

G3985

From *G3984*; to *test* (objectively), that is, *endeavor, scrutinize, entice, discipline:* - assay, examine, go about, prove, tempt (-er), try.

G3984

(through the idea of *piercing*); a *test*, that is, *attempt, experience:* - assaying, trial.

H2416 - Life

From *H2421*; *alive*; hence *raw* (flesh); *fresh* (plant, water, year), *strong*; also (as noun, especially in the feminine singular and masculine plural) *life* (or living thing).

H2421

A prim root to *live*, whether literally or figuratively; causatively to *revive:* -   keep (leave, make) alive, give (promise) life, (let, suffer to) live, nourish up, preserve (alive), quicken, recover, repair, restore (to life), revive.

H7522 - Favour

From *H7521*; *delight:* - (be) acceptable (-ance, -ed), delight, desire, favour, (good) pleasure, (own, self, voluntary) will, as . . . (what) would.

H7521

A primitive root; to *be pleased with*; specifically to *satisfy* a debt: - (be) accept (-able), accomplish, set affection, approve, consent with, delight (self), enjoy, (be, have a) favour (-able), like, observe, pardon, (be, have, take) please (-ure), reconcile self.

G3551 - Law

to *parcel* out, (especially *food* or *grazing* to animals); *law* (through the idea of prescriptive *usage*), generally (*regulation*), specifically (of Moses [including the volume]; also of the Gospel), or figuratively (a *principle*): - law.

G5015 - Troubled

to *stir* or *agitate* (*roil* water): - trouble.

G1168 - Afraid

From *G1167*; to *be timid:* - be afraid.

G1167

From *G1169*; *timidity:* - fear.

G1169

dread; *timid*, that is, (by implication) *faithless:* - fearful.

G3306 - Abide

A primary verb; to *stay* (in a given place, state, relation or expectancy): - abide, continue, dwell, endure, be present, remain, stand, tarry (for), X thine own.

G4336 - Praying

From *G4314* and *G2172*; to *pray to* God, that is, *supplicate, worship:* - pray (earnestly, for), make prayer.

G4313

to *precede* (as guide or herald): - go before.

G2172

to *wish*; by implication to *pray* to God: - pray, will, wish.

G4335 - Prayer

From *G4336*; *prayer* (*worship*); by implication an *oratory* (*chapel*): - pray earnestly, prayer.

H8159 - Dismayed

A primitive root; to *gaze* at or about (properly for help); by implication to *inspect, consider, compassionate, be nonplussed* (as looking around in amazement) or *bewildered:* - depart, be dim, be dismayed, look (away), regard, have respect, spare, turn.

H5826 - Help

A primitive root; to *surround*, that is, *protect* or *aid:* - help, succour.

H7503 - Fail

A primitive root; to *slacken* (in many applications, literally or figuratively): - abate, cease, consume, draw [toward evening], fail, (be) faint, be (wax) feeble, forsake, idle, leave, let alone (go, down), (be) slack, stay, be still, be slothful, (be) weak (-en).

H5800 - Forsake

A primitive root; to *loosen*, that is, *relinquish, permit*, etc.: - commit self, fail, forsake, fortify, help, leave (destitute, off), refuse.

H2865 - Dismayed

A primitive root; properly to *prostrate*; hence to *break* down, either (literally) by violence, or (figuratively) by confusion and fear: - abolish, affright, be (make) afraid, amaze, beat down, discourage, (cause to) dismay, go down, scare, terrify.

G2978 - Storm

Of uncertain derivation; a *whirlwind* (*squall*): - storm, tempest.

G2008 - Rebuke

to *tax upon*, that is, *censure* or *admonish*; by implication *forbid:* - (straitly) charge, rebuke.

G4623 - Peace

silence, that is, a *hush*; properly *muteness*, that is, *involuntary* stillness, or *inability* ot speak; figuratively to *be calm* (as *quiet* water): - dumb, (hold) peace.

G5392 – Be Still

(a *muzzle*); to *muzzle:* - muzzle.